RESHAPING CURRICULA

RESHAPING CURRICULA

Revitalization Programs at Three Land Grant Universities

Joyce Povlacs Lunde

with

Maurice Baker
Frederick H. Buelow
Laurie Schultz Hayes

Anker Publishing Company, Inc.
Bolton, MA

Reshaping Curricula
Revitalization Programs at Three Land Grant Universities

ISBN 1-882982-09-6

Composition by Deerfoot Studios
Cover design by Deerfoot Studios

Anker Publishing Company, Inc.
176 Ballville Road
P.O. Box 249
Bolton, MA 01740-0249

EDITORS

JOYCE POVLACS LUNDE, Associate Professor, Department of Agricultural Leadership, Education and Communication, and Educational Specialist, Office of Professional and Organizational Development, Institute of Agriculture and Natural Resources, University of Nebraska-Lincoln (UNL). Joyce served as a project codirector for New Partnerships in Agriculture and Natural Resources (NUPAGE). Coming to Nebraska in 1978, she was an instructional consultant in the UNL Teaching and Learning Center before becoming a faculty member in 1989 in the College of Agricultural Sciences and Natural Resources. She has been a grant writer and project leader for a number of projects in higher education, including such areas as professional renewal of faculty, rewarding teaching, and currently, food systems professions education. As a longtime member of the Professional and Organizational Development (POD) Network in Higher Education, she has contributed to the field of faculty development and teaching improvement in higher education. One of her current interests is in developing and implementing programs to prepare graduate students for college teaching.

MAURICE BAKER, Professor, Department of Agricultural Economics, University of Nebraska-Lincoln. In New Partnerships in Agriculture and Education (NUPAGE), Maurice served as a project codirector and faculty leader. He has over 35 years of college teaching experience, during which he has been concerned about effective teaching and how to institutionally organize to meet the needs of students. This concern led him to examine his own teaching approach and the research on alternatives to those he was using. He simultaneously studied the institutional organization within which teaching takes place. This study has led to significant changes in his own teaching over the years and to his acceptance of the codirectorship of NUPAGE.

FREDERICK H. BUELOW, Professor Emeritus, Agricultural Engineering Department, University of Wisconsin-Madison. Fred served as director of the project "Integrative Approach to Curricular Revitalization and Faculty Development—A Strategy for Change," in the College of Agricultural and Life Sciences at the University of Wisconsin. Before going to Wisconsin, he was on the faculty of the Agricultural Engineering Department at Michigan State University for ten years and served as Acting Director of Resident Instruction in the College of Agriculture there for one year. At the University of Wisconsin-Madison, he was professor of Agricultural Engineering for 28 years, serving as department chair for 17 of those years. While he was chair, he developed and gained approval for both the B.S. and Ph.D. programs in Agricultural Engineering.

LAURIE SCHULTZ HAYES, Associate Professor of Rhetoric and Associate Dean, Curricular and Student Affairs, College of Agriculture (now College of Agricultural, Food, and Environmental Sciences), University of Minnesota. Laurie was a full-time faculty member until March 1988, when she became Acting Assistant Dean for Academic and Student Affairs. In that role she led the final design and implementation of the College of Agriculture Portfolio (1988), and then, as chair of the newly organized Curriculum Committee (1989–1990), she facilitated the transition to the new all-college curriculum and the initiation of the new curricular management structure. She is an award-winning classroom teacher of speech communication and is recognized nationally for her role in developing courses for the hybrid discipline of scientific and technical communication and for designing and promoting undergraduate research programs.

CONTRIBUTORS

Maurice Baker is Professor of Agricultural Economics, University of Nebraska-Lincoln

Elizabeth Banset is Assistant Professor of Agricultural Leadership, Education and Communication, University of Nebraska-Lincoln

Mary Beck is Associate Professor of Animal Science, University of Nebraska-Lincoln

Virginia Book is Professor Emerita of Agricultural Leadership, Education and Communication, University of Nebraska-Lincoln

Lloyd Bostian is Professor Emeritus of Agricultural Journalism, University of Wisconsin-Madison

Dennis Brink is Professor of Animal Science, University of Nebraska-Lincoln

F. H. Buelow is Professor Emeritus of Agricultural Engineering, University of Wisconsin-Madison

Laura Casari is Associate Professor of Agricultural Leadership, Education and Communication, University of Nebraska-Lincoln

Dennis M. Conley is Associate Professor of Agricultural Economics, University of Nebraska-Lincoln

Terence H. Cooper is Professor of Soil Science, University of Minnesota

Ann Hill Duin is Associate Professor of Rhetoric, University of Minnesota

Jim Gosey is Associate Professor of Animal Science and Extension Beef Specialist, University of Nebraska-Lincoln

Laurie Schultz Hayes is Associate Professor of Rhetoric and Associate Dean, Curricular and Student Affairs, College of Agriculture (now College of Agricultural, Food, and Environmental Sciences), University of Minnesota

Glenn J. Hoffman is Head and Professor of Biological Systems Engineering, University of Nebraska-Lincoln

Emily E. Hoover is Associate Professor of Horticultural Science, University of Minnesota

Bruce Johnson is Professor of Agricultural Economics, University of Nebraska-Lincoln

David D. Jones is Assistant Professor of Biological Systems Engineering, University of Nebraska-Lincoln

Robert G. Kranz, Jr. of Middleton, Wisconsin, is formerly Curriculum Consultant on the Curricular Revitalization Project, University of Wisconsin-Madison

Joyce Povlacs Lunde is Associate Professor of Agricultural Leadership, Education and Communication, and Educational Specialist, Office of Professional and Organizational Development, University of Nebraska-Lincoln

Albert H. Markhart is Associate Professor of Horticultural Science, University of Minnesota

Patricia B. McConnell is Adjunct Assistant Professor of Zoology, University of Wisconsin-Madison

George Pfeiffer is Associate Professor of Agricultural Economics, University of Nebraska-Lincoln

Fahriye Sancar is Professor of Landscape Architecture, University of Wisconsin-Madison

Tom Scanlan is Associate Professor of Rhetoric, University of Minnesota

Jack Schinstock is Assistant Dean, College of Agricultural Sciences and Natural Resources, and Professor of Biological Systems Engineering, University of Nebraska-Lincoln

Steve R. Simmons is Professor of Agronomy and Plant Genetics, University of Minnesota

Rebecca L. Thomas of Fort Collins, Colorado, is formerly Outreach Coordinator of NUPAGE, University of Nebraska-Lincoln

Kenneth Von Bargen is Professor of Biological Systems Engineering, University of Nebraska-Lincoln

Steve Waller is Assistant Dean and Director, Agricultural Research Division, and Associate Dean, College of Agricultural Sciences and Natural Resources, University of Nebraska-Lincoln

Arthur E. Walzer is Associate Professor of Rhetoric, University of Minnesota

CONTENTS

FOREWORD

The W. K. Kellogg Foundation was founded in 1930, with an initial focus on children and the conditions necessary for a child to grow into a healthy, productive citizen. Hence, initial grantmaking focused on improving the total environment for well-being, which translated at the time to an emphasis on health, education, and agriculture. Agriculture was emphasized because of the child's need for a safe, wholesome, nutritious diet, and because agriculture symbolized the predominate life style of the era.

While much has changed since the establishment of the Kellogg Foundation, these same areas of emphasis still represent a context for programming with the foundation. However, the emphasis on agriculture is now the responsibility of the Food Systems unit, so named to reflect a broader emphasis on the social, economic, and political environment in which food and agriculture interact with people, whether it be at the local, state, national, or international level. Certainly colleges of agriculture and the food systems education components of our universities are significant parts of the total food system. Such institutions will continue to be a primary resource supporting professionals charged with addressing the significant agricultural and food systems issues of this and future generations.

Schools with agricultural and food systems education programs across the country find themselves in a unique situation. The contribution of agricultural research, extension, and teaching to the production of large quantities of safe, wholesome food for this country and a significant portion of the rest of the world remains a phenomenally successful story. The food production capacity of the U.S. has been significantly affected by higher education in agriculture and is the envy of the world.

Even with those successes, the professional educational system supporting the food system must change with the times. With the emphasis on environmental and long-term sustainability issues, curricula within the schools of agriculture and food systems must change to remain relevant. Smaller numbers of people are directly employed in the production of food and are therefore losing the economic and political influence needed to establish policy and solve their own problems. Fewer and fewer people within the general public are acquainted with agriculture and the food systems, resulting in growing numbers of uninformed consumers and policy makers. More and more people in the U.S. and around the world are having difficulty finding and affording food for their families on a daily basis.

It was the challenge of remaining relevant in an era of rapidly changing conditions and expectations that brought three unique curriculum change projects into being. The reports of these projects allows us an opportunity to learn about the commitment it takes to address significant issues within higher education. It also offers an opportunity to learn about innovation and creative curriculum revitalization efforts that may prove useful to institutions across the country.

These three major projects to revitalize curricula were funded by the W. K. Kellogg Foundation from 1986 through 1991. The University of Wisconsin-Madison conducted *An Integrated Approach to Curricular Assessment and Faculty Development* (1986–1990); the University of Minnesota established *Project Sunrise* (1986–1988); and the University of Nebraska-Lincoln implemented *New Partnerships in Agriculture and Education (NUPAGE,* 1988–1991). All three projects focused on how educational curricula could be enhanced through partnerships with community organizations and businesses. They also considered the need for continuous and proactive faculty development opportunities required for significant lasting change.

The W. K. Kellogg Foundation was pleased to be a partner with these institutions to address the current and future needs of professionals in agriculture and the food system. It is our belief that agriculture and food systems education programs in the U.S. must continue to evolve into the types of people-service institutions that will be responsive to the ever changing and complex needs of the global food system of the 21st century. Future efforts will, out of necessity, focus on new and innovative partnerships between the academy and the people and organizations it serves, collaborative efforts among institutions within the same state and/or region, and use of educational distance education and learning technologies that will allow access to information and resources around the world.

It is important that we learn from the experiences of faculty and faculty-partners from the Universities of Wisconsin, Minnesota, and Nebraska as they develop and implement new and innovative programming, just as it is important that we establish learning and sharing networks among all institutions. In this volume, faculty report their successes, as well as their false starts. It is important to realize that mistakes are not fatal; rather they offer an opportunity for reflection and refinement that only improves both process and product. Students and faculty greatly benefitted from these experiences, and you are invited to benefit as well.

We wish to express our deep appreciation to the project leaders and participants in each of these highly prestigious institutions for increasing our knowledge of curriculum change for agriculture and food systems education programs.

Rick Foster, Coordinator
Food Systems and Rural Development
W. K. Kellogg Foundation
Battle Creek, Michigan

PREFACE

In this volume we present an array of examples and materials drawn from curriculum revitalization programs in colleges of agriculture at Minnesota, Nebraska, and Wisconsin. With the resources provided to each university by grants from the W. K. Kellogg Foundation, Battle Creek, Michigan (1986–1991), faculty and administrators in our colleges were able to engage in developing new approaches to curricula and to teaching and learning. Although we are in colleges of agriculture, our focus on the dynamics of curriculum revitalization, faculty development, and student learning applies to any discipline in any higher education setting.

The projects on the three campuses did not begin as collaborations, but with the assistance of the Kellogg Foundation, we came together and discovered much in common. One overarching commonality is the dedication and persistence of those who moved ideas to action. New courses, new teaching strategies, and new approaches to curricula are not achieved without the actual workings of academia—e.g, attending countless meetings, discussing, scheduling, conferring, persuading, negotiating, investigating, attending conferences and workshops, preparing new materials, writing, reflecting, testing, revising, and, even during the earliest stages, recruiting students and motivating them to try new learning experiences.

The contributions here were written by 30 individuals who were among those deeply involved in the process of curriculum revitalization on each of our campuses. Their experiences are now set forth for consideration by readers across higher education. We believe that both individual and team experiences described in the following pages give a unique window into a means of changing higher education from within.

ORGANIZATION OF THIS VOLUME

We invite readers to examine the examples of curriculum change presented here and to consider what might be adapted to situations on their own campuses—across higher education as well as within colleges of agricultural sciences and natural resources. The collection is organized into seven sections and 25 chapters, with an overview and examples found in each section. Each chapter, written from the vantage point of one of our three campuses, tells about the innovations we tried, how processes were structured, and what happened as a result of our efforts. Section One contains descriptions of our goals, approaches, and the strategies we used to initiate change. Section Two focuses on developing "general education" or the core curriculum for each college. Sections Three to Seven each focus on one approach to teaching or one instructional method and contain chapters demonstrating how an approach or strategy was put into practice in different settings. The last chapter sets forth the significant lessons learned from our work. The reader will find that themes of student-centered instruction, active learning, and interdisciplinary teaching, as well as strategies of faculty development and outreach, are central to the changes we effected.

ACKNOWLEDGEMENTS

If we added everything up, hundreds of faculty, administrators, staff, students, and external partners made significant contributions ranging from idea generation, through implementation, to dissemination. We can mention only a few persons here, and, in particular, those who were in at the beginning of the projects and those who helped bring this publication to fruition.

Those in at the beginning include: at the University of Minnesota: C. Eugene Allen, then Dean, College of Agriculture, later Vice President for Agriculture, Forestry, and Home Economics, now Provost of Professional Studies; W. Keith Wharton, then Associate and later Acting Dean, College of Agriculture, now Professor of Rhetoric; Richard L. Jones, then Professor and Head of Entomology, Chair of Project Sunrise Task Force, later Dean of the College of Agriculture; Bonnie J. Pechtel, Mound Minnesota, then Director of Project Sunrise; at the University of Nebraska: T. E. (Ted) Hartung, then Dean of the College of Agriculture and Codirector, New Partnerships in Agriculture and Education (NUPAGE), now Associate Vice Chancellor for the Institute of Agriculture and Natural Resources and Director of Communication Information Technology; Donald M. Edwards, Dean, College of Agricultural Sciences and Natural Resources and project Codirector for NUPAGE (Don not only saw to it that NUPAGE became an essential part of the college's 1990–1993 action plan, but also encouraged us in disseminating results); Daniel W. Wheeler, Coordinator, Office of Professional and Organizational Development and project Codirector, NUPAGE; at the University of Wisconsin: George W. Sledge, then Associate Dean and Director of Academic Student Affairs, College of Agricultural and Life Sciences, now Professor Emeritus, Department of Continuing and Vocational Education; at the Kellogg Foundation: those who served our campuses as program directors include Dan E. Moore, now Vice President-Programs, and Thomas L. Thorburn, Program Director, Food Systems/Rural Development.

We also thank those who supported us in bringing this work to completion. In addition to the original grants to each campus, the W. K. Kellogg Foundation supported this effort with a dissemination grant. A special thanks goes to our current Kellogg program director, Richard M. (Rick) Foster, Program Director and Coordinator, Food Systems/Rural Development. Well-deserved recognition for service and assistance is extended to our outstanding technical editor, Elizabeth A. (Liz) Banset, Assistant Professor, Department of Agricultural Leadership, Education, and Communication, University of Nebraska-Lincoln. We are also appreciative of those who agreed to contribute and then did their part—the authors in this volume. Another thank you goes to our publishers, James D. Anker, President, and Susan W. Anker, Vice President, Anker Publishing Company for their patient assistance.

Lastly I offer profound gratitude to my three colleagues in this enterprise, the project codirectors and associate editors: Laurie Schultz Hayes, University of Minnesota; Maurice Baker, University of Nebraska; and Frederick H. (Fred) Buelow, University of Wisconsin. In addition to collaborating on concept and contents, Maurie, Fred, and Laurie were responsible for identifying authors on their campuses; they served as section editors, and, despite busy schedules, put a high priority on turning a grant project into a tangible outcome. Together, the four of us invite colleagues from across higher education to benefit, as we have, from the lessons learned in our attempt to reshape curricula at our universities.

Joyce Povlacs Lunde
March, 1995
Lincoln, Nebraska

SECTION 1

THREE PROGRAMS IN
CURRICULUM REVITALIZATION

Edited and with an introduction by
Joyce Povlacs Lunde
University of Nebraska-Lincoln

In the 1980s, it became increasingly clear across all of higher education that undergraduate education was in need of major revitalization. Higher education and its faculty were pictured as notoriously resistant to change. In this system, recognition, job security, and reward were seen as coming to faculty from research and publication, with teaching frequently treated as a necessity but not nearly as important an endeavor. The report *Involvement in Learning* (Study Group on the Conditions of Excellence in Higher Education, 1984) was the first of many publications calling attention to the neglect of teaching and undergraduate curricula, especially in comprehensive and research universities.

Programs of study in colleges of agriculture were not exempt from the general feeling that society was not being well served by higher education. In 1987, Keith Wharton, in the preface to *Curricular Innovation for 2005*, a report issued by the Higher Education Programs of the U.S. Department of Agriculture, said, "we do not question whether our curricula should be revised and revitalized; we accept as given that they should be...."

Land grant education appeared more and more isolated from society exactly when its expertise and programs of education were increasingly needed to address growing world-wide problems, not only in food and agriculture, but also in society, the environment, political structures, and the economy. If the traditional land grant mission of serving the citizens of our states were to remain viable, we needed to scrutinize our programs of study, renew our mission and goals, and revitalize our curricula. Instead of narrowly-trained graduates, our students must be educated to function as problem solvers not only in their professions in food, agriculture, and natural resources, but also in their roles and responsibilities as citizens.

With the assistance of the W. K. Kellogg Foundation, Battle Creek, Michigan, three land grant institutions in Wisconsin, Minnesota, and Nebraska initiated projects to revitalize traditional agricultural curricula. These programs were "An Integrative Approach to Curricular Assessment and Faculty Development" (1986–1990) at the College of Agricultural and Life Sciences of the University of Wisconsin-Madison; "Project Sunrise" (1986-1988) at the College of Agriculture of the University of Minnesota; and "New Partnerships in Agriculture and Education" (NUPAGE) (1988–1991) at the College of Agricultural Sciences and Natural Resources (formerly the College of Agriculture) of the University of Nebraska-Lincoln.

In each of these programs, the faculties of our respective colleges were regarded as the major agents of change in reforming curricula, renewing themselves, and improving instruction. All three programs, therefore, contained strategies to stimulate faculty involvement and influence the direction of change. In this first section, we set forth the major processes and strategies of change we selected or invented to reach the goal of designing curricula that would truly educate our students and thus serve society.

Each of the four essays sets forth and illustrates one major ingredient for change. Although in general the processes described here were found in all three of our programs, each essay is largely written from the perspective of one of the campuses. Robert Kranz describes models of curriculum development and gives the conceptual framework for Wisconsin's broad-based approaches to revitalization. My essay focuses on strategies of faculty development which were used at Nebraska to encourage faculty to work cooperatively to improve teaching and learning and thus make changes in curriculum. Maurice Baker, in the essay on partnering, a major strategy at Nebraska, describes how faculty inside and outside the College of Agriculture, students, and a broad spectrum of individuals from agribusiness, government, and the community served as working partners in the revitalization process. Organizational change and restructuring, as noted in the essay by Laurie Hayes, were both an impetus to change and an outcome of it at Minnesota.

In telling our stories, we report the underpinnings of curricular change and tell about what happened. We describe the what, who, and how of making complex and deliberate changes in curricula in higher education. Not all our strategies worked, however, and we say so. We discovered that the greater the magnitude of change, the more time it takes and the greater the risk. Nor will the task of revitalizing the curriculum ever be finished. These approaches and strategies (what we came to call the "process" essays) are offered to provide models, ideas, and stimuli as we continue to engage in the essential tasks of education.

Joyce Povlacs Lunde is Associate Professor of Agricultural Leadership, Education and Communication, and Educational Specialist, Office of Professional and Organizational Development, University of Nebraska-Lincoln.

REFERENCES

Study Group on the Conditions of Excellence in American Higher Education. (1984). *Involvement in learning: Realizing the potential of American higher education.* Washington, DC: Department of Education.

USDA (United States Department of Agriculture). (1987). *Curricular innovation for 2005: Planning for the future of our food & agricultural sciences.* Madison, WI: University of Wisconsin.

1

A THEORETICAL CONTEXT FOR DESIGNING CURRICULA IN THE AGRICULTURAL AND LIFE SCIENCES

Robert G. Kranz, Jr.
University of Wisconsin-Madison

Colleges of agriculture were founded on a democratic philosophy of education. Since their beginnings in the 19th century, they have attempted to meet the wide-ranging educational needs and interests of a broad, non-elite student clientele. This approach to higher learning has usually been served by a "learning product" theory of education, emphasizing specified knowledge and skills (Bjoraker, 1987). Armed with this conceptual tool, academic planners conceived curricular development models accentuating both rational analysis of educational needs, goals and objectives, and frequent testing of students to document the efficiency and effectiveness of the process. This development model led to a distinctive curricular design, in which the program of study typically resembled a pyramid, with a sequential, vertical arrangement of subject-centered courses (Sledge, 1974).

Learning product theory and its emphasis on a hierarchy of knowledge has always been viewed with suspicion by some within academe. In its most extreme form, this vein of commentary regards a sequentially-organized curriculum as a technique of control by social, economic, and professional elites. Moderate critics of learning product theory point to its lack of concern for individual interests and abilities and its failure to recognize the value of experiential learning. In the early 1980s, the criticism of learning product theory went mainstream, and calls for reform of the curricula were made on a regular basis by citizen groups and educators alike.

THE CASE FOR REFORM

This assault on undergraduate education was launched along two different fronts: cultural critics objected to declining emphasis on the humanities in undergraduate curricula, and members of the business community criticized colleges and universities for graduating students with poor problem solving skills and deficiencies in basic subject areas. Both lines of attack deplored what they regarded as paralysis and lack of vision among educators. Not surprisingly, these criticisms inspired college administrators to call for broad-based reform and curricular revitalization, if not exactly a full-blown revolution in educational theory and curricular development and design.

Calls for comprehensive reform in the agricultural sciences were sounded as early as 1985. At that time the North Central Curricular Committee Project, with George W. Sledge of the University of Wisconsin-Madison as chairman, initiated meetings around the country to discuss the issues underlying curricular change. These efforts eventually resulted in the publication of *Curricular Innovation for 2005: Planning for the Future of our Food and Agricultural Sciences* (1987). This document, featuring essays and research by some of the country's leading agricultural administrators, became the basic document outlining the conceptual, policy, and planning issues and concepts for curricular revitalization in the agricultural sciences in the latter part of the decade. It was followed two years later by another volume, *Educating for a Global Perspective: International Agricultural Curricula for 2005* (1989), that outlined the need and steps necessary for developing "globalized curricula" in the agricultural sciences. Even as the North Central Project unfolded, however, plans were already underway at the University of Wisconsin-Madison for an "institutionally specific" program of reform.

THE UNIVERSITY OF WISCONSIN-MADISON

The comprehensive revitalization of undergraduate instruction that took place at the University of Wisconsin-Madison can be understood only by first understanding the underlying conceptual issues at work on the Madison campus. What philosophy of education characterized the College of Agricultural and Life Sciences (CALS)? What theories of education were subscribed to by administrators and faculty? What curricular development and design models derived from these philosophies and theories? The Curricular Revitalization Project (CRP) attempted to shed light on these questions, and to realign the college's curricula in a way that reflected newly emerging insights on conceptual matters.

Like all other land grant institutions, UW-Madison is an embodiment of the democratic philosophy of education. Although somewhat selective in admissions, CALS aspires to give the "lion's share" of Wisconsin students an opportunity for a higher education, and, in fact, the college now serves a more demographically diverse population than at any time in its history. At the same time, however, access to the University has narrowed, principally because of rising tuition, but perhaps also because higher academic standards have been adopted as part of a university-wide enrollment management strategy.

Prior to the work of the Curricular Revitalization Project, CALS was for many years wedded to a learning product theory of education. During the 1950s, this gave rise to a curricular development model that relied on job analysis techniques, resulting in a curricular design emphasizing standardized, sequentially organized course requirements. Educational arrangements that promoted learning skills (such as internships), instead of an approved body of knowledge, were rare. In fact, administrators were at best reluctant, and in some cases opposed, to sponsoring faculty discussion on these matters. Nonetheless, the hegemony of learning product theory began to crumble during the 1960s and 1970s, although it continued to survive into the 1980s in individual classrooms.

By promoting the development of problem solving skills, broad-based curricula, and balance among fields of study, the CRP implicitly rejected the learning product theory. In its place, a "learning process" theory of education was advanced as the appropriate attitude for faculty and administrators alike. This theory sets the student at the center of the curricula, instead of subject matter, although the importance of transmitting cultural heritage and building a base of knowledge are acknowledged.

Curricular Development and Design Models

Prior to the work of the CRP, no comprehensive revitalization of the CALS curricula had been undertaken in almost a quarter of a century. Instead, the temper of the times dictated a policy of incrementalism whereby requirements and programs were added and deleted on a case by case basis. The CRP proposal to the W. K. Kellogg Foundation, Battle Creek, Michigan, was an acknowledgment of this fact, and the project was intended as an opportunity to pursue a systematic strategy aimed at changing the curriculum.

The CRP crafted an approach to curricular development with elements of both "mission-based" and "competency-based" models, as described by the North Central Project (Sledge et al, 1987). The main elements included development of an institutional mission statement, including identification of institutional parameters and definition of educational goals related to the mission (see Appendix A). The CRP model also included an analysis of future educational needs.

The curricular design that followed also was a hybrid of several models described by the North Central Project. The "core-based" model contributed the concept of a body of essential skills and knowledge common to all educated persons and professional activity in the agricultural and life sciences. As a student assimilates this part of the curriculum, breadth and depth of knowledge are achieved though study of an interdisciplinary core of knowledge related to study in the major. The "capstone-based" model contributed the idea of a final learning experience that allows the student to synthesize the skills and knowledge of core and major studies, under conditions similar to those found in the modern work place.

Implementation

The analysis of educational needs was crucial to developing the CRP curricular design. When the CRP began work, the evidence on student educational needs appeared mixed. For example, in a national survey conducted by two Pennsylvania State University investigators, agricultural educators were asked if they believed students attained minimum job or graduate school entry level skills in several basic areas (Love and Yoder, 1989). One of the areas surveyed was microcomputer and computer competence (i.e., competence in accessing the computer, word processing, creating spreadsheets, managing data bases, and programming). A fair number of respondents voiced skepticism of the need for such computer skills. This response was surprising, in light of the widely-made claim that computer skills are now virtually a prerequisite for employment.

Nonetheless, it echoed the findings of several earlier studies of agricultural employers that also underlined the relative unimportance of computer skills. For example, a national survey conducted by Texas A&M researchers found that agricultural employers voiced only mild enthusiasm for computers as a tool in decision-making (Litzenberg and Schneider, 1987). The ability to write computer programs, design programs, communicate with programmers, and understand artificial intelligence ranked near the bottom of 74 employee characteristics listed in the survey. Yet a majority of the students responding to the Penn State survey felt they were attaining less than entry level competence in word processing. Almost two-thirds felt less than proficient with spreadsheets. As many as three-quarters of the students surveyed felt deficient in data base management.

But if the evidence of student needs failed to provide much guidance in the areas of computer skills, it spoke clearly in other areas of the curriculum. Communication skills in particular, along with problem solving and capacity to work as part of a team, were commonly cited as areas in need of improvement. The CRP study of educational needs confirmed these findings. It also found that the college's client groups seemed to favor more emphasis in the natural sciences and were far more enthusiastic about increasing emphasis on computers than indicated by the national surveys of student educational needs. There was less consensus over the need to improve the breadth of the curriculum through study of foreign language, social science, and humanities, although client groups were critical of what they regarded as a lack of international focus in the undergraduate curriculum.

LESSONS LEARNED

The task of evaluating this evidence required a framework. If we see curricular revitalization as part of a dynamic social process reflecting group competition, and not simply as the outcome of a rational analysis of jobs and employment requirements, we shed a new and interesting light on differences over curricula. And if we discard our predisposition to see progress as given and recognize that interests supporting the old arrangements can derail progress at any moment, curricular change is then understood as a series of concessions to needs expressed by particular groups. Curricular revitalization is in fact a contest, with the outcome negotiated among faculty and various constituent groups by academic planners and administrators. This contest is based on a set of interrelated principles derived from Smelser (1985):

- Because educational institutions are dependent on society for support, they are unable to sustain or introduce programs that dominant groups oppose.

- Educational reform efforts must therefore focus on bringing institutions in line with the values and needs expressed by concerned groups.

- Thus, institutions are obliged to negotiate changes reflecting the conflicting values and needs of these groups, in some cases down to the pedagogical style of teachers and the content of particular courses.

Clearly, academic planners in the agricultural and life sciences competing in such a contest will do more than assess jobs and employment requirements. And they will do more than respond to technological advancement.

Winning the contest depends on careful examination of needs expressed by different groups—employers, farmers, environmentalists, students, college faculty and administrators, high school teachers, guidance counselors, and government officials, to name only a few. In some cases, groups will be in agreement, and the path to curricular revitalization will be clear. Academic planners and administrators must expect, however, that these groups will occasionally express different needs based on their own values. For example, groups may agree that their values and interests are best served by increased emphasis on verbal and written communication, problem solving, and team-work skills; other groups, however, may prefer to emphasize foreign language, breadth area, and work experience groups may disagree, and the path to revitalization will be less clear.

The CRP anticipated differing perceptions of student educational needs, and therefore incorporated two important guidelines into its curricular development model:

1. Carefully consider institutionally specific educational trends, and the unique ethos and strengths of the institutional and external environments.

2. At every step of the revitalization process, consult the stakeholders of the curriculum.

Two questions inevitably arise. First, does treating curricular revitalization as a contest merely invite conflict among faculty and client groups? Second, will these conflicts require bland compromises on curricular matters? The answers are not clear-cut and often depend on institutionally-specific factors.

As a general rule, though, it is safe to say that winning the contest depends largely on strong academic leadership. Strong individual efforts and a healthy tolerance (perhaps even a taste) for long, seemingly fruitless meetings and discussion also help. Luck, too, is important. Given these circumstances, curricular revitalization brings to the surface conflicts that already exist and offers a mechanism to resolve these conflicts on mutually agreeable terms.

At times, however, those responsible for the process will ask themselves if it is all worth the bother. In those moments, it is good to recall that conflicts over curriculum far more complicated than those we face today were resolved in the nineteenth century: the birth and development of the land grant system itself was the ultimate result. When viewed from this perspective, suffering through a little constructive conflict along the way is a small price to pay for advancing the land grant legacy into the twenty-first century.

Robert G. Kranz, Jr. is formerly Curriculum Consultant on the Curricular Revitalization Project, University of Wisconsin-Madison.

REFERENCES

Bjoraker, W.T. (1987). Concepts and philosophical issues in food and agriculture undergraduate education with basic guidelines for curricular planners. In *Curricular innovation for 2005: Planning for the future of our food and agricultural sciences.* Washington, DC: North Central Region RICOP Curricular Committee Project, U.S. Department of Agriculture, pp. 5–32.

Litzenberg, K., & Schneider, V.E. (1987). *Agri-Mass: Agribusiness management aptitude and skills survey.* Washington, DC: Agribusiness Education Project.

Love, G.M., & Yoder, E.P. (1989). *An assessment of undergraduate education in American colleges of agriculture.* State College, PA: Pennsylvania State University, College of Agriculture.

North Central Region Curricular Committee Project. (1989). *Educating for a global perspective: International agricultural curricula for 2005.* Washington, DC: U.S. Department of Agriculture.

Sledge, G.W. (1974). Curriculum strategies for agriculture: An analysis of problems relating to the choice, preparation and application of a curriculum. *Program and Methods in Higher Education in Agriculture,* Paris, Oct. 14–18, 1974. Fifth Working Conference of Representatives of Higher Education in Agriculture. Paris, France: Organization for Economic Cooperation and Development.

Sledge, G.W., et al (1987). Futuristic curricular models and designs for the food and agricultural sciences. In *Curricular innovation for 2005: Planning for the future of our food and agricultural sciences.* Washington, DC: North Central Region RICOP Curricular Committee Project, U.S. Department of Agriculture, pp. 115–130.

Smelser, N. (1985). Evaluating the model of structural differentiation in relation to educational change in the nineteenth century. In Jeffrey Alexander (Ed.). *Neofunctionalism.* Beverly Hills, CA: Sage, pp. 113–129.

APPENDIX A

A MISSION STATEMENT FOR UNDERGRADUATE EDUCATION IN THE COLLEGE OF AGRICULTURAL AND LIFE SCIENCES UNIVERSITY OF WISCONSIN-MADISON

The purpose of this mission statement is to provide a framework for continually examining and restructuring the college's curriculum to provide undergraduate education adequate to meet societal needs as we enter the twenty-first century.

First, this statement presents some general goals for undergraduate education in the college. Second, it lists further educational outcomes that a revitalized curriculum should achieve, along with some competencies all graduates should attain. Finally, it emphasizes the strengths and traditions that enable the college to provide superior undergraduate education on a campus providing an outstanding complement of curriculum and resources.

Goals

Through high quality, creative instruction, the college seeks to provide students with information and skills, and to help them develop attitudes and values that enable them to preserve, manage, and develop natural, biological, physical, and human resources for the benefit of the world.

Within at least one academic area of the college, students should understand and appreciate the current theories, principles, issues, and problems, and know where to find current information. All students should know how knowledge is generated, be able to critically evaluate data, and understand the contributions research can make to solutions of problems.

Above all, the college should provide an environment conducive to learning, one that stimulates intellectual curiosity, capacity for individual growth, and desire for lifelong learning.

Beyond curriculum, the college will provide students with opportunities to develop and display their leadership, citizenship and service.

Educational Outcomes

The college's goal is to further provide every student with these attributes:

- Specialized knowledge, including historical consciousness, in at least one discipline, but with educational breadth sufficient to meet the challenges of changing careers and opportunities

- Ability to think critically and creatively, to synthesize, analyze, and integrate ideas for decision-making and problem solving

- An international consciousness, and an appreciation for interdependencies among individuals and their work places, communities, environments, and world, and an understanding of the interrelationships among agriculture, technology, and society

- Ability to work with others, in small or large groups, to recognize civic and social responsibilities, and to appreciate the uses of public policy in a democracy

- Respect for truth, tolerance for diverse views, and a sense of personal and professional ethics

- Ability to communicate effectively through writing and speaking, by observing, reading, and listening, and in using appropriate technology for information management

Unique Strengths

The college will strive to provide educational programs of statewide, national, and international significance by emphasizing:

- A tradition of freedom of thought, search for truth, and belief in democratic processes and ideals

- A philosophy of instruction built on the land grant university strengths of research and public education, with administration and faculty dedicated to meeting the needs of society

- Curriculum diversity and flexibility that meet the educational needs and aspirations of students from every culture and nation

- Richness of extracurricular educational opportunities through student organizations, internships and career programs

- Faculty whose teaching and research place them at the forefront of knowledge and who contribute their expertise in the classroom and throughout the world

- Libraries and laboratories equipped to support the college's teaching, research, and public service goals

2

CHALLENGING FACULTY TO IMPROVE TEACHING AND LEARNING

Joyce Povlacs Lunde
University of Nebraska-Lincoln

Leaders of the curricular projects in the colleges of agriculture at Wisconsin, Minnesota, and Nebraska recognized from the beginning that if changes were going to be made, curriculum revision and faculty development had to go hand in hand. On each of our campuses similar questions were raised. How will faculty be motivated to participate? What new knowledge and skills do they need? How will they gain an understanding of broader issues and current trends in education? How can they better meet student needs and teach the competencies expected by employers? How will faculty learn about and implement new subject matter, new interdisciplinary approaches, and new instructional methods and strategies in their teaching? Each of our programs attempted to answer these questions by offering components which were designed to contribute to faculty development.

DIMENSIONS OF FACULTY DEVELOPMENT

In the last decade, the call to improve undergraduate education by improving teaching and learning across disciplines and institutions focused attention on the need for faculty development (e.g., Study Group on the Conditions of Excellence in Higher Education, 1984; Association of American Colleges, 1985; Katz and Henry, 1988; Boyer, 1987; Boyer, 1990). Faculty development to improve teaching has long been a feature of colleges of agriculture and natural resources, although few formal programs have existed (Simerly, 1990a; Simerly, 1990b). An assessment of faculty development in agriculture and natural resources found a "need for greater attention to

13

faculty development…, renewal, or redirection in teaching and research" (Chudzinksi, Simerly, and George, 1988, p.xv). In 1989, "Operation Change," a strategic plan to develop human resources, published by the National Association of State Universities and Land Grant Colleges (Hartung and Goecker, 1989), called for all colleges of agriculture and natural resources to have programs of faculty development by 1993. At a conference sponsored by the National Research Council of the Board on Agriculture in April 1991, the need for faculty development was a frequently-mentioned topic (Board on Agriculture, 1992).

Calls for faculty development across institutions of higher education are much in evidence. The meaning of the term "faculty development" may vary, however, and it has indeed been defined and refined in higher education over the past two decades. Originally, it signified funds for research and scholarship or support for sabbatical leaves. Today the term has come to designate one of three approaches to the improvement of the academic climate: faculty (or personal), instructional, and organizational development. The phrase "faculty development," in a restricted sense, denotes the provision of resources for the faculty member as teacher, scholar, and individual. Instructional development focuses on the course, the curriculum, and student learning. Organizational development includes the institutional structure and its components (POD, n.d.).

The Kellogg-supported projects on each of our campuses contained elements of all three kinds of development. Curricular revitalization was to be brought about by focusing on the faculty member as teacher, by designing new learning experiences, and by addressing changes in programs and organizational structure across our colleges and institutions. Activities associated with faculty development included workshops, seminars, retreats, grants, and face-to-face consultation about development of learning experiences and improvement of teaching. At the end of the projects, project leaders reaffirmed their commitment to faculty development. Our views, however, had been enlarged by our practices—by what went well and what did not go as well on our three campuses. This essay includes a brief description of programs at Wisconsin and Minnesota, followed by an extended example of the program at Nebraska and the lessons learned.

WISCONSIN: FACULTY DEVELOPMENT

In the Wisconsin Curricular Revitalization Project, faculty development was promoted as a means of increasing faculty awareness of the importance of undergraduate instruction and helping faculty members get started on effective professional development activities. When the curricular revitalization project was being formulated, the best opportunities for assisting faculty development seemed to be in increasing computer literacy, providing resources to manage academic stress, and financially supporting the development of new courses and curriculum revision.

Computer Literacy

Computer literacy was a problem for some instructors because they did not have access to computers in their offices, and because they also were reluctant to reveal their lack of knowledge and skill to other faculty and—especially—to students. Therefore a course was developed that would cover DOS, word processing, spreadsheets, graphics, data base management, statistical functions, and electronic communications. The Wisconsin College of Agricultural and Life Sciences (CALS) purchased eleven laptop computers for loan to instructors while they participated in the program. The curriculum project hired a computer instructor to conduct five series of sessions, each series being a once a week class for each week. In addition to these meetings, the instructor met privately with each participant in the participant's office to help with special difficulties. Ninety-seven instructors participated in the five series. Participants reported significant increases in their skills and confidence in using the computer as a teaching aid.

Academic Stress

The first approach considered for dealing with academic stress was to invite stress management experts to address faculty who were concerned about the problem of stress. It soon became evident that the persons most in need of assistance in stress management probably would not attend such sessions. Therefore a series of videotapes and related instructional materials were developed for distribution to departments and use by faculty members, spouses, and families, in the privacy of their homes or offices. The videotapes and related material draw on the expertise of Hamilton McCubbin, Dean of the School of Family Resources and Consumer Sciences and a nationally-known researcher on the effects of stress. The tapes also feature many CALS faculty discussing various aspects of stress in their lives (*Coping with Academic Stress,* 1989). This videotape series has been used on campus, and other universities have purchased copies for use on their campuses.

Course and Curriculum Development

The Curricular Revitalization Project also made funds available for mini-grants to faculty to develop course offerings and to promote curricular change throughout the college. As a result of these grants, undergraduates now can choose from revitalized or new courses in topics as diverse as applied demography, crop evolution and domestication, food service, forage management and utilization, insect ecology, media methods and advertising, and wildlife resource planning. In addition, new laboratory techniques, case studies, software, and computer-aided instruction have been incorporated into other existing courses.

In addition to the videotapes, a set of audiotapes titled *I Want to Learn, Not Just Remember* (1989) also was developed to enhance faculty teaching practices. In order to better serve a student population that includes a growing number of people over 25 years of age, the Curricular Revitalization Project produced a series of five audiotapes focusing on the older student in the classroom. Fifty copies of the tapes and accompanying booklet were distributed to all departments in the college for use by faculty.

MINNESOTA: FACULTY DEVELOPMENT

The faculty development component of Project Sunrise at Minnesota was linked to the mission statement in the grant proposal to Kellogg (1986): *To provide leadership and direction to a College of Agriculture effort, involving all faculty, in defining discipline-based curricula that focus on superior preparation of the student for today's technological, integrated and international society* (Project Sunrise First Annual Report).

The main strategy was to offer college-wide events consisting of workshops, seminars, and retreats in curriculum areas of the project. These covered such topics as leadership, communication, problem solving, interdisciplinary approaches, international perspectives, and societal values. In addition, a program of mini-grants provided opportunities for growth to individual faculty engaged in various course development projects. The project director was available to facilitate workshops and help faculty make changes.

Workshops and Retreats

Two curriculum retreats at the beginning of Project Sunrise provided organizational contexts for faculty development. At these retreats, the dean, department heads, and faculty representatives learned methods for reviewing and revising curricula, and considered issues of college-wide goals, learner outcomes, and areas for improvement. Participants returned home committed to bring about changes, as noted in the Project Sunrise First Annual Report.

During the first year of Project Sunrise, 162 faculty attended 40 retreats, faculty development seminars, and workshops. Many seminar and workshop leaders were nationally known authorities, and presentations usually were interactive. Topics included active learning, problem solving, cooperative learning, teaching, curriculum, writing, and thinking skills.

The faculty development emphasis shifted over the duration of Project Sunrise. Initial faculty development activities encouraged others to try new teaching methods and to apply for course development grants. In the second year of Project Sunrise, the seminars continued. Topics included ethics and values and leadership. These seminars were less well attended than those of the previous year, perhaps due to other activities in the project. The emphasis had shifted from learning to design and action. Also, most faculty were working on other Sunrise committees and projects and were learning by working with groups and implementing mini-grants. Faculty development also was shifted to two college-wide events: Computer Expo and the Global Perspectives Conference.

Mini Grant Projects

Throughout Project Sunrise, faculty members across the curriculum engaged in a total of 29 mini-grant curricular projects. These included projects which focused on: helping other faculty incorporate elements such as writing and historical perspectives in their classes; conducting research on thinking skills; instituting cooperative learning in courses in animal sciences and food sciences; developing a "strawberry patch" computer simulation; and initiating computer software projects and capstone courses in other disciplines and courses.

In the final year of Project Sunrise, faculty development was not a separate entity. Faculty development came in the form of consultations on the case study method, with 21 cases being developed by participating faculty.

NEBRASKA: FACULTY DEVELOPMENT

Faculty development in NUPAGE (University of Nebraska New Partners in Agriculture and Education) was an outgrowth of ongoing programs and opportunities. Faculty members in the college had (and continue to have) access to teaching improvement and professional development consultation. For more than a decade before the start of NUPAGE, the University's Teaching and Learning Center offered a program of workshops and individual consultation to improve teaching, as well as the services of an instructional consultant to work with both individuals and groups of faculty in the college in teaching improvement activities. In the 1980s, the Instructional Improvement Committee of the College of Agricultural Sciences and Natural Resources (CASNR) provided leadership in planning and implementing teaching improvement activities. A professional development program, which originated in the early 1980s as a cooperative program with the University of Minnesota College of Agriculture, focused on faculty careers in the context of institutional needs (Lunde and Hartung, 1990).

In NUPAGE, elements of faculty development and the other strategies designed to bring about curricular change were closely related. The goal for new curricula at Nebraska was to create new integrated learning experiences for students across the departments and disciplines of the college. We intended to include faculty, students, and external partners in these efforts. The major tools of change were grants to faculty to design new learning experiences in such areas of emphasis as communications, ethics and values, problem solving, interdisciplinary work, and active learning. The process of submitting and implementing NUPAGE grants and working with colleagues and students in teams also had faculty development effects (as reported below). The major strategy intended as faculty development was the NUPAGE Seminar required for those who had received NUPAGE grants.

The NUPAGE Seminar

In NUPAGE, faculty development was first conceptualized as teaching improvement. Project leaders proposed holding five semester-long seminars, meeting for two hours once a week, and convening a new group of participants each semester. The purpose was to encourage faculty to work cooperatively and to learn new approaches to teaching and instructional methods as they developed their learning experiences.

In addition, workshops co-sponsored with the university's Teaching and Learning Center were included as activities of the NUPAGE Seminar. Topics of workshops during the first seminars included "Approaches to Multi-Disciplinary Teaching," presented by Barbara Leigh Smith and Jean MacGregor, Evergreen College, and "Teaching Ethics Across the Curriculum," presented by Vincent Ruggiero, independent consultant, New York.

Topics introduced in the NUPAGE Seminar included: the systematic and conceptual filters models of curriculum design (Davis and Alexander, 1977; Stark et al., 1988); cooperative learning (Johnson and Johnson, n.d.); engaging students in the learning process (Study Group on the Conditions of Excellence in Higher Education, 1984; Chickering and Gamson, 1987; Chickering, Gamson, and Barsi, 1989); classroom assessment (Cross and Angelo, 1988); guided design and critical thinking (Wales, Nardi, and Stager, 1987); learning styles (Kolb, 1985); interdisciplinary teaching (e.g. Peters, 1982; Beckman, 1989); case studies (Christensen, 1987); and a systems approach using the learning spiral (Wilson and Morren, 1990). (The learning spiral recognizes different kinds of systems from reductionist to technological to hard systems to soft systems. The complexity of problems addressed by the application of these systems increases from the simplest at the reductionist level to the most complex at the soft systems level.)

The last several meetings of the seminar were reserved for presentations by participating teams, who presented their projects to the group as a whole and "taught" a lesson. Students were invited into the seminar to participate in the presentations and to give feedback to the faculty.

The first NUPAGE Seminar had 12 faculty participants, three leaders (two project directors and an invited faculty member who also was a member of the NUPAGE Board), and four students who gave feedback. The five projects represented by faculty participants covered these topics: critical thinking skills, a case study approach in food product development, the science of food, written communication in animal science courses, and an interdisciplinary internship in agricultural systems management (encompassing range management, animal science, and agricultural economics).

Participant evaluations of the first seminar were mixed. Sixty-nine percent reported gaining "new ideas, approaches, insights, or perspectives regarding teaching and learning in the seminar." Only about half of the participants, however, reported that what they learned in the seminar would have impact on their teaching. In the second year, which had nine individuals participating, the attitudes were slightly more positive (Selection Research, Inc., 1990). See Table 2-1 for a comparison of results of evaluations of the first two seminars.

As a result of feedback from the seminar the first time around, leaders revised the offerings and held fewer sessions. Altogether, five seminars were offered during the grant period. The last seminars met approximately three times during the semester. Student involvement and faculty presentations, however, were retained as features of all NUPAGE seminars. To compensate for fewer seminar meetings, more work was done with faculty in one-to-one consultations.

Other NUPAGE Support

Other parts of NUPAGE, beyond the seminar and workshops, were affecting faculty development. An evaluation specialist was made available to provide some assistance in designing evaluation procedures for the individual projects. This intervention was used for only a few projects; most project teams either had their own scheme for evaluation in mind, or they were concentrating on developing the learning experience almost exclusively.

TABLE 2-1

Faculty Attitude toward the NUPAGE Seminar

Question	1989 n = 10 Ave.*	1990 n = 5 Ave.*
1. I gained new ideas, approaches, insights, or learning regarding teaching and learning.	2.77	3.00
2. I accomplished what I set out to accomplish.	2.17	2.80
3. I had the opportunity to try out a new approach to teaching.	2.75	2.33
4. I can better see how my work fits into the curriculum of the college.	2.73	2.80
5. The undergraduate students made a positive contribution to the seminar.	3.15	3.50
6. Working with other faculty was a strength of the seminar.	2.92	3.00
7. I made better use of partners beyond the UNL faculty.	2.38	3.20
8. I am optimistic that the learning experience will contribute to the curriculum of the college.	3.77	3.80
9. Participating in the seminar will make little or no impact on what I teach.	2.54**	2.00**
10. The entire NUPAGE experience has been worth my time.	2.58	3.00

*Response: 4 = strongly agree; 3 = agree; 2 = disagree; 1 = strongly disagree
** Note negative item where strongly disagree is preferred response.

[Adapted from a table in End-of-Year Evaluation Report, NUPAGE Project (Third Project Year) (1991), The Gallup Organization, p. 21.]

The use of partners in the developmental stages, however, was becoming better understood and more consistent. The outreach coordinator, whose main task was to help identify partners, served as a facilitator for faculty, partner, and student meetings (as described elsewhere in this volume.)

NUPAGE FACULTY DEVELOPMENT: A STUDY

NUPAGE interventions were ultimately successful, but at the same time they created noise and disequilibrium. At the end of the project and after the external evaluation had been completed, project leaders conducted a study of all strategies of NUPAGE for their potential effects on faculty development.[1]

Method

We wanted to know if participants experienced "faculty development" and if so, what the effect was and how it was achieved. Participants were asked to what degree their participation in various components of NUPAGE enhanced their faculty development. The cover letter defined faculty development for participants (similar to the definition given above in this essay). The questionnaire was mailed to 66 individuals, and 40 usable responses were returned; of these, 35 came from the College of Agricultural Sciences and Natural Resources and five were from other parts of the university. Frequency distributions and a ranking of means was used to compare participants' responses on two dimensions: the degree of faculty development experienced for each activity and outcomes achieved.

Results

Results indicated that participants felt their faculty development was enhanced by NUPAGE activities (see Table 2-2), but all activities were not perceived to be of equal value. Not everyone participated in all components of NUPAGE, nor did individual projects contain identical elements.

The top 25 percent of experiences (mean scores of 3.30 to 3.50, with 4.0 being high) which enhanced faculty development included: the process of designing the learning experience itself; working on an interdisciplinary team; interacting with colleagues; and disseminating results of their project. The middle 50 percent (mean scores of 2.72 to 3.25) included such experiences as revitalizing a current course; designing a new instructional approach; disseminating project results at a meeting; proposal submission; and working with external partners. The bottom 25 percent (mean scores of 2.42 to 2.46) included activities related to NUPAGE administrative functions, receiving resource materials, working with NUPAGE staff, and attending NUPAGE-sponsored workshops.

These rankings are not surprising. Participants rated those elements which they themselves originated and developed more highly than ones imposed by the project. Pride of ownership and a sense of accomplishment grew as a result of extensive work, implementation, and sharing of work with others. When this survey was conducted, most participants were implementing their projects. As is often the case, faculty learn from each other; discovering new colleagues and relating to old colleagues in new ways produce both excitement and motivation. Also at the time this survey was conducted, the Curriculum Revitalization Task Force was meeting to integrate NUPAGE gains into the general education requirements of the college. Student partners had been included not only in the seminar but also in individual projects and in task force activity. The

NUPAGE outreach coordinator had been especially involved with individual projects in obtaining external partners and facilitating meetings. While these elements had not been designed as faculty development interventions, they had a faculty development effect, according to the respondents in our survey.

TABLE 2-2

Perceptions of Nebraska faculty regarding the degree to which NUPAGE project activities enhanced their faculty development (1989–1992)

Rank/Activity	Ave.*	N
Top 25 percent		
1. Designed a new course	3.50	16
2. Designed an interdisciplinary experience	3.41	24
3. Worked with project team	3.37	29
4. Designed a new major	3.30	16
5. Increased contact with colleagues	3.30	40
Middle 50 percent		
6. Revitalized current course	3.25	16
7. Designed new instructional approach	3.06	17
8. Disseminated information at a meeting	2.93	31
9. Designed other curricular innovations	2.91	22
10. Submitted final NUPAGE proposal	2.90	30
11. Worked with external partners	2.86	30
12. Submitted NUPAGE pre-proposal	2.83	30
13. Participated in curricular task force	2.72	22
Bottom 25 percent		
14. Used NUPAGE resource materials	2.65	26
15. Worked with outreach coordinator	2.60	28
16. worked with student partners	2.60	30
17. Worked with NUPAGE directors	2.51	37
18. Participated in required NUPAGE seminar	2.46	26
19. Attended NUPAGE workshops	2.42	26

*Response choices: [My faculty development was] 4 = greatly enhanced; 3 = somewhat enhanced; 2 = slightly enhanced; 1 = not enhanced

The items rated the lowest are NUPAGE structures. As noted, as a result of feedback, the NUPAGE Seminar had been reduced in scope and presentation. Participants in the last three semesters had far less "in class" time. Likewise, the use of workshops was reduced over time. In general, faculty have a difficult time recalling workshops, their contents, and who sponsored them.

The NUPAGE seminars and workshops, however, might have had more effect than first appears. The study also asked faculty to report the outcomes they experienced and observed. Of a list of 12 items, a majority of faculty who responded agreed that they experienced "faculty development gains" as a result of NUPAGE participation. (See Table 2-3.) They reported that they developed relationships with other colleagues in the university; encouraged student creativity; developed relationships with external partners; and integrated diverse material in teaching. They also reported that their students draw information from many disciplines; are active learners; communicate more skillfully; practice better interpersonal skills; and confront values and ethics.

TABLE 2-3

Outcomes reported by Nebraska faculty based on their involvement in NUPAGE (1989–1992)*

Rank/Outcome	Ave.	N
1. I developed relationships with other colleagues in the university	3.50	34
2. My students drew information from many disciplines	3.14	29
3. I encouraged student creativity	3.10	30
4. I developed relationships with business, industry, etc. partners	3.07	29
5. I integrated diverse material when teaching	3.00	29
5. My students became active learners	3.00	28
5. My students communicated more skillfully	3.00	28
8. My students gained interpersonal skills	2.96	28
9. My students confronted values and ethics	2.91	23
10. I shifted toward problem-centered from discipline-centered teaching	2.87	23
11. I am better able to deal with change	2.84	31
12. My students gained a global perspective	2.68	22

*Response choices: 4 = highly agree; 3 = agree; 2 = disagree; 1 = highly disagree

The achievements listed in Table 2-3 are self-reported and may be overly optimistic. However, they do reflect positive attitudes toward offering more student-centered instruction and requiring more interdisciplinary integration—two basic goals of NUPAGE.

While NUPAGE participants may not have seen administrative components as especially helpful, the behind-the-scenes activity was vital to project accomplishment. The resources of faculty development were supplied and linked to individual or team needs. Even the seminar, which caused much of the early disequilibrium, did provide the setting for teams to meet, timelines and goals to be established, and an infusion of ideas, approaches, and strategies to develop new learning experiences and improve classroom teaching.

FACULTY DEVELOPMENT: LESSONS LEARNED

Faculty development in the context of curriculum revitalization did prove to be a vital part of the projects on each of our campuses. Major changes in higher education will not happen unless learning resources are provided for faculty as they become instruments of this change. Some lessons we learned in the process of our curriculum revitalization projects are:

- Faculty ownership is built by developing direction and intention in dialogue with faculty and by empowering participants to control their own projects.

- Workshops without application, and concepts without integration into the teaching experience, will fade at best and be resented at worst.

- The facilitator role in providing faculty development is vital, but may not be obvious to participants. The work of planning, evaluating, developing materials, gathering resources, and communicating mostly occurs behind the scenes.

- Conflict and resistance, in faculty development as in teaching, may be necessary preconditions to change. It may be necessary for leaders to go against the flow while remaining open and flexible to solve problems.

- Special structures, such as seminars or interdisciplinary teams, give organization and encourage community building along new lines.

- Faculty development brings about institutional change—in academic programs and in the collective will of the organization.

- The tools of faculty development can be broadly conceived: grants and mini-grants alone may not be sufficient to change faculty approaches and behavior, but when combined with opportunities for learning new things and working with colleagues, faculty become re-energized.

[I wish to thank Nancy Jo Egly, Ph.D., for her assistance in designing the study of NUPAGE faculty development and outcomes, and for collecting the data. I also thank my colleagues Professors Robert C. Sorenson and Maurice Baker for their many contributions to the analysis of NUPAGE faculty development.]

Joyce Povlacs Lunde is Associate Professor of Agricultural Leadership, Education and Communication, and Educational Specialist, Office of Professional and Organizational Development, University of Nebraska-Lincoln.

REFERENCES

Association of American Colleges. (1985). *Integrity in the college curriculum: A report to the academic community.* Washington, DC: Association of American Colleges.

Beckman, M.P. (1989). Interdisciplinary teaching in economics: How is as important as why. *College Teaching,* 37(3), 101–104.

Board on Agriculture. (1992). *Agriculture and the undergraduate: Proceedings.* Washington, DC: National Academy Press.

Boyer, E. L. (1987). *The undergraduate experience in America.* Princeton, NJ: Carnegie Foundation for the Advancement of Teaching.

Boyer, E. L. (1990). *Scholarship reconsidered: Priorities of the professoriate.* Special report, the Carnegie Foundation for the Advancement of Teaching. Lawrenceville, NJ: Princeton University Press.

Chickering, A.W., & Gamson, Z. F. (March, 1987). Seven principles for good practice in undergraduate education. *AAHE Bulletin,* 39(7), 3–7.

Chickering, A.W., Gamson, Z. F., & Barsi, L. M. (1989). *Seven principles for good practice in undergraduate education: Faculty inventory.* Racine, WI: Johnson Foundation, Inc. Wingspread.

Christensen, C. R. (1987). *Teaching and the case method: Text, cases, and readings.* Boston, MA: Harvard Business School.

Chudzinski, L. Z., Simerly, C. B., & George, W. L. (1988). *National assessment of faculty development needs in colleges of agriculture.* Urbana, IL: College of Agriculture, University of Illinois.

Coping with academic stress. (1989). [Videotape series]. College of Agricultural and Life Sciences, University of Wisconsin-Madison: Board of Regents.

Cross, K. P., & Angelo, T. A. (1988). *Classroom assessment techniques: A handbook for faculty development.* National Center for Research to Improve Postsecondary Teaching and Learning Technical Report No. 88-A-004.0. University of Michigan, Ann Arbor: Board of Regents. (Now available as Angelo, T. & Cross, P. (1993). Second Edition. San Francisco, CA: Jossey-Bass.)

Davis, R. H., & Alexander, L. T. (1977). *Guides for the improvement of instruction in higher education.* East Lansing, MI: Michigan State University, Board of Trustees.

Hartung, T. E., & Goecker, A. D. (1989). *Operation change: An action agenda for developing human capital to secure American agriculture.* Resident Instruction Committee on Organization and Policy. Washington, DC: Association of State Universities and Land-Grant Colleges.

I Want to Learn, Not Just Remember. (1989). In *Third annual report: Integrative approach to curricular assessment and faculty development.* Madison, WI: College of Agricultural and Life Sciences, Curricular Revitalization Project. p. 22.

Johnson, D.W., Johnson, R. T., & Holubec, E. J. (n.d.). *Learning together and learning alone* [workshop material]. Minneapolis, MN: University of Minnesota, Cooperative Learning Center.

Katz, J., & Henry, M. (1988). *Turning professors into teachers: A new approach to faculty development and student learning.* New York, NY: ACE/Macmillan.

Kolb, D. (1985). *Learning style inventory.* Boston, MA: McBer and Associates.

Lunde, J.P., & Hartung, T.E. (1990). Integrating individual and organizational needs: The University of Nebraska, Lincoln. In Schuster, J. J. & Wheeler, D.W. (Eds.), *Enhancing faculty careers: Strategies for development and renewal.* San Francisco, CA: Jossey-Bass.

Peters, D.S. (1982). Interdisciplinary teaching. *Alternative Higher Education.* 6(4), 229–241.

POD (Professional and Organizational Development Network in Higher Education). (n.d.). *An informational brochure about faculty, instructional, and organizational development: Prepared for faculty and administrators.* Ames, IA: Iowa State University, Professional and Organizational Development Network in Higher Education.

Selection Research, Inc. (August 1990). *End-of-year evaluation report: NUPAGE project (second project year).* Lincoln, NE: SRI.

Simerly, C.B. (March 1990a). A national assessment: Faculty development needs in colleges of agriculture. *NACTA Journal,* XXXIV (1), 11–14.

Simerly, C.B. (June 1990b). Faculty development: A strategy for revitalization and change. *NACTA Journal,* XXXIV (2), 14–17.

Stark, J.S., Lowther, M.A., Ryan, M.P., Bomotti, S.S., Genthon, M., Haven, C.L., & Martens, G. (1988). *Reflections on course planning: Faculty and students consider influences and goals.* Ann Arbor, MI: University of Michigan, School of Education.

Study Group on the Conditions of Excellence in Higher Education (1984). *Involvement in learning: Realizing the potential of American higher education.* Washington, DC: National Institute of Education.

Wales, C.E., Nardi, A.H., & Stager, R. A. (1987). *Thinking skills: Making a choice.* Morgantown, WV: Charles E. Wales, Anne H. Nardi, and Robert A. Stager.

Wilson, K., & Morren E.B. (1990). *Systems approaches for improvement in agriculture and resource management.* New York, NY: Macmillan.

3

PARTNERS IN CURRICULUM DEVELOPMENT

Maurice Baker and Rebecca L. Thomas
University of Nebraska-Lincoln

Cooperative learning is the instructional use of small groups in which students work together to maximize their own and each other's learning (Johnson, et al, 1991; Johnson & Johnson, 1985; Holubec, 1993). It dates back at least to the first century and was the general basis for teaching for centuries. It was not until the late 1930s that schools began to emphasize competitive education (Johnson & Johnson, 1992). While cooperative learning has traditionally been looked upon as a classroom philosophy and application, it also is a useful model for understanding "partners" in other educational situations.

The idea of using students and external partners in curriculum development is based on the premise that much can be learned from others. Partners can be used in a variety of ways, as demonstrated by the Universities of Wisconsin, Minnesota, and Nebraska, who used student, faculty, and external partners in their curriculum revitalization projects.

UNIVERSITY OF WISCONSIN

The College of Agricultural and Life Sciences (CALS) at the University of Wisconsin enlisted students as partners in studying revitalization of the curriculum. Students were included on project steering committees, but scheduling conflicts and graduation frequently limited the students' contributions. Indirect student partnering at CALS occurred through a student survey and analysis of transcripts. The survey was sent to all December 1987 graduates of CALS. They were asked to respond to questions about the amount of emphasis given to core requirements and to provide input about a variety of other topics, including major requirements, the number of credits required to graduate, and electives in their programs. The students also were asked to consider the educational outcomes outlined in a draft mission statement and to judge the effectiveness of their educational experience in meeting these outcomes. Analysis of student transcripts provided information about how students currently were meeting the curriculum requirements.

CALS also invited agribusiness executives, employers of CALS graduates, and CALS alumni to participate in its "Executives in Residence" program to draw on the expertise of these external partners. These partners, in addition to high school teachers, gave their views on CALS' curriculum revitalization plans, and their comments were recorded and used in further study of the future curriculum.

Partners were used in a variety of learning experiences available for students, including the "Quest Fellowship Program" (a program for 20 very talented students who were invited to be part of a learning community). Partners in this program included representatives of businesses, who accompanied students on field trips, as well as faculty who were responsible for presentations in the seminar.

Faculty and external partners are regularly used as resource people in the "Human/Animal Relationships: Biological and Philosophical Issues" course. This course was designed and initially taught by a team of faculty from diverse disciplines, and faculty and external partners continue to be involved.

UNIVERSITY OF MINNESOTA

The University of Minnesota's "Project Sunrise" established partnerships with 29 employers of College of Agriculture graduates in reviewing and guiding the development of the curriculum. These partners participated in both group and individual interviews.

All partners were asked to respond to the following 10 questions:

1. What position(s) reports to you? or Whom do you recruit and supervise?

2. What majors do you recruit/want to hire? What major do you want to see on a resume?

3. What qualities do you seek in job applicants? What qualities are most important on the job?

4. We've heard that some employers are becoming more interested in hiring liberal arts graduates rather than graduates from the College of Agriculture. What is your reaction to this?

5. What, if any, is the value of arts and humanities in an undergraduate program? What kinds of courses are more important than others?

6. We've been told that leadership is an important quality employers like to see in job applicants. Please give specific examples of employees demonstrating leadership in your organization. How would you determine that an employee has leadership skills?

7. We've been told that problem solving is an important quality employers like to see in job applicants. Please give specific examples of employees demonstrating problem solving in your organization. How would you determine that an employee has problem solving skills?

8. We've been told that ethics/values awareness is an important quality employers like to see in job applicants. Please give specific examples of employees demonstrating ethics/values awareness in your organization. How would you determine that an employee has ethics/values awareness skills?

9. Does your organization have educational or training needs that the University of Minnesota College of Agriculture could help meet, on-the-job and/or through off-campus degree programs?

10. What else would you like to say to the University of Minnesota College of Agriculture?

It was clear that respondents welcomed the opportunity to participate as partners in the curriculum review and enhancement process and to be partners in a variety of other ways, including giving guest presentations and meeting informally with students. They also suggested students and faculty obtain more industry experience. While they did not explicitly volunteer to be partners in the latter activity, it is fair to conclude they would be willing to consider making opportunities available for such activities.

UNIVERSITY OF NEBRASKA

The University of Nebraska-Lincoln curriculum development project, New Partnerships in Agriculture and Education (NUPAGE), was aimed toward more integration across disciplines and problem solving skills in the curriculum. The objectives were both curriculum development and faculty development. The intent of the latter objective was to help faculty become familiar with new approaches to course and curriculum development and implementation for an integrated curriculum.

The proposal to the W. K. Kellogg Foundation was built around a conceptual model which included partnerships. The idea was to enhance existing partnerships and to develop new ones in order to restructure old courses and develop new ones. Focusing courses on integrative experiences for students would create a more integrated curriculum and enhance student problem solving skills.

Project Guidelines for Using Partners

It was not the intent to replace existing interdisciplinary courses, but to build on this partnership model. The guidelines for the project encouraged partnerships between faculty within the College of Agricultural Sciences and Natural Resources (CASNR) and between CASNR faculty and faculty from other colleges at the University of Nebraska. Project guidelines also encouraged the full participation of students and off-campus partners, drawn from production agriculture, agribusiness, government agencies, and other organizations, in the planning and development of learning experiences. These partners were to be active participants from the early stages of conceptualization and development to initial implementation—not merely reactors after a proposal had been developed.

The NUPAGE staff and board developed guidelines for submitting proposals for developing new learning experiences. These experiences could be either for credit or non-credit, and they could be either direct student learning experiences or faculty development efforts which would later translate into student learning opportunities. The proposal guidelines asked the proposers to "attempt creative and innovative educational approaches or curricular combinations." They further asked that the project "involve partners from other disciplines or from agencies and businesses external to the university when appropriate."

Resources Provided for Working with Partners

Funds were made available for faculty release time, to pay honoraria to students and off-campus partners, as well as to cover other miscellaneous expenses. This approach was used to reduce the inertia which often occurs in the modification and development of learning experiences. How many times have we heard the statement, "I would sure like to do this, but I don't have the time or money it requires."

A key ingredient in the implementation of this model was an outreach coordinator who worked with faculty teams who either were considering a proposal or had received a grant from the Kellogg funds, to help them visualize how to utilize student and off-campus partners. The outreach coordinator encouraged faculty teams to work with partners and, when necessary, helped identify and contact people who could make significant contributions toward development of the learning experience. During the project, the outreach coordinator was able to change faculty attitudes about the role of students and off-campus people in course and curriculum development.

While partners provided significant input to the curriculum revitalization project, the modification and development of all learning experiences were faculty-initiated. This is important since "ownership" is necessary to implement changes. It is also important because academic custom, if not bylaws, places control of curricula in the hands of the faculty.

Faculty are accustomed to peer review of research publications and course outlines; however, many are reluctant to permit their peers, much less students and off-campus people, to be closely involved with the development of courses. They hesitate to expose preliminary and intermediate products to others' scrutiny (what we came to call the "muddling through" or trial and error stage of curricular development). It is difficult to expose what we do not know, particularly to people with whom we have not established a trust through a previous working relationship. Through the outreach coordinator's efforts, many faculty teams were able to overcome the deterrents to developing meaningful partnerships.

TABLE 3-1

Number of partners directly and indirectly involved in the development of NUPAGE projects.

Item	CASNR[1]	UNL Faculty	Students	External Partners	Other[2]	Total
Direct						
Individual Projects	74	14	136	72	11	307
Council	10	8	2	8	0	28
NUPAGE Seminar	1	0	10	1	0	12
Total	85	22	148	81	11	347
Indirect[3]	369	68	1,710	0	0	2,147
Total	454	90	1,858	81	11	2,494

[1] College of Agricultural Sciences and Natural Resources
[2] Includes graduate students, teaching assistants and technical experts
[3] Includes ad hoc committees, faculty and student input groups, a number of pilot classes, and audiences at presentations

The outreach coordinator's willingness to make initial contacts, and even set up and facilitate meetings of the expanded project team, removed some of the disincentives which faculty felt in trying to use student and off-campus partners. The outreach coordinator's efforts as a facilitator of the first team meetings also removed the perception of additional barriers involved in adding student and off-campus partners to the team. The availability of funds to pay honoraria to these partners also counteracted the reluctance of some faculty to ask people to work with them. This process generally expanded the base from which partners were solicited, resulting in consideration of a greater breadth of ideas.

Meetings with NUPAGE Partners

The initial meetings of the teams were designed to generate ideas and views rather than to develop details of the course or other learning experience under consideration. The general format was to ask small groups of participants to react to a question regarding topics critical to the new or redesigned course, followed by feedback to the entire group before a new question was addressed. The composition of the groups varied depending upon the kind of information and reactions being solicited. Sometimes the groups included representatives from faculty, students, and external partners; sometimes each small group consisted only of faculty, students, or external partners. These sessions were largely idea-generating; therefore, the ideas were solicited but not judged at the time. Records of the ideas were made on flipcharts and displayed around the room so all could see, providing opportunity for input by everyone and not just the ones in each small group. This approach had the added effect of permitting greater input, since ideas were not immediately judged.

Value of the Active Partnership Model

The active partnership model provides opportunity for meeting the needs of students and prospective employers. Since faculty have no monopoly on intellectual ideas and concepts, a more broadly based team of partners to provide for an active intellectual exchange seems sensible.

The active partnerships model has been adopted by a significant number of faculty teams as they developed or modified learning experiences. Student partners helped a team of animal science and agricultural communications faculty understand the unworkability of their preliminary idea of asking students to spend considerable time on writing activities with no credit. This same team has extensively utilized off-campus partners, not only to help design the writing-across-the-discipline plan, but to explain its importance to the faculty and students.

External partners legitimize the actions of the team output since they are perceived by non-team faculty and students as having a practical view. One student said to a technical writing instructor "this stuff is useful" the day after hearing external partners explain the importance of good technical communications skills.

Still another use of partners is to have them help through classroom participation as resource people. An example of the latter is the agricultural ethics course developed at the University of Nebraska-Lincoln. (This project is described more fully in Section Six of this volume.) A team consisting of an agricultural communications specialist, an agricultural economist, and a philosopher drew upon the intellectual capital of an off-campus partner not only to help develop an agricultural ethics course, but to participate actively as an instructor the first time the course was taught. As the external partner's time permits, the team still draws upon him to assist in the classroom.

LESSONS LEARNED

While partners were used in a variety of ways, faculty were generally, but not universally, reluctant at first to include other faculty partners in course development. This reluctance was much milder than the opposition expressed when it was suggested that students and off-campus people could be valuable additions to the planning team. There seemed to be a feeling of loss of control rather than an addition to the intellectual capital available to develop a stronger learning experience. However, the addition of non-faculty team members generally was accepted enthusiastically once these people participated. Some of the strongest proponents of non-faculty partners were among the more reluctant at first.

NUPAGE faculty project leaders were encouraged to identify students, other faculty, and professionals external to the university early in their efforts, so they could draw from the knowledge and experience of all of the participants rather than rely solely upon the faculty experience. This also had the added advantage of conveying to the students and external partners that their input was critical to the project, rather than mere reaction to a nearly finished product.

In all cases, external partners welcomed the opportunity to participate in curriculum review and enhancement. Most of them participated in projects voluntarily or for a small stipend, such as $25–50 per visit, or for lunch or dinner only. External partners with both NUPAGE and the University of Minnesota expressed a desire to be involved more with the university;

therefore, faculty and administration should make more use of them in educational planning and implementation.

Maurice Baker is Professor of Agricultural Economics, University of Nebraska-Lincoln.

Rebecca L. Thomas is formerly Outreach Coordinator for NUPAGE, University of Nebraska-Lincoln.

REFERENCES

Johnson, D.W., & Johnson, R.T. (July–August 1985). Student-student interaction: Ignored but powerful. *Journal of Teacher Education, 37*(4), 22–26.

Johnson, D.W., & Johnson, R.T. (Spring 1992). Implementing cooperative learning. *Contemporary Education, 63*(3), 173–180.

Johnson, D.W., et al. (1991). *Cooperative learning: Increasing college faculty instructional productivity.* ASHE-ERIC Higher Education Report No. 4.

Holubec, E.J. (Spring 1993). How do you get there from here? *Contemporary Education, 63*(3), 181–184.

4

CURRICULUM REVITALIZATION AND ORGANIZATIONAL CHANGE

Laurie Schultz Hayes
University of Minnesota

W hen the University of Minnesota's College of Agriculture (COA) began to examine its curriculum in 1985, there were 18 undergraduate major programs listed in the college bulletin.[1] Four years later, the 1989-91 college bulletin listed ten undergraduate majors.[2] The process of reducing the number of majors from 18 to ten was not merely a process of subtraction, with some winners and some losers. The process was more synergistic, and the outcome was a mosaic of redesigned majors arranged within a new administrative structure. Structural change had not been a goal of the college's Project Sunrise, but its occurrence helped both to mark the emergence of a new curriculum and to sustain it.

The purpose of this essay is to describe what organization was used to change the curriculum and how the organization itself was changed in the process.

USING AN ORGANIZATION TO CHANGE A CURRICULUM

When C. Eugene Allen, then Dean of the College of Agriculture, met with the college faculty in October 1985, he asked several fundamental questions: "What do we want to be? What should be the nature of our programs? What needs should be addressed? How are we perceived by our disciplinary peers and external clientele groups?" Allen challenged the faculty to "beware of tradition and complacency," to consider the changes occurring in agriculture around the world, and to get ready for the twenty-first century.

To get things started, Dean Allen and Associate Dean W. Keith Wharton cast a wide net. They recruited faculty representatives from each department in the college to form an *ad hoc* Curriculum Task Force, and asked the task force to consider a long list of divergent issues—human learning and development, international perspectives, interdisciplinary programs, liberal education, ethics and values, and systems approaches to agriculture and the teaching of agriculture. Further, they charged the task force to work with college and department curriculum committees to develop strategies for incorporating these issues into current programs.

The college-wide task force moved slowly, but steadily. In November 1985, members attended a two-day retreat and workshop led by Robert Stake, Director of the University of Illinois Center for Instructional Research and Curriculum Evaluation. At this retreat, the task force reviewed the college assets, identified obstacles to curricular revision, and drafted a mission statement, a strategic plan, and a timetable. During the next few months, they met several times and developed and submitted to the W. K. Kellogg Foundation a pre-proposal for funding, advised the faculty of the task force mission and activities, met with departmental and college curriculum coordinators to discuss revision plans, and developed a full proposal for the Kellogg Foundation.

Project Sunrise Administrative Roles

Project Sunrise, the name given to the curricular enhancement project funded by the Kellogg Foundation, finally started in October 1986. During the first year of the grant, most activities centered around individual faculty development and the college-wide definition of educational objectives or learner outcomes. A key organizational feature introduced during this time was the role of project director. Grant funds provided for the 60% appointment of a person responsible for directing, planning, managing, supervising, and evaluating all aspects of the project; the director also was charged with involving as many college administrators, faculty, and students as possible.[3] Funds also were provided for a secretary (50–75% time) to assist the project director and to be the chief project contact person for all parties interested in or working on project activities. In retrospect, an important lesson learned was the value of having an experienced project director who was a "new face" in the college, who had no political debts to pay or enemies to avoid, and who had a task to finish by a firm deadline.

Support Structures for Project Sunrise

The project director looked to three administrative groups for advice and support. Each of these groups provided project guidance without additional funds or release time:

- The college-wide Project Sunrise task force that had worked originally to secure funding from the Kellogg Foundation continued to meet bimonthly and to act as the project director's advisory board.

- The College of Agriculture dean and associate dean met periodically with the project director to jointly plan strategy and to make final decisions on certain budget allocations.

- The College's executive team of deans and department heads included the project director in its bimonthly meetings, to hear progress reports and provide feedback on significant project issues.

This structure not only resulted in 100% participation by college administrators, heads of all college departments, and at least one faculty representative from each department, but fostered a reasonably open and active communication network, as well.

Another layer of college participation was introduced after an all-college retreat in September 1987. The deans, working together with the department heads and the college curriculum committee, appointed seven workgroups. Each workgroup included at least one department head, one undergraduate student, and several faculty members representing a cross-section of departments. The general charge for all groups was to identify issues, concerns, and objectives for the group's topic; develop recommended action plans and timetables; and bring the group's plans and recommendations first to appropriate college committees and ultimately to the Faculty Assembly for approval. The workgroups and their assignments included:

- *Learner Outcomes:* Recommend the learner outcomes appropriate for all COA bachelor's-level graduates; begin by consolidating results of 1987 COA curriculum retreat.

- *Majors:* Recommend a reduced number of COA undergraduate majors; recommend other appropriate majors-related revisions (e.g. names and/or descriptions of majors).

- *Senior Projects & Portfolios:* Recommend criteria, requirements, and examples of appropriate senior projects and portfolios of student work.

- *Category A & B Requirements:* Review and recommend appropriate revisions in COA's all-college Category A (communication, language, symbolic systems) and Category B (physical and biological sciences) requirements.

- *Category C & D Requirements:* Review and recommend appropriate revisions in COA's all-college Category C (psychology & social sciences) and Category D (literature, humanities, fine arts) requirements.

- *Nontraditional Educational Alternatives:* Recommend alternatives to daytime, on-campus courses for students of all ages to learn what we want them to learn, including industry experiences for students and faculty and use of technology as an alternative to face-to-face teaching.

- *Introductory Course Development:* Design one or more introductory course(s) for COA (and non-COA?) undergraduates and recommend ways to implement the course.

Outcomes of Workgroup Activities

The creation of these diverse workgroups widened the span of involvement in curricular change. Although administrators had initiated the process and broadcast their commitment to it clearly and frequently, in order for change to occur, more faculty would have to accept it, understand it, and have the opportunity to specify as much of it as possible.

Admittedly, the tasks of each workgroup differed in specificity and complexity. The activities of two groups—*Learner Outcomes* and *Senior Projects & Portfolios*—are summarized in this book in "Developing Learner Outcomes to Support a Curriculum" and "Student Portfolios for Academic and Career Advising." The *Category A & B* and *C & D* workgroups examined current general education requirements and scheduled focus group meetings to accomplish their tasks. The *Nontraditional Education Alternatives* and *Introductory Course Development* workgroups each held many meetings to discuss issues, goals, and objectives, but ultimately both were hampered by the lack of budget resources and immediately implementable action steps.[4]

The *Majors* workgroup, on the other hand, had a more concrete task and after several meetings was prepared to propose a new list of majors for the college. Aficionados of titles, labels, and course clusters might be interested in the evolution of the assortment of majors considered and discussed by college faculty between September 1987 and June 1989, but that linguistic trail will not be taken here. Instead, the narrative will continue to focus on the organizational features that led to June 1989.

In April 1988, three deans, eight department heads, and forty faculty members participated in a second all-college curriculum retreat sponsored by Project Sunrise. While the primary purpose of this retreat was to discuss the progress of each of the seven workgroups and aim for closure on their tasks, the retreat agenda showed a clear priority for reaching some agreement on the issue of college majors.

Two of the retreat's four small group sessions focused on discussion of the list of new majors proposed by the *Majors* workgroup. The first session was full of lively discussion, but little consensus was reached within and between the groups. The second session occurred on the retreat's second day with the same small groups responding to a revised list of majors proposed by the deans. The deans' recommendations addressed some of the concerns raised in the earlier session and continued to emphasize a desire for interdisciplinary majors not identified with a single department.

No conclusions were reached in these small group sessions, but retreat participants were reasonably satisfied. Retreat evaluations, in response to the questions "What did you like about this retreat?" included such phrases as "arriving at some consensus," "we are not that far apart in our thoughts—even though you may think so," and "we didn't get it all done but we're a lot closer." And in response to "What did you dislike about this retreat?" comments included "sometimes it felt like we were doing things over again," "we didn't get closure on majors," "we made only apparent progress," and "we still sat in our boxes and didn't move around."

Academic Program Committees

Following the retreat, the deans, project director, and chair of the COA curriculum committee formed new faculty committees to address the content of each proposed academic program. Each committee was asked to go beyond the name of the major and to reach consensus on such details as how the learner outcome goals of the college could be satisfied by the major, the appropriate courses for each category of requirements, and the total number of credits for the program. The end result was to be a definitive set of recommended majors to be reviewed by the curriculum committee.

Nine committees were charged in early May, gave progress reports to each other toward the end of June, summarized their activities and outcomes at a meeting of department heads in August, and met again as a group in late August. In early October the college sponsored another two-day retreat for approximately forty faculty members who shared information, ideas, and concerns about each major and discussed recommendations for the undergraduate curriculum as a whole.

A significant feature of this new committee process was the focus on academic programs, not academic departments. Each committee, composed of members from more than one college department, was responsible for designing a program and included representatives from the associate-level programs at the University of Minnesota's Crookston and Waseca campuses, as well as delegates from other University of Minnesota colleges as appropriate for the major.[5] This shift from departmental to interdepartmental ownership increased the anxiety-level of those who were used to departmental programs. Under discussion was the elimination of such traditional majors as animal science, agronomy, horticulture, and soil science and the introduction of majors with such wordy titles as: agricultural industries and marketing, animal and plant systems, natural resource and environmental studies, and science in agriculture. Would students and employers know what these mean? Others less caught up in traditional identities were still concerned about whether interdisciplinary curricula that look good on paper could withstand the political roadblocks of academic bureaucracy. How would we track and advise students who didn't have a department to call home? Who would support instructional costs in interdisciplinary courses?

To increase the degree of comfort with the new programs and minimize the concerns about adopting new curricula, the project director and chair of the curriculum committee met with the faculty and staff of each department during November. They also met with other stakeholders—the College of Agriculture Student Board, a group of employers,[6] and faculty at the Crookston and Waseca coordinate campuses. An important feature of these "road shows" was a document prepared by the project director that summarized for each of the ten proposed majors its intended audience, purpose, special features, and comparative advantages. For those who had been active participants in the curricular revision process, the document served a persuasive function, offering helpful comparisons among the proposed programs. For those who had not been involved and would be overwhelmed by more detailed curricular outlines, the document served an important informative function, summarizing the changes and their benefits at a glance.

At their fall quarter faculty meeting in December 1988, the College of Agriculture faculty unanimously passed the following motion:

That the COA Assembly approves the development and implementation of curricula for ten majors to replace the existing COA majors. (The proposed names for these new majors are: agricultural business management, agricultural education, agricultural industries and marketing, agricultural sciences, animal and plant systems, applied economics, food science, natural resources and environmental studies, nutrition, and scientific and technical communication.)

CHANGING AN ORGANIZATION TO INSTITUTIONALIZE A REVISED CURRICULUM

The curriculum approved by the COA faculty in December 1988 was supposed to be available for students in September 1989.[7] Effecting such an implementation required not only fast action, but structural change.

Major Coordinators and Coordinating Committees

The first changes that had to occur were related to the final design and eventual maintenance of the curriculum. The Dean, in consultation with the department heads, appointed a coordinator and a coordinating committee for each major. The position of major coordinator was new to the college. In the previous department-based curriculum, each department had a director of undergraduate studies who administered the department's program(s). The new role of major coordinator was to be college-wide with the selected faculty members reporting to their respective department heads, but also being responsible to the college deans and curriculum committee. More specifically, major coordinators were to coordinate all course offerings and advising in a major. Departments were encouraged to keep a director of undergraduate studies in their internal organizational structures to assume responsibility for overseeing the undergraduate courses taught in their department and for working closely with the major coordinators. The inter-departmental coordinating committees that had helped to generate the initial major programs were also empowered to work with the major coordinators to finalize the curriculum and to assist in future periodic reviews. Major coordinators were appointed for two-year terms, but long-term continuation of the major committees would ensure that a knowledgeable group of teaching and advising faculty were responsible for the curriculum.

Reconstitution of the College Curriculum Committee

Another systemic change was the reconstitution of the college curriculum committee. Up until March 1989, the curriculum committee was composed of one faculty representative from each department plus some student, staff, and administrative representatives. The committee's role was primarily reactive—most of its energy took the form of acting on department-generated course changes. At the Winter Quarter Assembly meeting, the college faculty voted to reform the curriculum committee, incorporating the ten major coordinators plus at-large faculty members from departments not represented by major coordinators, some student, staff, and administrative representatives, and non-voting representatives from each of the coordinate campuses at Crookston and Waseca. Beginning in May 1989, the new committee's work was immediate—finalizing the curriculum for the publication of a new college bulletin in June, and more proactive—sharing information across majors, reviewing college-wide requirements, and monitoring the quality of undergraduate advising. The committee's work would also include acting on many course changes as a result of the ongoing curricular revision process, but the activity would occur in more of a college-wide context than a department-specific context.

Changes in Advising

A more subtle, but equally significant, change occurred in the college faculty advising system. In the previous case of departmental majors, all student/faculty advising had taken place within an academic department. Department heads would recruit faculty as advisors and somehow monitor advising activities as a part of a faculty member's regular assignment. College officials would usually connect with a department's secretary or administrator to ensure that information was communicated and deadlines were met. In contrast, the creation of interdepartmental programs now allowed faculty in a single department (e.g. animal science) to advise in several different majors (e.g., agricultural industries and marketing, animal and plant systems, or science in agriculture), and new arrangements had to be made for communicating information to advisors through major coordinators and/or directly through an advising network.[8]

Response to Change

Many of these structural changes were viewed initially with suspicion; some still are. Overall, after five years, the majority of faculty and administrators are pleased with the reorganization. There are those, however, who think major coordinators have too much authority or not enough. There are those who wish the major committees met more frequently or less often. There are probably just as many who wish the curriculum committee would spend more time on programmatic details as there are those who would prefer more time on college-wide educational leadership. There are those who think the new curricula leave students "homeless" and those who wish students would be even more independent. Some advisors feel overwhelmed with paperwork and information, others feel isolated and uninformed. Nevertheless, most still agree that the new organization is for the best and provides the good will, cooperation, and energy necessary to hold the revitalized curriculum together.

CONCLUSIONS

Managing change in higher education is complicated, but not impossible. In the case of the University of Minnesota's College of Agriculture, a sufficiently large group of administrative and faculty leaders believed that change was in order, that a goal of change could be set and met. Because they were not heavily invested in the details of a particular outcome, however, their essential task was to keep a large enough group of people involved, informed, and oriented toward change so that change could happen.

To mark change, to make it real, things must be different when you are through. Retreat to previous habits should not be too easy. So, ultimately, change can only occur if there are also those who are willing to give painstaking attention to the small details and make necessary adjustments in the organization's structure. The College of Agriculture was lucky that a critical mass of people wanted to see the curriculum changed, implemented, and sustained and had the vision to keep the process focused, the stamina to care for the details, and the willingness to modify their behavior.

Laurie Schultz Hayes is Associate Professor of Rhetoric and Associate Dean, Curricular and Student Affairs, College of Agriculture (now College of Agricultural, Food, and Environmental Sciences), University of Minnesota.

NOTES

[1] Agricultural business administration, agricultural economics, agricultural education, agricultural engineering technology, agronomy, animal science, consumer food science, economics of public resource management, entomology, food science and technology, horticultural science, integrated pest management, landscape architecture, nutrition and dietetics, plant health technology, soil science, soil and water resource management, and technical communication.

[2] Agricultural business management, agricultural education, agricultural industries and marketing, animal and plant systems, applied economics, food science, natural resources and environmental studies, nutrition, science in agriculture, and scientific and technical communication.

[3] The person selected was Bonnie J. Pechtel, whose professional qualifications at the time included a Ph.D. in educational psychology, 12 years of training experience in a variety of settings, seven years of managerial experience, and five years of research experience in adult learning and problem solving/decision-making. She had worked with both NSF and NIE grants and was an active member of her local school board.

[4]Readers working on the development of an all-college introductory course might be interested to know that College of Agriculture faculty rejected course proposals for several reasons: unwillingness of faculty to make a commitment to teach such a course; disagreement about target audiences (agricultural vs. non-agricultural); disagreement about the purpose(s) of an introductory course; disagreement about appropriate learning experiences in such a course; cautions from interdisciplinary course faculty at Guelph University in Ontario; and concern that students already were over-burdened with requirements.

[5]At that time, several programs were offered jointly with other colleges: agricultural business management with the Carlson School of Management; agricultural education with the College of Education; natural resources and environmental studies with the College of Natural Resources; and food science, nutrition, and scientific and technical communication with the College of Home Economics.

[6]For a brief discussion of the many ways employers participated in Minnesota's Project Sunrise, see "Partners in Curriculum Development" elsewhere in this volume. A key feature of this partnership was the perspective employers brought to the issue of academic major programs. Employers told COA faculty and staff that they were willing to hire students with almost any college major for most entry-level jobs. In general, they were satisfied with the current programs and said the name of the major was less important than an applicant's experience and interests. Another valuable contribution was the endorsement by employers of the learning objectives integral to Project Sunrise. Instead of narrow specialization, employers emphasized their preference that students develop a general background with a blend of scientific and technical knowledge and business and communication skills.

[7]Beginning in the fall quarter of 1989, students entering the College of Agriculture were enrolled in one of the ten programs. Continuing students could follow their current program plans or transfer to a "new" major. Every effort was made to assure that students would not be penalized if they chose to make a transfer decision; all current credits would count toward the "new" major.

[8]Much of the preparation for this new advising system was embedded in several advisor training workshops connected to the College of Agriculture Portfolio. (See "Student Portfolios for Academic and Career Advising" elsewhere in this volume.)

SECTION 2

GENERAL EDUCATION AND CURRICULUM REVITALIZATION

Edited and with an introduction by
F. H. Buelow
University of Wisconsin-Madison

The general education requirement for undergraduate curricula has been a topic of debate on campuses for many decades. As the perceived needs for specific competencies and awareness of issues changed, the general education requirements were modified to reflect those needs. The recent curriculum revitalization projects in colleges of agriculture also addressed the need for pertinent general education requirements for all students in the various undergraduate programs.

In three of the four essays which follow, each of the universities conducting sponsored curriculum revitalization projects outline their rationale for and development of general education requirements. Although the requirements that resulted are "site specific," they are remarkably alike in what they perceive as the current and future needs of their graduates. The approaches for developing the requirements and means of accomplishing them vary from campus to campus. The fourth essay, by Laurie Schultz Hayes of Minnesota, demonstrates how general education requirements might be translated for academic advisors and students and applied to individual programs of study. Altogether, the essays give different approaches to establishing and implementing general education requirements and thus suggest possible ways that other colleges may develop their own requirements and implementation plans.

F. H. Buelow is Professor Emeritus of Agricultural Engineering, University of Wisconsin-Madison.

5

DETERMINING THE COMPONENTS OF A PROGRAM OF GENERAL EDUCATION

Robert G. Kranz, Jr.
University of Wisconsin-Madison

The course requirements for a program of general education represent an agreement among curriculum stakeholders about the knowledge and skills necessary for responsible citizenship in a free society. Any changes in curriculum must derive from general agreement about new directions in society that mandate mastery of new skills or acquisition of new knowledge. When the University of Wisconsin-Madison's Curricular Revitalization Project began, the first step was to explore old agreements about general education; the next was to come to agreement about the demands of the workplace into which students were graduating. With a solid grounding in both the past and present, the project could look more confidently to the future in designing a curriculum that would meet the needs of students and the expectations of employers.

General education course requirements fall into three broad categories: competency, advanced skills, and breadth. Courses that meet competency requirements give students college-level proficiency in basic skills, including English, mathematics, and foreign language. Advanced skills requirements are satisfied by courses that extend and refine basic competencies and establish a base for study in a major. Breadth requirements are met by courses in the humanities and social and natural sciences that provide exposure to disciplines outside the major field of study. Courses that satisfy breadth requirements differ from electives, which students use at their discretion to pursue personal interests or goals.

Trends in General Education

Campus debate often focuses on the nature of general education requirements. In fact, opposition to the liberal arts core curriculum of the nineteenth century shaped the early land grant system and led to the development of curricula in the agricultural and life sciences. As these curricular innovations became institutionalized throughout American higher education in the twentieth century, debate continued over the scope and content of general learning. In the immediate aftermath of World War II, academic leaders debated the value of educational experiences and courses focusing on "democratic living" and internationalism. By the late 1950s, curricular debate focused on increasing requirements in mathematics, science, and foreign language and on developing courses in area studies. In the late 1960s and early 1970s, many institutions reduced the number of general education requirements (because they were irrelevant to student interests) and increased electives. During this period, the proportion of the undergraduate curriculum reserved for electives grew from about 24% to 33% (Carnegie Foundation for the Advancement of Teaching, 1976).

In each of these examples, the debate over general education reflected events taking place outside the college classroom. Harvard faculty leaders and the President's Commission on Higher Education gave birth to the democratic living movement of the late 1940s as an alternative to both America's old money elite and communism. In the 1950s, the National Science Foundation and provisions of the National Defense Education Act prompted an emphasis on science, mathematics, foreign language, and area studies. This was part of a strategy to combat Soviet emergence in the natural sciences and win allies in Africa, Asia, and Latin America. Finally, student demands for personal relevance and a generalized distrust of authority were often the rationales for reducing the size of the core curriculum during the 1960s and early 1970s.

When the Curricular Revitalization Project began work at the University of Wisconsin-Madison in 1986, many academic leaders sharply disagreed over the form and substance of general education. A study released in 1984 by the National Endowment for the Humanities (NEH) portrayed undergraduates as isolationist and ignorant of traditional Western values, since they took few courses in history, literature, and foreign language (Bennett, 1984). The NEH recommended increasing general education requirements in the humanities. Meanwhile, a report issued by the National Institute of Education found that the structure and delivery of college courses contributed to poor learning skills and the inability to relate theoretical knowledge to real life problems (Study Group on Conditions of Excellence in American Higher Education, 1984). Finally, the American Association of State Colleges and Universities advocated community service projects, foreign language instruction, and international studies as the nucleus of the college core curriculum (National Commission on the Role and Future of State Colleges and Universities, 1986).

In the agricultural and life sciences community, concern over American economic competitiveness framed many discussions of student educational needs and appropriate general education requirements. Some claimed, for example, that conditions such as farm debt and world over-production of foodstuffs created new needs for knowledge of international trade, finance, currency exchange rates, agricultural output in major producing regions of the world, processes and linkages in public policy implementation, and basic science concepts connected to agriculture (Harl, 1985).

NEW MISSION STATEMENT FOR
UNDERGRADUATE GENERAL EDUCATION

After considering the historical trends and the current state of the national debate over general education requirements, the Curricular Revitalization Project began work on a new mission statement for undergraduate instruction. This statement provided "a framework for continually examining and restructuring the college's curriculum" (University of Wisconsin-Madison, 1990) and outlined general goals for instruction, expected educational outcomes, and the strengths and traditions of the college. Faculty task forces then began assessment of student educational needs in core curriculum subject areas.

The task forces recommended a set of general education requirements, which then were discussed with different client groups of the college and individual academic departments and finally adopted at an all-faculty meeting in late 1990. Overall, the new core curriculum comprises about 40% of the 124 credits required for graduation.

The task forces also drafted rationales for requirements in several key areas of the core curriculum, including the natural sciences; social sciences and humanities; mathematics, statistics, and computer science; and communications and foreign language (*An analysis of core curriculum*, 1988).

Natural Sciences

Students should be exposed to a broad range of subject matter in the natural sciences, including the agricultural, biological, and environmental sciences. Biology is "the unifying discipline" in the agricultural and life sciences regardless of subject matter specialty, since all graduates working in their chosen fields will deal directly or indirectly with living organisms. For students majoring in fields such as agricultural journalism, agricultural economics and agricultural engineering, this link with living organisms distinguishes their training from more general programs in other colleges. The study of chemistry is essential for understanding the working of nature. The use of chemicals also plays an increasingly important role in the agricultural and life sciences. Graduates must have a basic understanding of chemistry in order to understand when and how chemicals should be used and how they can be administered safely and effectively (Task Force on Agricultural, Biological, and Environmental Core, 1988).

Social Sciences and Humanities

Educational breadth stimulates intellectual curiosity, individual growth, and the desire for lifelong learning and encourages tolerance for diverse views. The study of history involves students in the unique human enterprise of discovering the past and understanding the present. The humanities showcase values, understanding, and wisdom. The social sciences provide insight into human behavior, social structure, and the interrelationships between technology and society. Courses in international and ethnic studies provide necessary information on contemporary cultures outside the Judeo-Christian tradition and on the consequences of racial differences within the United States (Task Force on Humanities and Social Sciences, 1988).

Mathematics, Statistics, and Computer Science

Computer literacy is both a liberal and a useful art. As knowledge expands, access to knowledge becomes the determining factor in public policy debates and a crucial ingredient in the quality of life. Computer skills are already required for employment in some fields, and profitability in agriculture is increasingly linked to decisions based on computer-generated information. Advanced skill in computers also contributes to effective teaching and learning, through the use of tutorials and expanded access to information. The importance of statistics increases as more aspects of life are quantified. Familiarity with basic statistics is essential if students are to understand how knowledge is generated and how to evaluate data (Task Force on Mathematics, Statistics, and Computer Science, 1988).

Communications and Foreign Language

The rationale for acquiring skills in oral and written communication is self-evident. Students should complete basic and advanced competency requirements in communication within the first two years of study.

Learning a foreign language sharpens reading and writing skills in English. Minimal fluency in any second language also provides the experience necessary for learning an occupationally relevant language later and opens a door to international involvement in agriculture, business, education, government, and science. Knowledge of another tongue also contributes to the understanding and appreciation of racial and ethnic diversity and erodes chauvinistic attitudes rooted in stubborn monolingualism (Task Force on Communication Arts and Foreign Language, 1988; Task Force on International Studies, 1988).

Capstone

A successful program of general education is not confined to the first two years of college study. Students should have the opportunity to focus the skills and breadth of knowledge provided by the core curriculum on problems related to their specific disciplinary interests. A required "capstone" course or experience is a logical conclusion to four years of undergraduate study (Task Force on Agricultural Systems, 1988).

CONCLUSION

These general education requirements, which are a part of all undergraduate curricula in the College of Agricultural and Life Sciences, give the students and their advisors flexibility in course selections that meet the requirements. At the same time, students can change their majors if they desire to do so without losing any or many credits for courses they have taken to meet the general education requirements. The incoming freshmen appreciate this flexibility so they can adjust their career direction after they have taken some college courses, and not be penalized for it.

Robert G. Kranz, Jr. is formerly Curriculum Consultant on the Curricular Revitalization Project, University of Wisconsin-Madison.

REFERENCES

An analysis of core curriculum in the College of Agricultural and Life Sciences, University of Wisconsin-Madison (1988). Madison, WI: University of Wisconsin-Madison, CALS Curricular Revitalization Project, Office of Student Academic Affairs.

Bennett, W. (1984). *To reclaim a legacy: A report on the humanities in higher education.* Washington, DC: National Endowment for the Humanities.

Carnegie Foundation for the Advancement of Teaching (1976). *Missions of the college curriculum.* San Francisco, CA: Jossey Bass.

Harl, N. (1985). *Implications of farm debtor distress: A challenge for land grant universities.* Paper presented at the Council of Agricultural Research, Extension, and Teaching. Arlington, VA.

National Commission on the Role and Future of State Colleges and Universities. (1986). *To secure the blessings of liberty.* Washington, DC: American Association of State Colleges and Universities.

Study Group on the Conditions of Excellence in American Higher Education (1984). *Involvement in learning: Realizing the potential of American higher education.* Washington, DC: National Institute of Education.

Task Force on Agricultural, Biological, and Environmental Core. (1988). *Final recommendations of the task force on agricultural, biological, and environmental core.* Madison, WI: University of Wisconsin-Madison, CALS Curricular Revitalization Project, Office of Student Academic Affairs.

Task Force on Agricultural Systems. (1988). *Agricultural systems task force policy statement.* Madison, WI: University of Wisconsin-Madison, CALS Curricular Revitalization Project, Office of Academic Affairs.

Task Force on Communication Arts and Foreign Languages. (1988). *Draft report: Final recommendations of the communication arts and foreign language task force.* Madison, WI: University of Wisconsin-Madison, CALS Curricular Revitalization Project, Office of Academic Affairs.

Task Force on the Humanities and Social Sciences. (1988). *Draft proposal three: CALS humanities and social sciences requirement.* Madison, WI: University of Wisconsin-Madison, CALS Curricular Revitalization Project, Office of Academic Affairs.

Task Force on International Studies. (1988). *Report of the international studies task force.* Madison, WI: University of Wisconsin-Madison, CALS Curricular Revitalization Project, Office of Academic Affairs.

Task Force on Mathematics, Statistics, and Computer Science. (1988). *Report of the task force on mathematics, statistics, and computer science core requirements.* Madison, WI: University of Wisconsin-Madison, CALS Curricular Revitalization Project, Office of Academic Affairs.

University of Wisconsin-Madison. (1990). *A mission statement for undergraduate instruction in the UW-Madison College of Agricultural and Life Sciences.* Madison, WI: CALS, Office of Student Academic Affairs.

6

SHIFTING THE CURRICULUM PARADIGM IN A LAND GRANT COLLEGE

Bruce Johnson, Kenneth Von Bargen, and Jack Schinstock
University of Nebraska-Lincoln

In today's world, mission statements and strategic planning permeate virtually every organization. Academic institutions are certainly no exception as they struggle to adapt to the demands of a resource-constrained and volatile world. But moving from a mission statement to its successful application is seldom a smooth process. Forces of status quo can often be extreme, and well-articulated goals and objectives can soon degenerate into little more than literary platitudes.

In the university community, those who attempt to set a new direction for undergraduate education can encounter considerable institutional inertia. Faculty beliefs, perceptions, and interests can be so fixed that any attempt to redesign and redirect a college curriculum is viewed with considerable skepticism, if not outright fear. It has been said that "throwing out the existing curriculum and redesigning a new curriculum are such traumatic and convulsive processes that most faculty can tolerate the experience no more than once or twice in their careers" (Miller, 1989).

The University of Nebraska College of Agricultural Sciences and Natural Resources (CASNR) was fully aware of this when it developed a four-year action plan titled *Project Scholar: Priorities and Plans For Excellence in Learning*. Released in late 1990, this action plan contained ten mission statements, one of which specifically addressed the curriculum: "The Integration of New Study and Student Learning Outcomes Into The Curriculum." Its two objectives were to: 1) design programs of study to include broader perspectives of the social, economic, and cultural forces shaping our lives, and 2) develop new disciplinary and interdisciplinary curricula.

But rather than being an amorphous decree by college administration, this action plan had fortuitous timing. The Kellogg-funded New Partnerships in Agriculture and Education (NUPAGE) was fully "on line" and visibly successful on several fronts. A solid cross section of college faculty were involved in various NUPAGE projects, enthusiastic about the creative opportunities they afforded in undergraduate education, and interested in seeing their innovations sustained through incorporation into the learning outcomes of the college. Moreover, faculty who were not directly involved with NUPAGE were aware of a new environment for positive change within the college which NUPAGE seemed to foster. In short, a subtle but discernible shift in mindset by the majority of faculty had occurred, which allowed for embracing curriculum reform.

DEVELOPMENT OF THE REVITALIZATION TASK FORCE

It was in this environment that a small group of faculty met with the college dean and began to devise a strategy for comprehensive curriculum review. What ensued was the Project Scholar Revitalization Task Force, comprised of individuals from all departments within the college. Several who were asked to serve were already involved with some aspect of the NUPAGE program. However, others were invited to participate based upon evidence of their commitment to educational excellence and their desire to improve the college's undergraduate program.

Participants were assigned to one of three working groups, each with unique responsibilities: the Conceptualizer Group, the Implementer Group, and the Outcomes Group. The Conceptualizers' charge was "to explore as widely as possible what undergraduate education should be, to identify or create a model for curricular renewal, to make recommendations for curricular renewal, and to set directions and frame the ideas for undergraduate minimum requirements in the college." The Implementers' task was "to implement a curricular plan to renew the college's minimum or core requirements." The Outcomes Group was charged to "ensure that NUPAGE outcomes be systematically incorporated into the college's minimum requirements and to integrate the multiple, innovative ways of involving students, faculty, and external partners in the process of curricular renewal."

As these working groups developed, the steering committee gave careful attention to their membership, considering the particular strengths each individual offered. For the Conceptualizer Group, "idea" people were chosen, individuals with vision and enthusiasm who could provide a total perspective of the forest without being lost in the trees. As these free thinkers were brought together from a full cross-section of academic disciplines and departments, conditions were ripe for a spirited think tank.

The Implementer Group was built around the qualities of organization and clarity. These were the people who could pay close attention to detail. They understood the trees in the forest and how to effectively organize and implement change within the existing institutional structure. They provided a much-needed reality check for the Conceptualizers, pointing out specific alternatives to accomplish curricular reform.

The Outcomes Group was comprised of people with demonstrated skills in group process and networking. Their focus was upon the process of curricular reform and the elements and activities necessary to successfully carry it out. For example, they promoted the partnering of faculty, students, and external partners in the overall effort, seeing that broad-based input occurred with built-in checks and balances. In essence, this group instigated a form of Total Quality Management within the curricular revitalization process, which promoted a sense of shared ownership and responsibility.

THE REVITALIZATION PROCESS

The steering committee designed a work plan and schedule for completion. As a first step, a one-day retreat was held just before the 1991 fall semester began, for all members of the working groups, staff assistants, and external partners. Under the leadership of a professional facilitator, small-group brainstorming sessions led to ideas which were organized into a systematic framework to serve as initial input for the three working groups. Not only did the retreat result in specific ideas, but the task force as a whole regarded this as an official and positive launch of curricular revitalization. A general vision was established as well as a sense of shared responsibility. If participants brought to the retreat any cynicism regarding curricular revitalization, they left without it. Indeed, the three working groups were energized.

Conceptualizing

For the Conceptualizer Group, work started immediately, since the general framework for a 21st century curriculum needed to be addressed before detailed work could proceed. Using initial ideas developed during the task force retreat, the conceptualizers met in weekly brainstorming sessions to address the basic question: "What attributes does the undergraduate student need to be successful as a professional and as a member of society in the 21st century?" Using "zero-based" planning, members considered process as well as content of the educational experience. For example, aspects of process included course sequencing, use of capstone experiences, team teaching, multi-dimensional learning experiences, systems versus reductionist educational philosophies, etc.

As members gathered information from both the literature and their own teaching experiences, ideas continued to grow. General themes quickly began to weave through the discussions which pointed to key elements necessary for excellence in the educational experience. The result was a list of ten competencies the conceptualizers believed were important to the college educational experience in general and to this College specifically:

1. Professional and technical competence with focus on agricultural sciences and natural resources

2. Higher order problem solving and critical/creative thinking skills

3. Broad communication competence

4. Skills in information management

5. Understanding of values

6. Relational skills

7. Adaptation skills to life's changes

8. Leadership/followership skills

9. Understanding of systems in the context of issues and challenges facing both the individual and society

10. A cosmopolitan view of the world

Initial Feedback

But were we on track? The conceptualizers needed feedback. So, the first of several iterative steps was launched in November 1991 with a mail survey of teaching faculty, students, and external partners. The tenor of the survey itself was a sincere plea for input—a Delphi Survey in which information and discovery flow in both directions through successive iterations. Respondents first were asked to rank how well they believed the current undergraduate program was preparing students in each of the ten competency areas, and, second, to rank how important development of each competency should be in future undergraduate programs. Open-ended questions were also asked so respondents could freely offer unique ideas and directions.

The survey responses proved most enlightening. Respondents regarded the current undergraduate program deficient in all areas except for its ability to develop students' professional and technical competence. Moreover, they ranked all competencies high in importance for future undergraduate programs. In addition, their open-ended responses further confirmed this list of ten competencies, with no new elements surfacing. There were no significant differences in responses across the groups surveyed, which further substantiated the validity of the initial set of competencies.

The survey results were presented and discussed in a college-wide workshop in January 1992. This discussion was significant in the process of curricular revitalization for several reasons. First, it provided timely and provocative feedback to all faculty and others regarding their input via the survey, broadening the sense of shared ownership in the process as well as the mission. Second, the open-forum nature provided another iteration of the feedback process by fostering rich discussion in a group context. Finally, and perhaps most important, college-wide consensus was reached regarding the basic conceptual building blocks of true curricular revitalization. Any disagreements that surfaced later about the details of revitalization were resolved by returning focus to the foundation already built.

In the next few months, the conceptualizers continued to meet with various groups to share information and solicit input, not just about the educational objectives but also about the educational process. The refinement continued and, in time, an "Educational DNA" emerged (see Figure 6-1) revealing that all ten educational outcomes essentially weave together in an interdependent and progressive fashion throughout a student's educational experience. No longer were we thinking about piecemeal issues, but rather were beginning to see undergraduate education as a systematic whole. Linkages and interfaces became evident; models for active student learning surfaced; and innovative teaching methods were revisited with enthusiasm. In short, the educational paradigm was undergoing metamorphosis.

Implementation

Concurrent with the conceptualizers' activity, the implementers also were researching the current status of requirements and the institutional parameters within which the curriculum revitalization process would occur. Frequent interaction in the early months occurred between the two working groups, as the implementers kept the conceptualizers from going too far afield. Once general consensus regarding educational objectives/outcomes was reached, the implementers moved into full swing to explore various alternatives for carrying out these objectives.

Several components of the implementation process needed considerable research. For example, the subcommittee assigned to the question of

FIGURE 6-1

An Integrated-Synergistic Curriculum

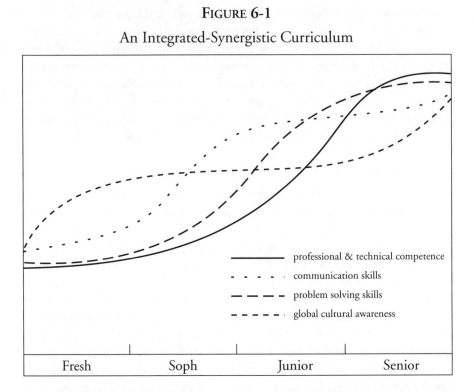

communication competence identified and evaluated several alternatives before recommending inclusion of communication-intensive disciplinary courses as part of the minimum requirements. Likewise, the concept of integrative educational experiences was investigated in depth before the group recommended a first-year integrative course and a senior capstone educational experience.

While individual components were being developed, the implementers also were working with the college's minimum educational requirements block, since this represented the basic framework for reform. Because there are only so many credit hours with which to work, the group had to grapple with this constraint in trying to achieve the desired outcomes. Here the detail skills of the implementers were tested as various tradeoffs were analyzed. In time, a particular configuration of course requirements was developed and presented to faculty, students, and external partners for discussion.

Outcomes

Through a series of public forums and thorough communication, the college gradually moved toward consensus regarding the minimum requirements block and the specific emphasis components. While debate was spirited and opinions and preferences often differed, a reasoned democratic process prevailed. The Outcomes Group had effectively met its responsibilities of insuring a broad-based participatory process, and collective decision-making occurred in a spirit of common vision and mutual regard. When the final mail ballot was completed, the new general requirements for the college were approved by an overwhelming margin. In approximately two years, the formal process of revitalization of the undergraduate curriculum was completed.

LESSONS LEARNED

While the process generally proceeded effectively, there still were lessons to be learned. The primary one was that the concept of partnering may be intriguing in theory but difficult in fact. The involvement of external partners and students in the revitalization process was a continual struggle, not because these groups were unwilling to participate (they were, in fact, most enthusiastic), but rather because faculty appeared not to be acclimated to working closely with them. In almost every aspect of partnership—from the scheduling of meeting times workable for the external and student partners to the flow of discussion—the faculty sometimes seemed to forget these partners and essentially "take over." Covertly, faculty seemed to want to maintain a sense of ownership over the curriculum and ultimately make the final decisions. Only by the deliberate and persistent efforts of the Outcomes Group in coordinating the partnering process did interaction occur. Even then it often fell short of the original intent. The implication is obvious: deliberate formalization of partnering with a framework for accountability is an absolute necessity. Otherwise, faculty governance and control will quickly dominate the revitalization process.

A second lesson learned is that a sense of dissonance due to time constraints will occur among the participants in the revitalization process, but that dissonance can create quite different perspectives. For the Conceptualizer Group, time was too short to explore all the rich literature and interesting concepts relating to curriculum. Yet the Implementer Group, which felt the pressure of a specific time deadline "to make the catalog," believed too much time was being eaten up by the conceptualization process. In reality, there was some truth in both perspectives which neither group appreciated at the time. Now, hindsight would suggest that a detailed planning schedule is crucial from the very start, but with sufficient time allocated to explore important conceptual aspects. In that case, dissonance due to time can be creative rather than destructive.

THE PRODUCT

Have we accomplished what we set out to do? Is the new CASNR curriculum really designed to provide an educational experience appropriate for the 21st century? Only time will give a definitive answer; but, for several reasons, we have confidence in the new program.

First, the new curriculum addresses the identified student educational objectives and outcomes both directly and indirectly. For example, more hours are available to the individual majors which should enhance professional and technical competence. Communication skills have greater attention through the initiation of communication-intensive disciplinary course requirements. Likewise, requirements for at least one cross-cultural course and one international course will enhance students' understanding of values and the global community as well as teach adaptation skills to life's changes. Higher order problem solving and critical/creative thinking skills as well as the understanding of systems will be emphasized throughout the undergraduate program, but with special emphasis in the beginning integrative course and the capstone educational experience designed by the individual departments. Because of its applied nature with a team orientation, the latter will also provide opportunity for developing relational skills. Indirectly, the new curriculum addresses the desirable outcomes and places greater emphasis on lifelong learning skills, problem solving, and adaptation, in contrast to time-limited knowledge. The new paradigm calls for preparing students to access, integrate, and apply information and knowledge in their professional and personal paths, rather than merely "filling them up" with information.

A second reason we have confidence in the new curriculum is that it conforms well with the recently-proposed new general requirements for the total university. In essence, the college preceded the rest of the university in visionary revitalization of its curriculum. As a consequence, it is positioned well to operate effectively within the emerging university framework, a situation envied by other colleges that still remain in a status-quo mode.

Third, the new curriculum and the process through which it evolved appears to have created a renewed vigor within the college in attitudes toward undergraduate education. Individual faculty are actively developing communication-intensive designated courses. Faculty teams within each department are constructing innovative capstone experiences for their respective majors. An interdisciplinary team of faculty is completing the design of a first-year integrative course which will eventually be team-taught. In other words, momentum to change and effectively implement curriculum reform appears to be well under way.

Finally, the curriculum revitalization effort within the college holds considerable promise of success since it is essentially an open-ended process. We have launched the process, but the evolution and development are ongoing.

To be sure, we had to take definitive steps and establish specific time horizons for enactment. Likewise, educational experiences have been designed in considerable detail to carry out some of the objectives. But we do not have all the answers as to how to best carry out the new curriculum. Much remains to evolve before the vision for educational excellence within the college is even approached.

However, instead of creating a level of anxiety and ambiguity, the revitalization process seems to have created an atmosphere of teamwork, trust, and shared responsibility. The need to guard the status quo has diminished as the energy for and commitment to positive, innovative change rises, both individually and corporately. Indeed, a paradigm of an evolving system of educational excellence is now in place, and within the framework of that paradigm we look with confidence and anticipation to the challenges of the 21st century.

Bruce Johnson is Professor of Agricultural Economics, University of Nebraska-Lincoln.

Kenneth Von Bargen is Professor of Biological Systems Engineering, University of Nebraska-Lincoln.

Jack Schinstock is Assistant Dean, College of Agricultural Sciences and Natural Resources, and Professor of Biological Systems Engineering, University of Nebraska-Lincoln.

7

DEVELOPING LEARNER OUTCOMES TO SUPPORT A CURRICULUM

Laurie Schultz Hayes
University of Minnesota

An expectation for the University of Minnesota's "Project Sunrise" was set out early for the College of Agriculture faculty, staff, and students by the college deans: we need "to carefully define the professional qualities and the skills that our students should have at graduation." But how do you do that? How do you identify the core of a new curriculum? Are the answers on stone tablets somewhere? There is probably no one sacred list of outcomes that is seen as universally acceptable for grounding an undergraduate education. To be successful, however, the challenge is to include as many people in the preliminary discussions as possible so that in the end there will be consensus about the outcomes that are adopted.

The next few pages contain a brief history of the steps followed by the College of Agriculture faculty at the University of Minnesota to develop a final list of fourteen learner outcomes. This list became the template for the college's new curriculum. The narrative concludes with some comments about the process.

PRELIMINARY LEADERSHIP MEETING

A few months after the Curriculum Task Force had been appointed by the college deans, the task force members met with the leaders of the departmental and college curriculum committees. At this meeting, the participants completed a "Skill Ranking Form," a questionnaire asking them to rate the importance of eight skills for student education:

- communication
- problem identification and solution
- teamwork skills
- interdisciplinary approaches
- environmental awareness
- historical perspective
- international perspective
- social values and ethics

While most agreed that all these skills were important, the forced rating yielded the following:

	Rank	*Average*	*Range*
problem identification and solution	1	1.7	1–4
communication	2	2.3	1–5
teamwork skills	3	4.3	2–8
interdisciplinary approaches	4	4.8	1–8
social values and ethics	5	4.9	1–8
environmental awareness	6	5.1	2–8
historical perspective	7	6.3	4–8
international perspective	8	6.3	4–8

This list and the accompanying ranking procedure led faculty leaders early in the curriculum revision process to think more about educational outcomes for all undergraduates and less about what courses students should take.

ALL-COLLEGE RETREAT

During the first year of Project Sunrise, most faculty in the college were involved in assorted seminars and workshops on active learning, cooperative learning, problem solving, and teaching. But toward the end of the first calendar year, attention was focused once again on college-wide goals.

Before classes began in the fall, a retreat was held at a site about 45 miles from campus. From noon one day until noon the next, representatives from each department in the college gathered to learn a common method for reviewing a curriculum and to discuss curriculum-related issues in light of Project Sunrise. At a 90-minute afternoon session on the first day, interdepartmental groups of four persons answered the question,

"What are appropriate learner outcomes for all College of Agriculture graduates?" (For those who are interested in meeting strategies, 38 faculty, at least two from each of 11 departments, were assigned to one of four large groups, identified by a different color name tag. For some portions of the retreat, participants worked in large "color groups"; at other times they worked in base groups of four, composed of one person of each "color.")

During the session, four-person groups generated lists of outcomes and put them on flip charts that were later posted for viewing. The assorted flip chart content demonstrates the previous claim that "no one sacred list of outcomes…is seen as universally acceptable for grounding an undergraduate education." Samples of the group products, transcribed from their flip charts, are offered in Appendix A.

These examples represent considerable variety. Although careful readers will find among them recurring themes, even similar language, it is important to note that the original intent of this retreat activity was not to reach consensus. Rather, a group of faculty were encouraged to think about educational outcomes and not disciplinary courses. Participant satisfaction was high. Of the five sessions at the retreat—Essentials, Majors, College of Agriculture (COA) Issues, Leadership, and Planning/Reporting—this one, COA Issues, received the highest participant evaluation mean of 4.3 out of 5. (The only higher evaluation for the retreat went to Accommodations with a score of 4.9!)

TASK FORCE SYNTHESIS

Two months later, the College Task Force met to decide on a list of six to ten learner outcomes from the possibilities generated at the retreat. There was early agreement on six outcome areas: communication, critical thinking/problem identification/solving, teamwork, international awareness, specialized learning, and environment. There was less agreement on leadership (was this a goal or an outcome?) and information management (was this a separate category or a sub-topic of other outcomes?).

A four-person team was then selected to write a draft of a goal statement for the college and a general statement to go with the selected learner outcomes. The draft was prepared and mailed to task force members for review prior to their next meeting in two weeks. Feedback at the next meeting helped the four-person team revise yet another draft that was prepared for the college curriculum committee.

CURRICULUM COMMITTEE DELIBERATIONS

The curriculum committee, composed of representatives from each of the college's academic departments, discussed the draft document given to them by the task force (Appendix B) and, after several meetings and some wordsmithing, adopted a revised version of the statement. Their revised draft was circulated for review among members of the task force and curriculum work groups (groups with varied assignments in the curriculum revision process), and, after a few more adjustments, another version was ready for presentation to the college faculty (Appendix C).

FACULTY ENDORSEMENT

In late winter that academic year, the curriculum committee presented its statement to the Faculty Assembly (an all-college meeting that occurs three times a year) and, with only a modest amount of large-group editing, a final statement was adopted. What had happened? Six months after an all-college retreat, a list of professional qualities and skills that students should have at graduation had been generated, synthesized, revised, and endorsed. Of the fifteen outcomes, three were linked with traditional educational goals ("demonstrate fundamental knowledge of the biological and physical sciences," "demonstrate specialized expertise in at least one collegiate major," and "develop expertise in additional areas"). The remaining twelve outcomes represented a general education core. Faculty agreed that by the time students graduate from the college, they should be able to:

- Demonstrate fundamental knowledge of the biological and physical sciences

- Demonstrate specialized expertise in at least one collegiate major

- Develop expertise in additional areas

- Solve problems in a profession

- Appreciate and interpret works of literature and the arts

- Retrieve, analyze, and use information

- Work effectively as a team member

- Manage human resources and provide leadership

- Communicate effectively and use communications technology

- Evaluate and integrate diverse viewpoints or data

- Make responsible judgments on ethical and policy issues in agriculture

- Apply an historical perspective to the role of science and technology in agriculture
- Apply global perspectives to food and agricultural issues and decisions
- Make responsible judgments about management of natural resources and the environment

The College of Agriculture held its second all-college retreat six weeks later, to discuss the progress of the seven college-wide work groups formed to address issues that had surfaced at the first retreat. The new list of fourteen learner outcomes was available for the retreat's participants to use as building blocks for the assembly of a new curriculum.

CONCLUDING OBSERVATIONS

The successful experience of Project Sunrise at the University of Minnesota's College of Agriculture in developing a list of learner outcomes as a first step in creating a new curriculum leads to these observations:

1. It is possible for a large faculty group to agree on some educational outcomes if they have all had a chance to participate in the process.

2. Some people can edit forever. It is important to keep the process of inclusion, synthesis, and endorsement moving along a timeline.

3. A list of learner outcomes is not generated in a vacuum. Faculty will be active and more imaginative contributors during the process if they have also been participating in seminars whose focus is the development of professional skills and lifelong learning abilities.

4. Close contact with alumni and employer advisory groups helps faculty focus less on what they want to teach students and more on what students need to learn.

5. Faculty in the food and agricultural sciences are remarkably generous in their willingness to consider the wide-reaching and long-term needs of student learners.

Laurie Schultz Hayes is Associate Professor of Rhetoric and Associate Dean, Curricular and Student Affairs, College of Agriculture (now College of Agricultural, Food, and Environmental Sciences), University of Minnesota.

APPENDIX A

SAMPLE LISTS OF OUTCOMES
GENERATED BY GROUPS AT ALL-COLLEGE RETREAT

Graduates from the COA will have:

- Interpersonal skills such as self motivation, ethics, work attitude and a team player
- Communication skills: listening, speaking, writing
- Scientific and technical training (competence) in chosen discipline
- Critical thinking and problem solving skills
- Quantitative and computer skills
- Ability to continue their education through graduate school, continuing education, and self-education
- Awareness of profession and industry through work experience, extracurricular activities, etc.

COA Learner Outcomes:

- Acquire knowledge independently
- Synthesize data and results
- Speak and read a foreign language
- Appreciation of humanities
- Develop historical perspective
- Communication of technical ideas
- Working knowledge of descriptive statistics and hypothesis testing
- Understanding of ag/environmental policy

Learner outcomes:

- Communication—different levels, different forms
- Technically competent in one of the following:

        Business/management

        Science/technical service

        Production

        Marketing/Distribution/Service

- Interpersonal skills
- Problem solving skills from personal to professional
- Socially, ethically, culturally, historically aware

The student will be able to:

- communicate succinctly and effectively in problem solving, on scientific and technical aspects of the field, and on social and cultural issues
- interact effectively with individuals and groups
- demonstrate a systems perspective in problem solving, situation improvement, decision-making and forming judgments
- use fundamental scientific methods and skills to identify problems and devise acceptable and feasible solutions
- demonstrate that he/she has learned how to learn
- have an understanding and appreciation of the arts and humanities
- think and function in a global environment
- demonstrate professional competence
- know *E. coli*

What are proper COA learner outcomes?

- Conceptual skills and knowledge

    Mathematics

    Values—Know what I believe

    Creativity

    Curiosity/interest

    Knowledge synthesis

    Fundamental sciences

    Logic/common sense/awareness, e.g., ethics, logic, calculus, independent study

- Technical skills and knowledge

    Telecommunications/computers

    Skills/knowledge within the discipline(s)

    Historical perspective

    Experience (internships, extracurricular)

- People skills and knowledge

    Verbal communication

    Humanities, social science

    Flexibility/ability to cope—get along with others

    Leadership management skills, e.g., art, literature, history, extracurriculars, psychology

APPENDIX B

MISSION STATEMENT FOR THE CURRICULUM OF THE COLLEGE OF AGRICULTURE, UNIVERSITY OF MINNESOTA

Introduction
This mission statement is intended to provide direction to the College of Agriculture in evaluating and redefining a curriculum to prepare students to meet current and future educational needs.

Goal
The mission of the College of Agriculture is to provide students with the educational experiences and environment that promote discipline competence, the capacity to attain career success in agriculture, food, or related professions, and a sense of civic responsibility.

Learner Outcomes
Students graduating with a College of Agriculture degree should be proficient and current in discipline knowledge and be able to apply this knowledge to make sound professional analysis, judgment, and decisions. They should be critically aware of contemporary and historical issues, particularly those concerning food, agriculture, and the wise use of natural resources. They should be able to discern relationships among current issues and be capable of participating constructively in discussion and resolution of these issues. Students should develop an appreciation of, and affection for, music, literature, and the arts. They should be able to communicate effectively. Students should be motivated and equipped to continue to learn and provide professional leadership for the benefit of agriculture and society.

Specific Objectives
Upon completion of a degree in the College of Agriculture students will be able to:

- demonstrate fundamental knowledge of the biological and physical sciences
- demonstrate specialized expertise in at least one agricultural discipline
- develop specialized expertise in other disciplines as needed
- apply their knowledge to solve problems in their chosen profession
- appreciate and interpret works of art, literature, and the humanities
- retrieve, analyze, and manage information
- work in a team and manage human resources
- communicate effectively (speak, write, listen, telecommunicate)
- critically evaluate and integrate diverse viewpoints or data

- make sound, responsible judgments on the ethical policy issues involved in the production of food and fiber
- apply an historical perspective to the role of science and technology in agriculture
- apply an international perspective to agricultural issues and decisions
- act as responsible stewards of the land, natural resources and environment

(Revised December 3, 1987)

APPENDIX C

GOAL FOR THE UNDERGRADUATE CURRICULUM
OF THE COLLEGE OF AGRICULTURE, UNIVERSITY OF MINNESOTA

Introduction
This statement is intended to provide direction to the College of Agriculture in defining an undergraduate curriculum that prepares students for personal growth and to address current and future needs of agriculture and society.

Goal
The goal of the College of Agriculture is to provide students with varied educational experiences and an environment that promotes professional competence, the capacity to attain career success in agriculture, food, or related professions, and a sense of social responsibility.

Learner Outcomes
Students graduating with a College of Agriculture degree should be proficient and competent in a major and make sound professional analyses, judgments, and decisions. They should be able to communicate effectively. They should be aware of contemporary and historical issues and be able to critically relate these to food, agriculture, and the use of natural resources. They should be able to discern relationships among current issues and be capable of participating constructively in discussion and resolution of these issues. Students should develop an appreciation and understanding of creative expressions through literature and the arts. They should be motivated and equipped to continue to learn and to provide professional leadership for the benefit of agriculture and society.

Specific Objectives (not ranked):
Upon completion of a degree in the College of Agriculture students should be able to:

- demonstrate fundamental knowledge of the biological and physical sciences
- demonstrate specialized expertise in at least one collegiate major
- develop expertise in additional areas
- solve problems in their profession
- appreciate and interpret works of literature and the arts
- retrieve, analyze, and use information
- work effectively as a team member
- manage human resources and provide leadership
- communicate effectively and use communications technology
- critically evaluate and integrate diverse viewpoints or data

- make responsible judgments on ethical and policy issues in agriculture
- apply an historical perspective to the role of science and technology in agriculture
- apply global perspectives to food and agricultural issues and decisions
- make responsible judgments regarding natural resources and the environment

(Revised February 15, 1988)

8

STUDENT PORTFOLIOS FOR ACADEMIC AND CAREER ADVISING

Laurie Schultz Hayes
University of Minnesota

In early 1988, the College of Agriculture faculty adopted a list of 14 specific objectives that each undergraduate student in the college should be able to reach upon completion of a Bachelor of Science degree. Since then, these "learner outcomes" have provided the framework within which ten new college majors have been defined and each undergraduate student has been advised. The following essay outlines how the learner outcomes were designed into the "College of Agriculture Portfolio," describes how the portfolio was introduced to faculty advisors and to students, and discusses both lessons learned during the process and current practices.

HOW THE LEARNER OUTCOMES WERE DESIGNED INTO THE PORTFOLIO

In June 1988, the Project Sunrise Workgroup on Student (Senior) Projects and Portfolios submitted its final report. This committee, formed in the fall of 1987 and composed of five faculty and two students, was one of seven college-wide workgroups. The workgroup's specific charge was "to recommend criteria, requirements, and examples of appropriate senior projects and portfolios of student work," and in their final summary, the workgroup reported that they had "considered student projects, portfolios, and job placement course activities that 'cap off' students' collegiate educational experience and launch them into careers."

In addition to making specific recommendations about student projects and the job placement course, the workgroup report proposed two forms or phases of a portfolio. The first was an advising portfolio to be used during a student's career at the university. It would enable students to plan and monitor their progress in satisfying the learner outcomes. Students and advisors would use this portfolio to track course credits and co-curricular experiences. The second phase was a senior portfolio that would be used to document and provide examples of a student's educational and work experiences. This portfolio would serve as a communication aid during the job placement process.

To get the two-phase portfolio off the pages of a workgroup report and into the hands of students and advisors by the end of August 1988, I formed a three-person design team. B. Katherine Maple, at that time the College of Agriculture Coordinator of Administrative and Student Affairs, worked with me quickly to retain the services of a professional designer. By the time Maple and I were ready to have our first meeting with the designer, we had established several key guidelines for the project:

1. All pieces of the portfolio project should have a uniform identity: each piece should be seen as part of a package.

2. The design should give an identity to the College of Agriculture and link it with pre-existing University of Minnesota design elements (school colors, preferred typefaces, etc.).

3. The advising portfolio should have separate parts to be kept by the advisor and the student.

4. Each piece should be useable: of manageable size, compatible with the size of regular office files and student notebooks.

5. Each piece should be durable: printed on substantial paper stock that will last for several years as it is carried around by students and filed and refiled by advisors.

6. The advisor's portfolio for each student should have a place where the advisor can keep other documents connected with the student and another place to write notes recording comments from meetings with the advisee.

7. The student's advising portfolio should have a place to keep additional college-related documents.

8. The senior portfolio should have a "more professional" look to it: students will use this in the presence of potential employers and the portfolio should leave a distinct, positive impression.

9. The learner outcome part of the advising portfolio should:

    -   be adaptable to a variety of students, from freshmen to transfer students, enrolled in any academic major program

    -   be easy to use, understand, and work with

    -   serve as a "stand alone" portfolio for students, including some explanatory or historical material and a place to put the student's name, address, and telephone number in case it should be misplaced

    -   track both course work and non-curricular experiences

    -   provide enough space for recording non-curricular experiences, because while course work can be noted with a course title and number, experiences need several words to describe them

10. Costs for the entire project should be kept low, but the products should not look cheap; all the pieces should reflect the significant value given to the project by the college faculty and staff.

DESCRIPTION OF PORTFOLIO

The outcome of this development process was a four-piece portfolio. Three pieces—the portfolio for the student, the learner outcome booklet, and the portfolio for the advisor—constitute the advising portfolio; the fourth piece serves as the senior portfolio.

Advising Portfolio

The simplest of the three components of the advising portfolio is the *portfolio for the student,* a 9" x 12" single-fold piece of marble-textured paper stock with two inside flaps glued on the outside edges, similar to many two-pocket folders available in most office supply stores. The cover bears the identifying words: "University of Minnesota" and "College of Agriculture PORTFOLIO."

The *learner outcome booklet* is made of marble-textured paper of slightly lighter weight than the portfolio for the student. It is identified by the words "LEARNER OUTCOMES: Meeting the Objectives," and sized at 8 3/4" x 11" to fit comfortably in one pocket of the portfolio. Printed on the inside front of the booklet's cover are the college goal statement, a summary of the college philosophy about the learner outcomes, and blank lines for the students to write their name, address, and phone number(s).

The booklet itself consists of 14 pages, one for each of the 14 college learner outcomes. The pages increase in width by 1/4" increments from 5 inches to 8 3/4 inches. Each page is printed on only one side and separated into two sections labeled "COURSE WORK" and "EXPERIENCES." The "COURSE WORK" section is scored with 10 lightly printed lines for recording notes; the "EXPERIENCES" section has 30 lines.

Printed at the head of each page is one of the 14 college learner outcomes:

- Demonstrate fundamental knowledge of the biological and physical sciences
- Communicate effectively and use communications technology
- Evaluate and integrate diverse viewpoints or data
- Make responsible judgments about management of natural resources and the environment
- Make responsible judgments on ethical and policy issues in agriculture
- Apply global perspectives to food and agricultural issues and decisions
- Apply an historical perspective to the role of science and technology in agriculture
- Retrieve, analyze, and use information
- Manage human resources and provide leadership
- Appreciate and interpret works of literature and the arts
- Solve problems in a profession
- Demonstrate specialized expertise in at least one collegiate major
- Develop expertise in additional areas
- Work effectively as a team member

Printed along the right margin of each page, parallel to the page's edge, is a key term or phrase which identifies the outcome that heads the page:

- Biological and physical sciences
- Communication
- Data & evaluation
- Environmental concerns
- Ethics and policy
- Global perspectives

- Historical perspective
- Information analysis
- Leadership
- Literature & arts
- Problem solving
- Specialized expertise
- Supporting expertise
- Team work

When the booklet is opened to the first page, with all 14 pages in increasing size in view, the margin labels for each page are visible. Because the learner outcomes have no special priority ranking, they are merely arranged alphabetically.

The most complex piece is the *portfolio for the advisor*, which measures 12" x 9" when closed and 12"x 26 1/2" when open. An extended tab on the portfolio's longest side allows it to be used as a regular file folder when it is closed, useful for identification and recovery from a file drawer. When open, the advisor's portfolio has three sections separated by two folds: the left and center sections are lined for recording handwritten notes; the right section is blank, but has a glued flap for document storage. Stapled to the second fold, separating the writing and pocket storage sections, is a slightly altered version of the learner outcome booklet described above: a 4 3/4" x 11" cover followed by 14 pages each increasing in size. When the advisor's copy of the student portfolio is opened flat, two pages for notes are visible on the left and at center, and on the right is the 14-page display of learner outcomes.

Senior Portfolio

The fourth piece of the project is almost the same as the portfolio for the student (a 9" x 12" folder with two inside flaps and the words "University of Minnesota" and "College of Agriculture PORTFOLIO" printed on the cover). The major difference is that the senior portfolio for the student has the words "College of Agriculture PORTFOLIO" overprinted in gold foil. While each student receives an advising portfolio upon entry into the College of Agriculture, the senior portfolio is given when the student nears graduation. This fancier folder was designed to hold materials, such as a resume, the learner outcomes booklet, an academic transcript, and work or product samples that the student can carry to interviews for prospective employment or advanced study.

How The Portfolio Was Introduced To Faculty Advisors

During spring quarter 1988, the deans of the College of Agriculture had reported to the faculty their intention to improve the undergraduate advising system in the college. Central to this initiative was a core of faculty members who had volunteered to be advisors, who had been accepted by their departments and department heads as advisors, who understood advising to be a regular component of their faculty assignment, and whose performance as advisors would be evaluated and rewarded as other components of their assignment.

All faculty advisors choosing to be a part of this Certified Advisors Program were expected to participate in a series of workshops, seminars, and related activities leading to their certification. Forty-seven faculty members attended the first day-long workshop, held in August and covering these topics: the college advising system; the advisor's role; orientation—the student's view; the advising portfolio; orientation—the advising tasks; legal issues in advising; and communicating with students. For advisors who could not attend this workshop, two additional sessions were offered in late October and early November.

When the advising portfolio was introduced to the faculty at the August workshop, it was literally "hot off the presses." Few had seen it before the discussion began. Most of the time was dedicated to reminding the advisors about the content and origin of the 14 learner outcomes and giving them ideas about how they could complete the booklet with their advisees. Attention also was directed to the lined spaces in the portfolio, where advisors could write comments about miscellaneous advising matters, and to the pocket for storing assorted papers on each student. Some time also was spent on the logistics of when and how faculty advisors would get copies of the advising portfolio as a part of the upcoming fall orientation and registration period for new students.

Part of the workshop discussion was, of course, focused on the advantages of the portfolio for advisors. The advising portfolio was promoted as offering: 1) a somewhat uniform and user-friendly means for advisors to track students; 2) an opportunity for faculty to use advising sessions to focus on the discussion of educational issues rather than administrative details; 3) an opportunity for advisors to get acquainted quickly with advisees by together using the learner outcome booklet to make preliminary inventories of the courses and experiences students have already had; 4) a means for advisors and advisees jointly to develop plans for filling the gaps in a student's course work and experiences; 5) a basis for helping advisees prepare a résumé or a statement of skills, experiences, accomplishments, and interests that could be presented in a senior portfolio to a prospective employer; and 6) as advisees prepare their senior portfolios, an opportunity for faculty to learn more about the world of work that today's students are entering.

HOW THE PORTFOLIO WAS INTRODUCED TO STUDENTS

It was decided early that formal implementation of the advising portfolio would happen only with new students. If advisors wanted to share the concept and practices with continuing students, that was their prerogative, and extra materials were delivered to each department to be available as needed.

Prior to their registration in the College of Agriculture for the first time in fall 1988, new students were greeted by letters of welcome. They were told that the college was in the midst of a major curriculum revitalization project from which they would derive several immediate benefits. One of these, they were told, was the advising program—the college tradition of faculty advising for all students was being given a boost and this year everyone was working to make sure that advisors in the college were the knowledgeable, caring, accessible people that everyone wants them to be. Students also were told they would be working with their advisors to track 14 different objectives in an advising portfolio. The letter didn't list the learner outcomes, but it did inform students that they could achieve the outcomes by taking classes and participating in extracurricular and co-curricular activities.

The letter also advised new students that, while some of the objectives might be entirely new, the students may already have had considerable experience—both inside and outside of the classroom—that would contribute to the achievement of other objectives. The overall goal was to communicate to new students that the college was eager to meet them and ready to work with them, from wherever they were starting, to reach mutually desirable goals.

When students arrived on campus for their formal two-day orientation to the University of Minnesota and the College of Agriculture, they were introduced to the advising portfolio on the morning of the second day, just before they were prepared to select and register for classes. The introduction to the advising portfolio was in four parts. The first part was a brief historical narrative, giving background to the project and showing students the four pieces of the project.

The second part was more interactive. Many faculty had been suspicious during the development of the list of learner outcomes that students would not understand all the objectives. My intent as I worked with each group was to see how much they already knew. Using an overhead projector, I listed each of the 14 outcomes and asked them to brainstorm with me on ways they might satisfy the outcomes both in and out of class. I also helped them to reveal to the larger group what kinds of experiences they had already had that would satisfy the objectives. These sessions were actually quite lively, for entering freshmen as well as transfer students, seeming to spark the students' imaginations.

In the third part of the portfolio introduction, each student used a worksheet to inventory his or her progress on each of the objectives. Jotting notes on what they already knew, what they already knew how to do, and what they had already done, helped students prepare in advance for their first meeting with their advisors.

In the final part of the introduction, I summarized the advantages we saw for students in the advising portfolio and the learner outcomes booklet: 1) a way to engage their faculty advisors in conversation and begin a relationship with them; 2) a way to give their advisors autobiographical information, so valuable for later letters of reference, without seeming immodest; 3) a way to start thinking about the importance of breadth in their education (technical expertise in a major is only one of the 14 outcomes); 4) a way to monitor their progress in accomplishing certain goals by graphically highlighting what is done and what is left undone; and 5) a way to think about their education less in terms of what they have learned (a transcript of courses taken) and more in terms of what they know how to do (a list of 14 active verbs phrases beginning with such words as "solve," "develop," "manage," "integrate," and "apply").

LESSONS LEARNED AND CURRENT PRACTICES

Physical Structure of Portfolio Pieces

Some of the lessons we learned during the duration of this project were connected with the actual *physical structure* of the portfolio pieces.

- The portfolio for the advisor was not large enough for those advisors who like to keep numerous materials for each student.

- The tab on the portfolio for advisors made the folder too large and unmanageable for those who use a hanging folder system.

Current Practice

Once the supply of advisor portfolios was depleted, we replaced them with standard stock three-fold manila expansion folders. We lost the physical identity that comes with uniform covers, colors, and labels, but the advisors were much happier with the usability of the alternative. The substitute also meant that we would no longer have to print different learner outcome booklets for advisors and students; all now have the same full cover.

Advisor's Use of the Learner Outcome Booklet

Many of the lessons were connected with the *advisor's use of the learner outcome booklet:*

- Those faculty advisors who are convergent thinkers had difficulty imagining different ways students might satisfy learner outcomes inside and outside the classroom. To help them think more divergently, they asked for reference lists of possible courses and experiences. They also requested samples of completed learner outcome booklets as models.

- While the advising portfolio offers a uniform means for tracking student progress, it assumes that all advisors were already tracking student progress, but in a more random fashion. In fact, some advisors had not been keeping active advisee files, and for them the advising portfolio seemed to demand an investment of time and energy (both intellectual and emotional) they were not prepared to make.

Current Practice

It was deemed impractical to prepare sample portfolios for advisors and students to view and model, but by the summer of 1990, an 8 1/2" x 11" *Learner Outcomes Reference Manual* was created and distributed to all faculty advisors. This 37-page manual was not meant to burden busy advisors with more reading, but to offer quick answers for those who wanted help for brainstorming with their advisees.

The manual has some introductory pages, reminding advisors of the purposes and values of the learner outcome booklet, but the majority of the space is dedicated to ten separate lists, one for each of the college's ten majors. Each list, prepared after consultation with faculty advisors in that particular major, suggests appropriate courses and experiences for the 14 different learner outcomes.

The lists were updated and revised in 1992, and recent practice is to give new advisors only the introductory pages of the Learner Outcome Reference Manual and the pages for the major program(s) they advise. Some advisors duplicate this list and give it to their advisees. In any event, all students are now also given three pages of the reference manual at their orientation. These pages contain paragraph-long descriptions for each of the outcomes and offer general suggestions for students to follow in reaching them.

Strength of the College's Commitment to the Advising Portfolio

Many other lessons were related to the *strength of the college's commitment to the advising portfolio*. Throughout the life of the portfolio, numerous questions have challenged the faculty and staff:

- When a student is in academic difficulty, is there value in an advisor's still working through the learner outcomes booklet with the student, or should advising time be devoted to the student's more immediate needs?

- If an advisor and advisee are satisfied with their advising relationship, but they don't work together on the learner outcomes booklet, should the advisor be replaced?

- Some major programs have introductory courses where the portfolio is the basis of a student project. Should all majors have a similar unit in some course?

- Should a student be required to show a completed learner outcomes booklet in order to be granted a degree from the college?

- If a student gives you a blank stare when you mention the words advising portfolio or learner outcomes booklet, has the college effort been a failure?

Current Practice

While some faculty have been disappointed to learn that the college administration has decided not to require a completed learner outcomes booklet from each student as a degree requirement, most have been relieved. The current college position is that the advising system is important enough to make a substantial capital investment in printing the portfolio pieces and an equally significant human investment in the time and energy necessary to explain the system to advisors and students. Ultimately, however, the ongoing success of the advising portfolio is a function of the commitment of the college faculty to the project. External motivation—either threat or promise—will not guarantee success. Students and faculty have to see the value of the system for themselves.

Faculty and students are frequently reminded of the portfolio's advantages. Students are especially urged to be mercenary, using the portfolio to get the most for their educational dollar. Faculty advisors are often reminded of the practicality of having a record of diverse information about students who will be asking them to write recommendations. Testimonial endorsements by enthusiastic faculty advisors who use the portfolio have been valuable features of advisor training sessions.

Integration of the Advising Portfolio and the Senior Portfolio

Another lesson learned was about the *integration of the advising portfolio and the senior portfolio.*

- While the advising portfolio has had a natural distribution time— whenever students first enter the college—student services staff in the college have never been able to find a satisfactory time to deliver the senior portfolio to students.

Current Practice

When we had exhausted our supply of regular portfolios for students, the gold embossed senior portfolio was substituted and used in its place. This action has saved the cost of printing more folders, but it also has reduced the need for faculty advisors to focus on career advising. Perhaps the purpose of the senior portfolio, limited to a folder, was partly responsible for its disuse. Whatever the cause, recent discussions with faculty new to the college and the advising portfolio have generated helpful suggestions for integrating the learner outcomes booklet into the résumé-building process that is a part of the college Career Services Office.

The original Project Sunrise Workgroup on Student (Senior) Projects and Portfolios had proposed that a job search course be added to the college curriculum. That did not happen. But we have recently implemented a computerized résumé system, where students are prompted to provide certain data and the program simultaneously enters information into a data base and prepares a résumé for the student. It is probably time to review the connection of what students are asked to produce as a part of that résumé process with the 14 learner outcomes in their advising portfolios.

CONCLUSION

On balance, the College of Agriculture portfolios for academic and career advising have been a successful experiment in personalizing and individualizing the undergraduate educational experience. Rather than seeing faculty advisors only to secure a signature on a registration form, students now have the opportunity for more substantial faculty contact. Rather than overemphasizing the specialized subject matter of a disciplinary major, students are constantly reminded of the necessity for educational breadth. Rather than feeling like a small part of a big machine, where personal interests and needs are irrelevant, students are encouraged to discover that their individual past experiences and future goals are the appropriate focus of an academic advising conversation.

Laurie Schultz Hayes is Associate Professor of Rhetoric and Associate Dean, Curricular and Student Affairs, College of Agriculture (now College of Agricultural, Food, and Environmental Sciences), University of Minnesota.

SECTION 3

INTERDISCIPLINARY COURSES

Edited and with an introduction by
Maurice Baker
University of Nebraska-Lincoln

Interest in interdisciplinary courses has increased in recent years for a variety of reasons. These include a reaction to the narrowing of experience and interest of students and faculty, as well as the ever-increasing complexity of agricultural production and utilization systems. Students of the agricultural sciences come to universities with less understanding about the agricultural and utilization systems which characterize modern society. They may have little or no experience directly related to their areas of study, either because they come from non-agricultural backgrounds or because their agricultural experience is narrowly based. This makes it more difficult for students to identify and understand the connections among information received in different courses.

The knowledge explosion also has added to the need to provide more interdisciplinary experience. Disciplines (as, for example, molecular biology) have become more specialized as the ability to study smaller units in more detail has become the norm. That specialization often implies that instructors are less knowledgeable, not only of interactions across disciplines, but even of other specialties within their own disciplines. Specialization can make it difficult for students to find common ground with which to connect the various pieces of the system. In turn, higher-order thinking skills of synthesis and evaluation may never be reached.

Production and utilization systems have also become more complex as scientific discoveries permit manipulation of more components. Potential spillover effects multiply. With the increased manipulative ability of science and technology today, it is more difficult to accurately predict the outcomes.

This means there is a need for more specialists to interact, to lessen the chance of undesirable outcomes.

Interdisciplinary courses provide this interaction, alerting students to look for the complexity in other situations and to appreciate the value of a holistic perspective. Students gain guided practice at integrating diverse subject matter in interdisciplinary courses. They also have the opportunity to learn how specialists in various disciplines may view the same situation differently and at the same time observe how they may resolve conflicting views. From this experience, students are able to see much more of the system under consideration.

Many interdisciplinary courses are capstone courses for the student's program. Some of these are team taught by faculty. Others draw on external partners as resources for helping students integrate the subject matter. Still others broaden existing courses with the same instructor providing the integration.

While interdisciplinary courses help students understand the complexities of the world which they are studying, only through these courses, in combination with those which are more discipline-based, do they receive a broad-based education. It is this approach which the University of Wisconsin-Madison used in reshaping the undergraduate curriculum from one which was strongly professionally-based to a broad-based one. The following chapters represent different topics and approaches to interdisciplinary courses and broad-based curriculum, but they all stress the importance of helping the student view learning as a system rather than a series of loosely-related learning experiences.

Maurice Baker is Professor of Agricultural Economics, University of Nebraska-Lincoln.

9

A BROAD-BASED CURRICULUM

Robert G. Kranz, Jr.
University of Wisconsin-Madison

In the early 1960s, the University of Wisconsin College of Agricultural and Life Sciences (CALS) pioneered a flexible undergraduate curriculum featuring five different curricular options oriented to student occupational interests. The original intent was to provide a curriculum that allowed students to cross disciplinary boundaries as their talents and interests developed. With guidance from the faculty, students would choose the building blocks of their higher education. Inherent in this approach was a well-defined core of courses for all students as a starting point, and strong communication among the faculty across disciplinary boundaries.

By 1986, new occupational and social demands, competition for enrollment among institutions and between academic departments, and the flexibility of the option system itself promoted the proliferation of increasingly differentiated programs in all fields of study. General education requirements in the college were minimal, due partly to the evisceration of all requirements during the troubles of the 1960s and early 70s. But curriculum change was slow in coming also because faculty, pursuing their own professional interests, had little motivation or time for defining an educated person, and then taking the necessary steps to bring about a revitalized, broad-based curriculum.

On the other hand, the faculty did have the time and interest to refine its definition of an agronomist, a food scientist, a journalist, a wildlife biologist, and practitioners of all of its other specialties. As a result, specialized major requirements grew as a proportion of the total curriculum throughout the 1970s and 80s at the expense of electives and core requirements. This narrowing of scope highlighted the growing isolation between departments and contributed to the fragmentation of knowledge. The rise of vocationalism among students during the same period also contributed to increasingly narrow preparation among the college's graduates. Lost in the shuffle was any sustained faculty effort to define a set of goals and outcomes for all undergraduates.

UNDERGRADUATE MISSION STATEMENT

As a first step in defining a curriculum that would result in an educated rather than a merely trained person, the Curricular Revitalization Project (CRP) convened a task force to write a mission statement for undergraduate instruction. Bewildered and frustrated at first, task force members objected to the general nature of the task at hand and to any potential encroachment on departmental prerogatives. This mood of skepticism, although potentially disruptive, actually proved to be a constructive part of the task force's learning process. Different educational philosophies and theories were considered with a critical eye, and early drafts of the mission statement were debated, amended, discarded, and then brought back to life.

Within six months, the CRP task force identified the unique strengths of the college and developed a set of broad, interdisciplinary educational goals and outcomes for undergraduate instruction. Over the course of the project, the educational outcomes envisioned by the Mission Statement Task Force gained acceptance as the college's vision of the educated person. Due to their central role in the subsequent development of the college's broad-based curricula, the educational outcomes bear repeating here:

- Specialized knowledge, including historical consciousness, in at least one discipline, but with educational breadth sufficient to meet the challenges of changing careers and opportunities

- Ability to think critically and creatively, to synthesize, analyze, and integrate ideas for decision-making and problem solving

- An international consciousness; an appreciation for interdependencies among individuals and their workplaces, communities, environments, and world; and an understanding of the interrelationships among agriculture, technology, and society

- Ability to work with others (in small or large groups), to recognize civic and social responsibilities, and to appreciate the uses of public policy in a democracy

- Respect for truth, tolerance for diverse views, and a sense of personal and professional ethics

- Ability to communicate effectively through writing and speaking, by observing, reading, and listening, and in using appropriate technology for information management

Widely distributed and debated by the entire faculty, the CALS Mission Statement for Undergraduate Instruction was adopted in 1991, with only a handful of dissenting votes.

CERTIFICATE PROGRAM IN AGRICULTURE, TECHNOLOGY, AND SOCIETY

Once the mission statement was written, the college faced a crucial fork in the road. The project could simply have commissioned several courses specifically addressing the outcomes in the mission statement. The faculty could have scrapped all requirements, including departmentally-based majors, and evaluated the students against the outcomes described in the mission statement. The mission statement itself could have been put on a shelf and ignored.

Instead, the CRP developed a new interdisciplinary certificate program in Agriculture, Technology and Society (ATS). Available to all undergraduates with a major in CALS, the ATS program provides a framework for students to explore and understand the interaction between technologies and techniques of agricultural production, as well as the social, economic, political, and environmental contexts in which production takes place. In order to earn the certificate, a student must complete 18 credits among courses offered by a wide variety of departments (Appendix A). A number of these courses were developed through the CRP expressly for the ATS program and gave faculty from different disciplines an opportunity to teach together.

DEGREE STRUCTURE REFORM

But the outcomes outlined in the mission statement were so general and so ambitious, a new interdisciplinary certificate program and a limited number of new and revitalized courses among the hundreds offered by the faculty could not begin to address them all. Nor could a relative handful of courses succeed in meaningfully affecting all the college's students. In order that all CALS students might benefit from a broad-based interdisciplinary curriculum, the CRP chose to reform the basic degree structure of its entire undergraduate instructional program.

The college core curriculum was reconfigured, and, beginning in the 1992–93 academic year, a broad-based set of college requirements was adopted. (See Figure 9-1.) After lengthy discussion among the departments, the faculty agreed to set aside the old system of vocationally-based curricular options. Instead, students now complete a broad-based set of college requirements prior to study in the major. This broad-based education extends into professional areas of preparation including: agricultural business management, agricultural engineering, agricultural sciences, construction administration, dietetics, landscape architecture, natural resources, and natural sciences. Faculty interest in international issues also led to a new interdisciplinary B.S. degree in International Agriculture and Natural Resources with majors in 20 different CALS departments.

LESSONS LEARNED

A broad-based curriculum is essential for creating the educated rather than the merely trained person. It is important to recall, however, that interdisciplinary programs such as the Agriculture, Technology, and Society program developed by the CRP are only complementary to a degree program. Interdisciplinary programs like ATS can give color to and enhance undergraduate education, but they are no substitute for general education or in-depth study in the major.

Broad-based curricula like the one developed by the CRP can meet all the interdisciplinary outcomes outlined in an institution's mission statement. One cautionary note: dividing the curriculum into segments that produce specific outcomes is problematic. Such an exercise simply fragments the curriculum in another way, undermines the faculty, and can potentially lead to micromanagement of the classroom. It is instead preferable that the entire degree program be evaluated by the faculty with the understanding that outcomes can and will be addressed at many different points. A grid such as that shown in Figure 9-1 is a useful tool for informally assessing whether a curriculum meets all the desired interdisciplinary outcomes.

Robert G. Kranz, Jr. is formerly Curriculum Consultant on the Curricular Revitalization Project, University of Wisconsin-Madison.

FIGURE 9-1

Courses in the Degree Program That Provide Knowledge/ Skill In:

DEPT.	COURSE NO.	TITLE	CR.	personal and professional ethics	historical consciousness	understanding the contribution of research to problem solving	evaluation of data in the major field	how knowledge in the major field is generated	finding current information	current issues and problems	current theory and principles

APPENDIX A

COURSES THAT HAVE BEEN ACCEPTED FOR THE CERTIFICATE
PROGRAM IN AGRICULTURE, TECHNOLOGY, AND SOCIETY

Agricultural Economics/Agricultural Journalism 479. Agricultural development in Latin America. 4 cr. Recent research on the peasant (campesino), a group that comprises the majority of the Latin American agricultural labor force.

Agronomy 300. Cropping systems. 3 cr. Comparisons and implications of specific cropping systems with emphasis on environmental, management, and economic considerations. Tillage systems and ecological constraints as related to agronomic crop production are also emphasized.

Agronomy 377. Cropping systems of the tropics. 3 cr. Crops and cropping systems of the tropics. The environmental requirements of the major crops, their botany, and how they fit into local farming systems will be emphasized. For students with broad interests in tropical agriculture and food production.

Entomology 324. Use of insects as food and animal feed. 1 cr. A variety of insects constitute a traditional and extensively-used food resource among many Third World rural populations. The course examines the biologies of the species used and experimental approaches for increasing supplies. Environmental implications are discussed.

History of Science 201. The making of modern science. 3 cr. Major trends and developments in the sciences from the 17th century to the early 20th century. Emphasis on those with broad cultural and social implications.

Environmental Studies/Environmental Toxicology/Preventive Medicine 507. People, chemicals, environment. 2 cr. An interdisciplinary approach to problems related to the presence of biologically active substances and potentially hazardous synthetic chemicals in the environment. Principles of toxicology, drugs and drug abuse, pesticide chemicals, radiation hazards, industrial chemicals, food poisoning, and problems related to exposure to foreign compounds such as carcinogenesis, mutagenesis, and teratogenesis.

Environmental Studies/Philosophy 441. Environmental ethics. 4 cr. Adequacy of ethical theories in handling such wrongs as harm to the land, to posterity, to endangered species, and to the ecosystem itself. Exploration of the view that not all moral wrongs involve harm to humans. Inquiry into the notion of the quality of life and the ethics of the "lifeboat" situation.

Rural Sociology/Sociology 612. Agriculture, technology, and society. 3–4 cr. Interaction between agricultural technologies and the social, political, economic, and environmental contexts in which production takes place. Issues such as agricultural sustainability, the social impacts of biotechnology, and technology development in both advanced industrial nations and developing countries.

Agricultural Journalism 340. Contemporary communication technologies and their social effects. 2 cr. Explores the growth of the information industry. Looks at the characteristics and spread of new communication technologies. Evaluates their social, economic, and political effects. Attention is given to rural-urban differences.

Agronomy 338. Gene transfer in crop improvement. 3 cr. Principles of transferring plant genes by sexual, somatic, and molecular methods, and the application of gene transfer in plant breeding and genetic engineering to improve crop plants.

History of Science 201. The origins of scientific thought. 3 cr. Emergence of scientific method and scientific modes of thought out of ancient philosophical and religious traditions; the impact of ancient science on medieval Christendom; the origins and development of the Copernican-Newtonian world view.

History of Science 203. Science in the twentieth century: A historical overview. Major themes in the physical and biological sciences from 1890 to the present, with attention to conceptual development, interaction of science and society, philosophical issues, and personalities in science.

History of Science/Rural Sociology 230. Agriculture and social change in western history. 3 cr. Agricultural practices and social history from prehistoric times to the present. Topics include origins of agriculture, feudalism, agriculture and the Industrial Revolution, farming in America, and the consequences of the Green Revolution.

Plant Pathology/Botany 123. Plants, parasites, and people. 3 cr. The course will explore the interaction between society and plant-associated microbes. Topics include: the Irish potato famine, pesticides in current agriculture, role of economics and consumer preference in crop disease management, and the release of genetically engineered organisms.

Soil Science/Environmental Studies 324. Soils and environmental quality. 3 cr. Interaction of soils with environmental contaminants and the role of soils in pollution control.

Wildlife Ecology/Zoology 335. Human/animal relationships: Biological and philosophical issues. 3 cr. An interdisciplinary approach to our complex and often contradictory relationship with non-human animals, including information about the nature, needs, and behavior of human and non-human animals in relation to our personal and professional interactions with them.

10

TEAM TEACHING WITH CASE STUDIES: ON-CAMPUS INTERNSHIPS

Jim Gosey, Steve Waller, and George Pfeiffer
University of Nebraska-Lincoln

T raditionally, facts and independent discipline-based solutions to segments of complex agricultural problems have been taught in agricultural courses. Rarely has consideration been given to the impact of such solutions on the farm/ranch system as a whole. Even more important has been the failure of students to thoroughly understand and integrate the values and ethics that ultimately define managerial decisions. The farm/ranch enterprise influences and is influenced by its social, economic, and biological environment. There is a relationship between the individual enterprise and its social environment, and this relationship must be considered in making general management decisions (Learned, 1987). Students, therefore, must develop a better sense of how to use a wide array of technological and value-based information to develop decision-making skills within an interactive system.

RATIONALE FOR INTERDISCIPLINARY LEARNING

Students must actively participate in the learning experience to develop confidence in their ability to cope with a constantly changing economic and technological environment. They also must be able to establish priorities and balance profit potential with risk to achieve both short- and long-range goals for an enterprise. The goal of this course in agricultural systems management was to provide an interdisciplinary learning experience which integrated knowledge of plant/animal biology and economics with aspects of the other social sciences.

Traditional Internships

Internships have been an accepted methodology for integrating the academic experience with the management and decision-making realities of practical applications. Internships provide students with the opportunity to work with and appreciate the decision-making rationale of producers. However, traditional internships have several drawbacks. Most are restricted to summers or a summer plus an academic semester; such a seasonal view limits the student's perspective of decision-making by farmers and ranchers. The number of agricultural producers willing and/or capable of providing a worthwhile internship is limited; in addition, internships may not be available close to home and students usually must relocate to participate in them. Finally, internships can provide only a day-to-day management view of a single enterprise, limiting the range of decision-making situations a student may experience.

On-Campus Class Internships

To capitalize on the benefits and minimize the drawbacks of traditional internships, a campus internship in agricultural systems management was developed, based on team teaching and the use of case studies. This approach was desirable for several reasons:

- It recognizes financial and/or family considerations which often restrict student access to off-campus internships.

- It allows all students in a class to learn from several of the best agricultural producers in the state.

- The case studies focus on real enterprise problems which students address in collaboration with their fellow students, instructors, and business and industry external partners.

- It allows a variety of different internship activities to occur within a semester.

- Including faculty partners in each case study broadens the perspective of the students to challenges and opportunities and sharpens their critical thinking and problem solving skills.

- The on-campus internship provides the flexibility for instructors to identify and bring external or internal resource people to the class debate on any case study.

- On-campus internships emphasize collaborative learning rather than individual efforts.

Interdisciplinary, Problem-Based Focus

Previous experience with integrative courses confirmed the importance of involving faculty partners and studying "real-life" problems. However, most synthesis courses are discipline-based and offer limited exposure to farm/ranch owners and managers. In addition, most students are not highly skilled in asking the right questions to obtain necessary information to solve a specific problem within a well-defined context. Student creativity seldom exceeds the ideas of the faculty or the student's perceived notion of a safe textbook answer. But interdisciplinary courses cannot be bound by the disciplines of the faculty. An important feature of this course was its emphasis on the uniqueness of each problem and the understanding that there are no textbook answers.

DESCRIPTION OF THE BEEF CATTLE MANAGEMENT DECISIONS CLASS

"Beef Cattle Management Decisions" was developed as an interdisciplinary course (integrating the disciplines of animal science, agronomy, and agricultural economics) designed to teach students how to identify problems, propose solutions, and evaluate possible outcomes. All students were required to state their positions or conclusions (Learned, 1987). A major focus was the development of appropriate communication skills to interact with producers.

Demographics and Logistics

Eleven students with a variety of backgrounds enrolled. Students were required to complete a course and subject matter inventory and a personal goals statement, which provided the faculty with important information on selection of external partners and case studies.

Each student analyzed and wrote reports on two farm/ranch case studies dealing with beef cattle. The first case study also was used as an instructional model to help students understand the case study process and to illustrate faculty expectations. Consequently, a draft was graded (10% of course grade), and students were allowed to rewrite the report (25% of course grade). The second case study was weighted more heavily (40%) for the semester grading. Students also were graded on their personal goals statement (5%), completion of the subject matter inventory (10%), and class attendance and participation (10%).

Description of Cases

The first case study focused on a diversified farm in eastern Nebraska and the need to make beef cattle decisions related to opportunities in the

Conservation Reserve Program. The second case study involved a ranch in the Nebraska Sandhills with significant financial problems resulting from excessive leveraging against land and cattle, poor hay quality, and a high proportion of open cows in the fall.

One producer visited the class, while the second interacted by telephone conference calls with the class. Both openly discussed a number of aspects of the farm or ranch, including current financial status, management, and personal and enterprise goals. Producers were encouraged to integrate their own values and ethics into class discussions as appropriate.

Four external partners also were consulted during the semester; they represented banking, extension (agricultural economics), and the ranching industry. Again, the values and ethics of land ownership and the professional responsibilities of those servicing agricultural producers were emphasized. The external partners also were challenged to provide a long-range vision of the beef industry and future opportunities, focusing on the impacts of the five most critical issues facing the beef industry in the 1990s.

FINDINGS

The course ran for one semester and became the model for a new course in animal systems analysis that is currently offered in the Animal Science Department. An evaluation of several components of the course led to conclusions that proved helpful in refining the course design and focus. The following discussion describes our findings in the areas of student characteristics, faculty, selection of case studies and external partners, teaching methods, and evaluation strategies.

Student Characteristics

The success of this integrative instructional approach depends on investing appropriate time and thought in defining the class composition and student abilities. The class "chemistry" strongly influences the development of an effective course; therefore, defining appropriate prerequisites to ensure that students understand the relevant disciplines is essential. Since it is unlikely every student will have had all the relevant prerequisite coursework, it becomes critical that the students collectively have a breadth in coursework and experience and that no one major be over represented. A class inventory of skills and previous coursework allows instructors to define the types of case studies that will be appropriate in any given semester.

It was apparent that our upper-division students did not have the problem solving skills essential for this type of instruction. Their problem solving skills depended on a discipline-based rationale in a sterile, technological environment. Students seldom included relevant questions on producer goals (personal and enterprise). Individual and societal values and professional ethics were not concerns.

Faculty

A team-taught course can be successful only if each faculty member attends and enthusiastically participates in every class discussion. Faculty interaction tends to define the limits of students' creativity. Dialogue between faculty and students must be open and accessible, and faculty must be willing and anxious to take the dialogue beyond their areas of expertise. Often, faculty are faced with problems for which they lack immediate knowledge upon which to base a solution; but it is important to allow students to observe and participate with faculty in areas where information is lacking. In such cases, students can see how problem solving leads to understanding the relevant process, to asking appropriate questions, and to discovering where and how to find additional information.

The success of interdisciplinary courses is not in mandated teaching teams, but in the evolution of a group of faculty who enjoy each other, both personally and professionally, and value the opportunity to teach and learn together. In this type of course, the faculty are also learners; and this duality of roles, more than anything else, defines the learning environment for the students. Faculty serve as role models of the active learner, learning from each other, the external partners, and the students.

Selection of Case Studies and External Partners

Instructors should develop an inventory of well-documented case studies prior to the beginning of any class, but should select case studies to use in the course based on the class expertise. While a single case cannot represent the entire decision-making process, a good decision case should include the essential information on which a decision about the issues would be based (Stanford, 1992).

The selection of class partners is just as important as selecting students and faculty. External partners must be comfortable visiting with students and answering some very probing questions. They must value the importance of education and have a personal interest in enhancing the students' educational experience.

External partners must share values, goals, and sources of information to provide insight into their decision-making. It is the personal input of the external partners that directly contributes to the students' education and sets this class apart from others.

Involving key producers in classroom instruction indicates that their abilities and contributions are valued and lends credibility to course content as viewed by the students. Such involvement also creates curricular owner-ship by our partners and may lead to other forms of support such as off-campus internships or permanent employment for students.

Recommendations for Methodology

The deficiencies in students' problem solving skills were underestimated by the faculty. It is important to provide some instruction on problem solv-ing strategies since most students do not understand the process.

The first case study should be relatively simple and straightforward, to serve as an example of faculty expectations of the problem-solving process and to model "what if?" thinking. A second way to reinforce understanding of process and development of creativity is to use the individual student solutions to each case study as components of a summary of the case.

As might be expected, we underestimated the time required to conduct a thorough case study. We had planned three case studies per semester and felt rushed completing two. This type of instruction would be constrained by a rigid course syllabus. If a sideline is potentially important, it should be developed if there is time (Learned, 1987), but both faculty and students must be comfortable with a flexible semester plan.

A grading system based on process rather than a "correct" solution is appropriate. Students should be recognized for their efforts in creative prob-lem solving rather than graded on their specific solutions. Creativity and problem solving can be encouraged only if students feel comfortable prob-ing beyond the textbook and/or anticipated faculty solutions.

Roundtable discussion is the only desirable format for classroom work, requiring a classroom facility which will accommodate this format. All class participants—faculty, students, and external partners—must be on an equal basis in the classroom. However, it is the responsibility of the faculty to avoid non-directed interviews (Learned, 1987). We scheduled external part-ners in the evenings and/or late afternoons so discussions would not be lim-ited by the time constraints of a scheduled period. We often included a meal as part of this process to further encourage the informal setting. Of course, faculty and students should prepare in advance for meetings with external partners to make the most efficient use of their time.

Evaluation

Pre- and post-evaluations were important to characterize the potential improvement in critical thinking and problem solving. An evaluation team of three faculty peers representing the three departments (animal science, agronomy, agricultural economics) was formed at the beginning of the semester.[1] This team met with the class at the beginning and end of the semester to assess changes in students' critical thinking skills and to arrive at a general evaluation of the course.

The pre-class evaluation was conducted to determine student expectations for the course and to assess their ability to approach complex problems relating to beef management. Expectations varied, but there was a consensus regarding integrating animal science, agronomy, and agricultural economics into "real-life" problem solving. Students also expected a focus on animal management. Based on some example case studies, the class was able to identify traditional, discipline-based considerations in problem solving, but often in a random pattern. This ability appeared to be based on recall stimulus rather than deliberate and stepwise approaches to a problem.

The post-class evaluation indicated that students had developed a broader perspective as they approached problems. The strong discipline-based focus students exhibited at the beginning of the course was no longer evident. The questions students used to frame the problem solving were much clearer and the class appeared to have a more deliberate and open process to problem solving.

The pre- and post-evaluations were critical components of this course. They resulted in student ownership of the course content and process. Students had to consider their expected learning outcomes and to create a process to achieve those outcomes. Students became active learners and collaborators with the faculty. The comparative nature of the evaluation scheme and its realistic basis provided students with a much stronger sense of academic accomplishment than a grade on a final examination. Students enjoyed the satisfaction of applying their knowledge to practical problems. In many cases, the course provided the only assurance to students that they had developed meaningful, marketable skills. The evaluation program provided evidence that their education was evolving from component, disciplinary knowledge to professional wisdom.

OUTCOMES

This class was used as a model for the development of a new course, "Animal Systems Analysis," currently being taught in the Animal Science Department. In addition, components and strategies of this course were incorporated into synthesis courses in the other major disciplines. The external partners and producers who participated in the case studies have maintained a relationship with the faculty involved as well as some of the students in the class.

NOTE

[1] The authors express their appreciation to the evaluation team: Professors Lowell Moser (agronomy), Doug Jose (agricultural economics), and Dennis Brink (animal science).

Jim Gosey is Associate Professor of Animal Science and Extension Beef Specialist, University of Nebraska-Lincoln.

Steve Waller is Assistant Dean and Director, Agricultural Research Division, and Associate Dean, College of Agricultural Sciences and Natural Resources, University of Nebraska-Lincoln.

George Pfeiffer is Associate Professor of Agricultural Economics, University of Nebraska-Lincoln.

REFERENCES

Learned, E.P. (1987). Reflections of a case method teacher. In C.R. Christensen & A.J.Hansen (Eds.), *Teaching and the case method* (pp. 9–15). Boston, MA: Harvard Business School, Publishing Division.

Stanford, M.J. (1992). How to prepare decision cases. In M.J. Stanford, R.K. Crookston, D.W. Davis, & S.R. Simmons (Eds.), *Decision cases for agriculture* (pp. 42–48). St. Paul, MN: College of Agriculture, University of Minnesota.

11

A DUAL-PATH COURSE IN EQUIPMENT SYSTEMS

Kenneth Von Bargen and David D. Jones
University of Nebraska-Lincoln

As career opportunities become more diverse for students, educators must explore options to effectively meet diverse educational needs within existing constraints. One method of accomplishing this task is to offer dual-path courses. Such courses generally take advantage of "practical" or laboratory sessions to address the specific needs of two distinct groups of students within the same course. Usually, however, some needs of these students overlap and common elements can be addressed in a single lecture setting. The application of these elements can then be specialized to meet specific interest needs in the laboratory.

In the Mechanized Systems Management (MSM) major (formerly Mechanized Agriculture) at the University of Nebraska-Lincoln, traditional students are interested in the operation and management of mechanized systems for the production of crops and livestock. Today, expanding opportunities exist for an additional group of students in the management of equipment systems for producing and processing food, feed, fiber, and fuel.

Within the Mechanized Systems Management major, the challenge was to provide application experiences for both groups of students through a single senior course, MSM 462, Equipment Systems. The general objective of the course is to enable students to study and apply techniques for planning, scheduling, and controlling equipment systems. Obviously, many common elements exist between the management of equipment systems for crop and livestock and the management of processing systems.

A dual-path approach was proposed to explore the possibility of meeting student needs in two areas within the scope of the existing equipment systems course and of experimenting with a dual-path delivery of material. Common elements in the two areas relate to the performances of machines that are functional, mechanical, ergonomic, capacitive, and economic in nature. Senior-level proficiency in problem solving, information gathering, assessment and utilization is common for all students.

BACKGROUND AND BASIS FOR THE DUAL-PATH COURSE

Prior to the dual-path approach, the course was totally oriented toward a capstone experience in which students were guided through the process of analyzing, selecting, and evaluating a set of tractors and machines for a crop production system. The flow of topics progressed through the logical steps needed to develop an equipment plan for a farm. Throughout the semester, students worked on individual projects, usually related to their family farms or farms with which they were familiar. At the end of the course, students completed an abbreviated equipment system evaluation using linear programming analysis (Krutz, et al., 1980). The course concluded with an oral exam on the results of this analysis, in which each student presented results to the client (instructor). This approach was successful because students usually studied their home farms and their results could be validated by comparison with existing equipment systems.

A strength of the course was that the individual projects involved existing equipment systems. This realism made it possible for students to validate the results of their planning activities and also made the course more interesting to students because of their personal knowledge of the situation.

Using this project approach as a basis for the dual-path course in which both crop production and processing systems applications were to be used caused some difficulties. Students had little experience with processing equipment systems other than that which they picked up from academic courses. Most students had toured processing plants as elementary or high school students, but never had toured with the perspective of an equipment systems manager. Because students had no real connection to a processing plant (in the same way they had connections to crop production operations), we developed partnerships with local processing plants which offered opportunities for student projects and for one-on-one partnership with an equipment manager. Fortunately, a number of processing plants are within a 30-minute drive from campus.

Dual-Path Course Development

Because instructional expertise was needed in both crop and processing equipment systems, the initial dual-path offerings were team taught. The instructor primarily responsible for the course had extensive experience in crop equipment systems. The second instructor provided the expertise for processing systems.

The initial processing equipment systems team consisted of four students. Because their experience with processing systems was minimal, students and instructors visited several processing plants. These visits familiarized both the students and the instructors with processing plants and established contacts for future projects. The students toured a food processing pilot plant at the University, a feed mill producing dry and liquid feeds, a potato chip plant, and a pet food factory producing both canned and dry pet foods.

Students described these plant visits and identified problems in a project notebook or journal in which they recorded their observations, information, questions, and partner comments. Outside reading summaries, information sources, contacts, etc. also were entered into the notebook. The notebooks had duplicate pages, and carbon copies of the student entries were submitted to the instructors.

After the first offering, the success of the dual-path approach warranted continuation. In two subsequent offerings, three processing equipment teams have undertaken projects. In cooperation with a potato chip processing plant, a team gathered information to determine if the capacity of a dryer would be adequate for a corn puff line if the extruder were replaced with another unit with greater capacity. In another project, students examined equipment options for controlling dust when grains were processed with a roller mill in a mini-brewery. Another team developed a plan for the feed handling and delivery equipment for a cattle feedlot.

Student Responses to the Dual-Path Course

Following the initial offering of the dual-path course, students were surveyed to assess their view of the course. The survey asked to what extent (strongly or moderately) respondents agreed or disagreed with each of five questions. The results summarized below indicate the percent of students who agreed or disagreed.

Question/Prompt	Response	
	Agree	Disagree
Dual-path applications were detrimental to the course. (One student stated that sharing between the crop and processing equipment groups would be desirable.)		81%
Separate recitation periods for different applications are best for the dual-path approach.	91%	
Crop equipment applications were neglected.		81%
Continue offering the course as a dual path.	70%	
Self-management of scheduling of project activities by the students was detrimental to learning.	54%	

The students supported continuation of the dual-path learning experience. The most negative feedback did not relate specifically to the dual-path approach, but to the method of teaching. Fifty-four percent of students did not favor self-management of projects because they were accustomed to having the instructor set deadlines and make up the course schedule. Instructors required individual time management, however, because of the management nature of the course and the need for students to learn to use time effectively and responsibly. Obviously, some students did not schedule their activities for their course projects on a weekly basis and quickly fell behind.

COMMENTS ON THE DUAL-PATH APPROACH

The course continues to be offered as a dual-path course with two recitations, one for each topic. The course call number is suppressed so that during early registration students must come to the instructor to obtain the computer call number. This arrangement allows the instructor to clearly communicate the course requirements to students and to arrange ahead of time for industry partners for the processing group projects. For the course to succeed, it is important that the project objectives be determined the first week of the semester. Students in the crop equipment area now identify their project topic before the beginning of the semester. The course is advantageous to students in several ways, beyond providing experience with equipment systems in their area of primary interest, because it:

• Broadens experience in working with real projects and industry partners

• Places learning on a real problem basis and allows students to apply their knowledge to specific projects

- Allows instructors to teach general equipment fundamentals and to key problem applications to student career interests

- Provides a means to offer a variety of applications within a single course

- Provides for specialization to match the career interests of students without duplicating courses

A dual-path offering is not without disadvantages. At times it seemed to the instructors that two courses were being offered in one course. Continued contact with industry partners is essential because their situation may change on short notice. In one instance, a prospective partner agreed to establish a project for a team. The week before the semester began, a change in company plans made it impossible to continue and an alternate project needed to be found. Other disadvantages are:

- Dual-path offerings require instructors to diligently manage time to prevent one-on-one instruction for each individual project.

- Evaluation is more difficult because there is not one homogeneous set of activities for all students.

- Dual-path offerings may require individualized input for each recitation or project group, which may require consultation from other faculty in a department.

Challenges

While we are proponents of the dual-path approach for offering specialized subject matter within existing courses, some challenges remain. These are to:

- Get students ready to begin projects on the first day of the semester

- Develop skills in time management for the instructor and students

- Provide feedback and interaction with students to keep the project moving to completion in 15 weeks

- Maintain industry partnerships and an inventory of possible projects

- Instill in students the need to write a high quality project report for the course and the industry partner (C-level reports are not good enough to retain industry partners for future dual-path projects)

- Maintain nearly equivalent projects among several project groups

SUMMARY

We believe the dual-path approach has merit in meeting the diverse needs of our students because it allows specific individual career needs to be met with a minimal number of courses. The dual-path approach has been extended to a second course in the College of Agricultural Sciences and Natural Resources, an irrigation course offered as a dual-path course with two laboratory sections. One laboratory emphasizes the equipment for farm irrigation, while the other emphasizes turf irrigation. Faculty from the Department of Horticulture assist in this laboratory.

Kenneth Von Bargen is Professor of Biological Systems Engineering, University of Nebraska-Lincoln.

David D. Jones is Assistant Professor of Biological Systems Engineering, University of Nebraska-Lincoln.

REFERENCES

Krutz, G.W., Combs, R.F., & Parsons, S.D. (1980). Equipment analysis with farm management models. *Transactions of the ASAE* 23(1):25–28.

12

AN INTERDISCIPLINARY MAJOR AND COURSE DEVELOPMENT: LESSONS LEARNED

Terence H. Cooper
University of Minnesota

This essay describes the activities and lessons learned at the University of Minnesota's College of Agriculture during a period of interdisciplinary curriculum and course development from 1987 to 1990. The three goals of the project were to: 1) incorporate computer-assisted instruction, environmental activities, and cooperative learning strategies into the introductory soil science course; 2) coordinate the planning and development of needed courses on environmental issues related to water; and 3) develop an interdisciplinary major that deals with the environment.

INTRODUCTORY SOIL SCIENCE

The goals for the introductory soils course were: 1) develop computer-assisted instruction (CAI) programs for use in the auto-tutorial laboratory; 2) help students learn the Soil Survey Information System (SSIS) computer program for their land use project; and 3) incorporate cooperative learning strategies into the recitation sections, especially using environmental examples. All the goals have been met and are now integrated into the course.

Development of CAI Programs

When course design is the sole responsibility of a single faculty member who controls content, delivery style, and format, accomplishing change requires time beyond that usually available for regular teaching duties. I completed the computer-assisted instruction component during a quarter leave, purchasing programs developed with Pilot, a computer program authoring system from North Dakota State, and adapting them to Minnesota examples. Additional programs from Purdue were obtained and modified to better suit Minnesota. I discovered that it would have been useful to hire a computer programmer to assist in program development. Without the benefit of a programmer's expertise, the programs I developed, while useful, were not as elaborate as many of the current CAI programs currently on the market.

The CAI programs provide a means for students to review the material being covered in laboratory or lecture. Students are encouraged, but not required, to use these programs during a weekly, two-hour self-paced autotutorial laboratory. Students currently find the programs useful and fun. It is estimated that by the end of the quarter all students have attempted to complete some of the programs, and over half have done all of them.

Use of the Soil Survey Information System (SSIS)

With the assistance of the Soil Survey Research Group, the Soil Survey Information System was added to the programs available in the computer laboratory. The SSIS program is a tool to help determine the potential of a given section of land. It provides a rapid inventory of the soils data from a soil survey and can label soil maps with soil ratings for various land uses. This program allows students to rapidly assess the potential of the land, which they need to do for a land use project.

The land use project requires students to determine environmentally sound agricultural practices for one quarter section and determine how the remaining quarter sections can be adapted for various urban uses. The project teaches students the importance of determining the soil's potential for a specific land use. Students enjoy the project because it allows them to use many of the concepts they have learned during the quarter; it is a real-world, practical application of the knowledge they have gained about soil science.

Students are not required to have computer skills prior to the course, so even computer novices can learn and use the programs. It has been our experience that using the computer has not been a problem for the students although the lack of computers (5 work stations in the lab) has been. To compensate for the scarcity of computers, we now allow the students to copy the SSIS program and use it at home.

Cooperative Learning

The incorporation of cooperative learning strategies was accomplished after I attended two workshops and visited with other faculty members about what might work for the weekly 50-minute recitation periods. Each recitation is divided into teams of 3 to 4 students. Assignments, each of which focuses on at least one environmental problem, are sets of questions that the students must answer as a team, since the team is allowed to turn in only one paper. Frequently teams are asked to present their answers orally to the class in addition to turning in the assignment.

Two out of three parts of the land use project also are group-based. The project requires the students to make land use decisions based on soil properties. They are required to use the SSIS computer program to generate soil interpretation maps and to carefully consider many environmental issues in making their decisions. By working as a team, the students engage in a great deal of discussion about environmental dilemmas.

Lessons learned about the use of cooperative learning strategies in a recitation revolve around group dynamics. Some individuals are not yet ready to work in groups and resist the chance to cooperate with their classmates. Fortunately, because so many of our classes are using these strategies, the number of these students has steadily declined. Most of our students now accept the fact that they will be working in teams and do try to get the most out of the experience. The main lesson is that if ten questions can be answered by an individual in a 50-minute period, then only five can be answered by a team because of the interaction and discussion that takes place.

The changes in the introductory soils course have made the course more integrated into the environmental curriculum. The course improves or enhances students' computer skills, as well as their teamwork skills.

WATER COURSES AND THE ENVIRONMENT

A full-day workshop to coordinate the current course work in the area of water resources was planned when all involved faculty (24 from four departments and two colleges) had indicated they were available. Workshop planning was undertaken by the coordinator of the College of Agriculture's Natural Resources and Environmental Studies Program to better address the needs of the students in the area of water resources.

Each person was allocated time to explain his or her course and how that course (hydrology, soil physics, climatology, etc.) fit into the current water resource curriculum. Unfortunately, three faculty members, representing two of the core courses in water resources, discovered at the last minute they were unable to attend. However, the meeting did provide an opportunity for the attending faculty to discover, through course outlines distributed at the meeting, the content of the courses currently offered and to discuss both the courses and the need for additional course work.

As a result of the meeting, everyone attending had a clearer picture of current course offerings. Participants concluded that a course was needed to incorporate environmental factors related to water quality, and a subcommittee was formed to develop an outline for such a course.

A few weeks later, the subcommittee met for half a day to develop an outline for a course in environmental water resources. This outline was circulated to all faculty in the departments that were represented at the previous meeting. Response from these faculty indicated approval of the concept, but none were interested in further developing the course or in teaching it. For lack of an instructor the course was never offered. We had never had the full support of the administration in guaranteeing that after a course was developed, an instructor would be appointed.

From this experience we learned that while interdisciplinary committees may be uniquely capable of developing courses, without full administrative support in appointing instructors (if one does not volunteer) the course may never actually be offered. Just determining the need for an integrated, cross-disciplinary course will not be sufficient incentive for getting the course taught.

Later the Soil Science Department held a half-day workshop to coordinate courses in soil physical properties, soil water resources, and soil classification. As a result of this meeting, two new courses were developed as modifications of existing courses: Environmental Biophysics and Field Study of Soil for Environmental Assessment.

In addition, in the last year two new courses related to water resources have been developed by faculty who were invited to the original meeting. One course, Wetland Soils, is offered by the Soil Science Department, and another, Water Quality in Natural Resource Management, is offered by the Forest Resource Department. These two courses cover much of the information in the original outline developed by the committee, yet each course was developed independently without benefit of the committee's outline, and only minimally overlaps the other. A need for the new courses was perceived by a faculty member who was willing to modify or drop existing courses to allow room for the new ones. Thus, new courses were introduced, and old ones were dropped and the process of curriculum revision continued.

INTERDISCIPLINARY MAJOR

The interdisciplinary major dealing with the environment (now called Natural Resources and Environmental Studies or NRES) was developed to attract students into the College of Agriculture to replace those traditional agriculture students who were pursuing studies in fields outside of agriculture. The idea was to develop a strong science-based major that resembled current programs in soil and water resources but was broader in covering environmental issues.

The original committee, consisting of two members of the College of Agriculture faculty and one person with a water science background from the College of Natural Resources, developed a major for Project Sunrise that was approved in theory at one of the final meetings. It was decided that the new major should be offered as a joint program between the two colleges, and a new committee was appointed by the deans of the two colleges.

With the reconvening of the new committee, a slightly different outlook emerged for the new major. The strong science base was removed since the College of Natural Resources did not want to create a major that would directly compete with current majors in Forest Resources or Forest Products. College of Agriculture committee members argued against the deemphasis on science but were voted down in the final program plan. During this same period, the name for the major was determined and shortly thereafter the College of Forestry changed its name to the College of Natural Resources. The new major was approved and students were accepted into the program in the fall of 1989.

During early discussions about how students who had selected NRES as a major were to select their college of admission, we determined that students would be sent a card and asked to select their college: either Agriculture or Natural Resources. In most cases this was confusing to students, most of whom assumed all NRES majors were in the College of Natural Resources. Most new students were unaware that the College of Agriculture also had a major in NRES. Consequently, a committee established in the College of Agriculture to revise its majors ended up developing a major that had over 250 students enrolled in a competing college.

The number of students majoring in NRES increased from 100 the first year to over 350 during 1993, with 15 to 20 percent of the total registered in the College of Agriculture. The number of NRES students in 1993 in the College of Agriculture was about the same as the number of students in the former Soil Science and Soil and Water Resources majors prior to the decline in enrollment. Thus, the development of the NRES major was successful in increasing College of Agriculture enrollment to previous levels.

The rapid increase in the total number of students in the program, however, has affected many of the courses required for the major. These courses have seen dramatic increases in numbers and have felt the problems associated with this growth. The problem has especially been acute in NRES 5100, which is the capstone course for the NRES major.

NRES 5100 requires that students tackle real world problems and report on them to the community. Two faculty (one from College of Natural Resources and one from College of Agriculture) have been working with this course during the past 4 years, during which time course enrollment increased from 20 students per year to 80 without any increase in assigned faculty. Faculty teaching this course can work comfortably with 20 to 30 students but become frustrated when the class is larger. Students are assigned to teams of 4 or 5 persons, and with previous enrollment levels, each faculty member worked with 2 or 3 teams. When a faculty member must advise more than three teams, the ability to adequately assist the teams in their problem solving process is diminished.

Because NRES 5100 is not considered the administrative "property" of any department, faculty who teach it must do so in addition to regular teaching duties. Thus, when the call goes out for more faculty to help teach the course, no one volunteers, since their teaching load would not diminish in other areas. Problems also have arisen in assigning teaching credit and in providing funding for the team-taught course.

Some of the problems related to class size have been partially solved by offering the course during the summer and by allowing students to substitute other problem solving courses for NRES 5100. The latter, however, are not equivalent to NRES 5100, and students may opt to take those courses because they seem to be easier and require fewer credits, even though the NRES 5100 experience is really the better option.

Another problem can be attributed to advising difficulties that stem from development of identical curriculum and areas of concentration in two colleges, with faculty expertise concentrated in only one. A student may not consult with an assigned advisor, but instead seek assistance from a faculty member who is more familiar with the student's area of interest. This practice places additional demands on the time of an unofficial advisor who receives no administrative credit for his or her effort, while the official advisor receives credit without actually investing advising time. This dilemma results from a system that centralizes accountability for faculty time, which may be a problem on other campuses, as well.

The program was more successful than expected in attracting students, and the number of NRES graduates in both colleges now exceeds the number of career positions available. However, the number of students in each college needs to increase or at least be maintained if support dollars from central administration are not to be cut. Thus the problem now is how to scale back a program that was too successful in attracting students and still allow them to find gainful employment, without losing basic support dollars.

Problems with the administration of the NRES major resulted from non-parallel administration and faculty involvement in the undergraduate affairs of the two colleges. In the College of Agriculture, faculty were given responsibility for administering the program and advising all students, while in the College of Natural Resources, these are the responsibilities of the dean's office staff, with minimal input from faculty. Consequently, the program in the College of Natural Resources remained fairly rigid after development, while the College of Agriculture program, with constant faculty input, continued to mold to the needs of the students. Thus over time some parts of the program were no longer identical.

The NRES program continues to be successful in terms of attracting students and in providing a well-rounded education in environmental issues. The College of Agriculture will continue to make changes in the program as we adapt our majors to meet the liberal education requirements of the University. The NRES major will gradually become more science-based, and areas of concentration will emphasize the expertise of the faculty in the College of Agriculture.

ADVICE

Anyone who plans to develop an interdisciplinary major available to students in more than one college should:

- seek complete administrative support from both colleges
- work out the way student numbers are counted if student numbers are an important criterion in determining funding from central administration
- establish guidelines for curriculum revision and follow similar procedures in both colleges
- plan to establish areas of concentration only in the college where related areas of expertise are located and have faculty advisors advise only students in their areas
- solicit faculty input to determine who should teach capstone or interdisciplinary courses and include such assignments not as overload, but as part of regular teaching activities.

Terence H. Cooper is Professor of Soil Science, University Of Minnesota.

SECTION 4

AN INTRODUCTION TO CAPSTONE EXPERIENCES

Edited and with an introduction by
F. H. Buelow
University of Wisconsin-Madison

Discussion about capstone experiences in education often is rooted in a set of values about school and society, curriculum, pedagogy, and student-teacher relations usually associated with the philosopher John Dewey (1975):

1. School is not preparation for life, it is part of life; therefore problems addressed should be real and not pretend exercises.

2. Emphasis should be on skill development, not acquiring a subject matter.

3. Instruction is interactive, not didactic.

4. Relations between students and teachers are relaxed, and faculty facilitate student interests and values.

Employers of agricultural and life science graduates (according to several sources, including group interviews conducted as part of the UW-Madison Curricular Revitalization Project), believe that students seldom are given sufficient opportunity to apply their education under conditions found in the modern work place; to relate their education to real life problems; or to communicate professional findings and recommendations to persons outside their field. In short, executives typically expect agricultural science programs to fill the occupational need for:

1. Teamwork skills: interaction with colleagues, leadership, and problem solving initiative

2. Critical thinking skills: identification, assimilation, integration, application, and display of information

3. Experience with current issues and problems, not textbook examples

Capstone experiences provide students the opportunities they need to develop the workplace skills employers expect. They also encourage interactive learning, based on the processes necessary to solve real problems within a framework of the students' own skills, interests, and values.

GUIDELINES FOR DEVELOPING CAPSTONE COURSES

Although many approaches to capstone course development are possible within colleges of agriculture, some guidelines are common to most of them. Some of the more significant ones are:

1. Every experience should be under a course number that is approved for an integrated learning experience course.

2. Each major may make available several possible capstone experiences for its students.

3. Faculty should organize the experience, guide (mentor) the students, and evaluate the performance of each student.

4. Capstone experiences may be spread over several semesters.

5. Coordination and collaboration with other departments are encouraged.

6. Cases must describe actual (not simulated) situations that advance understanding or teaching of decision-making.

7. Cases must be thorough and well-documented.

8. Suggested deadlines and final grade weights for reports:

    a. Submit proposal — Week 1 (5%)

    b. Submit progress report — Week 6 (5%)

    c. Oral presentation — Week 12 (25%)

    d. Submit final report — Week 14 (65%)

9. Since new professionals rarely have the opportunity to select specific projects, teams should be permitted only a general choice of the field within which they will work. They need to learn to become experts on very short notice.

10. Periodic meetings with students are necessary to keep in touch with the

project contents and to make certain that proper caliber study is being undertaken.

11. Design is crucially important as a method to teach holistic thought. One goal of design is to encourage the student to use higher levels of cognition, as in Bloom's (1956) learning hierarchy of analysis, synthesis and evaluation, and to rely less on the lower levels of recall, translation and manipulation.

12. The most important, least appreciated, and most often mismanaged resource available to the student is time. The capstone experience should help students develop the ability to segment a large problem or project into a series of smaller and more manageable tasks.

CAPSTONE COURSE MODELS

Educational literature gives examples of capstone course models that faculty may find useful for developing a capstone experience. Some of these are:

Guided Design Model. The instructor defines a contemporary problem that requires students to formulate a problem objective. The students, individually or as members of a team, list constraints, assumptions, and facts out of which are generated possible solutions to the problem objective. The student or team is then required to choose, analyze, and evaluate the solution, and report the results to the class. A key feature of the guided design model is instructor feedback at every step in the problem solving process.

Algorithmic Process Model. The instructor presents a contemporary problem and student teams employ a ten-step problem solving process: 1) goal-setting; 2) translation of goals into objectives; 3) data collection; 4) data analysis; 5) generation of alternative solutions; 6) forecasting of the outcome of solutions; 7) evaluation of alternative solutions; 8) selection of optimal solution; 9) implementation of the selected solution; 10) inspection of the implementation process.

Problem Analysis Model. Through lecture, students are introduced to basic problem solving techniques, such as defining a problem, identifying alternatives, evaluating alternatives, creating a plan of action, carrying out the plan, and evaluating results. Students then are presented with broad disciplinary approaches including the scientific method; social science modifications (e.g., distinguishing between behavioral and humanistic, quantitative and qualitative approaches); and the humanities (e.g. distinguishing between artistic and critical problems). Finally, individuals are assigned to small teams and work on a complex contemporary public policy problem.

The team divides research tasks among the members, and the group shares and evaluates the findings. Each team member then writes a separate analysis of the problem.

Diversity Model. Students are presented with a well-defined contemporary problem and asked to role play persons with conflicting policy interests. Each player must present to the class coherent, substantial arguments supporting his or her position. Students' presentations are sequenced by the instructor to insure that conflicting/divergent positions are heard by all, and the instructor explicitly challenges and questions each position to consider alternatives.

Creative Thinking Model. Students are presented with a multi-sided approach to a contemporary problem using books, films, and debates. Students then write personal essays describing, if possible, a "eureka" experience they had in the course.

Social Transmission Model. Students are asked to conduct laboratory experiments based on unfamiliar concepts. During classroom discussion, students generate inferences and hypotheses from the experiments and confront the differing ideas of others.

Direct Experience Model. Students are guided through different out-of-classroom experiences in order to dispel stereotypical notions of a contemporary problem. This is accomplished through a well-structured professional internship, study-abroad program, or participation in a community-based service project. As part of the experience, students interview various experts and write reports discussing the different viewpoints.

CAPSTONE COURSE DESIGN IDEAS

None of the models described above are mutually exclusive, and with some modification all of them can be designed as interdisciplinary capstone experiences. Some possible approaches include:

Modular Format. The first module defines a contemporary problem from different viewpoints for students enrolled throughout the college. Each student then enrolls in a second module taught by his or her major department, focusing on a disciplinary approach to the problem. In the third module, students from different departments are assigned to an interdisciplinary team, and expected to provide a solution to the problem.

Case Study Format. Students receive instruction in problem solving techniques, followed by case studies presented from different disciplinary viewpoints. The instructor for the course serves as coordinator and enlists other faculty to help with the case studies.

Seminar Format. Students from different departments approach a well-defined topic from their own disciplinary viewpoints and make class presentations.

Senior Thesis Format. Students attend two lectures a week during the fall semester on problem solving techniques and design. During the spring semester, each student produces, evaluates, and modifies an individually-designed project pertaining to a contemporary problem. Presentation of a final report on the student's project is made to an appropriate public agency.

EXAMPLES OF CAPSTONE EXPERIENCES

The three chapters that follow give examples of capstone courses developed at the Universities of Wisconsin-Madison, Minnesota, and Nebraska-Lincoln. These examples show how the objectives and guidelines of capstone courses can be met in three different disciplinary areas, and how the courses are conducted. As you review these course descriptions, remember the statement Dean George Sledge used to conclude his paper, *Capstone Learning Experiences in Agricultural and Life Sciences:*

It is natural, and expected, that faculty members and administrators have many concerns about initiating new or innovative educational approaches. The same is true for capstone learning experiences. Faculty members might, at the outset, feel a degree of apprehension, in a learning situation which is "student-centered, student-involvement" rather than in the didactic mode. These concerns need to be overcome with the realization that "learning" is the real objective in teaching (directing/facilitating learning), and new paradigms are needed. R.P. Rohrback, of North Carolina State University, in an ASAE Paper No. 89-5502, said it so well: "Meaningful learning demands involvement." With awareness and an understanding of alternative paradigms and formats for capstone learning experiences, faculty and administrators will discover that there are several ways to achieve an integrative, synthesizing, problem solving learning experience for students. Students should not be passively involved in their education. They need to be highly active participants in the learning environment. As faculty and administrators in the agricultural and life sciences, we share a responsibility in determining how best to provide the very best learning environment possible for graduates who will be the future leaders in the 21st Century.

F. H. Buelow is Professor Emeritus of Agricultural Engineering, University of Wisconsin-Madison.

REFERENCES

Bloom, B.S. (Ed.). (1956). *Taxonomy of educational objectives, handbook I: Cognitive domain.* New York, NY: Longmans.

Bruffee, K.A. (1987, March-April). The art of collaborative learning. *Change,* 42–47.

Dewey, J. (1975). *Moral principles in education.* Carbondale, IL: Southern Illinois University Press.

Hart, F., & Turkstra, C.J. (1979, April). Senior projects supervised by consulting engineers. *Engineering Education,* 747–748.

Sledge, G.W. (n.d.). Capstone learning experiences in agricultural and life sciences. In *Capstone notebook.* Madison, WI: University of Wisconsin-Madison, College of Agricultural and Life Sciences.

Stonewater, J.K., & Stonewater, B. (1984). Teaching problem solving: Implications from cognitive development research. (ED 240–918). *AAHE-ERIC Higher Education Research Currents.* Washington, DC: American Association for Higher Education.

Whiteman, N. (1983). Teaching problem solving and creativity in college courses. (ED 226-650). *AAHE-ERIC Higher Education Research Currents.* Washington, DC: American Association for Higher Education.

13

USING DECISION CASES IN A CAPSTONE COURSE

Steve R. Simmons
University of Minnesota

> *While learning cannot of course take place devoid of subject matter, how that subject matter is experienced is what concerns us here...To reason well, to recognize when reason and evidence are not enough, to discover the legitimacy of intuition, to subject inert data to the probing analysis of the mind—these are the primary experiences required of the undergraduate course of study.*
> (from *Integrity in the College Curriculum*, 1985)

No external factor had a greater influence on the early formation of the Project Sunrise curriculum revitalization effort at the University of Minnesota than the publication *Integrity in the College Curriculum* (Association of American Colleges, 1985). This brief report, authored by a select committee of American educators, was highly critical of contemporary higher education with its emphasis on factual knowledge and its neglect of important process and higher order outcomes.

When Project Sunrise began, none of us involved in the early phases fully comprehended the journey upon which we were embarking—a revolutionary journey that would change our perspectives on the very nature of education. While much has been said about the structural revisions of the collegiate curriculum through Project Sunrise (such as the reduction in the number of majors), I believe that the project has had a more profound and lasting effect on the way students engage their disciplinary subject matter, especially in upper division courses. This is where the capstone course has made its mark.

THE NEED FOR CAPSTONE COURSES

I don't recall the first time I heard the term *capstone course* used in conjunction with Project Sunrise. Some faculty early in the process expressed a desire to enhance students' problem solving and critical analysis skills, stemming from criticism by employers who were dissatisfied with some graduates' capabilities to apply technical knowledge, solve problems, and analyze unfamiliar situations. Closer evaluation of these criticisms revealed that the employers were seeking graduates who had a better capacity to exercise judgment and make sound, reasoned decisions when faced with difficult dilemmas to which there were no clear-cut answers and no experts to provide the answers. I remember one person noting, "They [students] need to learn that life doesn't present itself in a series of multiple choice questions."

It became evident that much of the undergraduate experience in the College of Agriculture had emphasized knowledge accumulation with only limited exposure to problems with "no right answer." One of the most important needs of our undergraduate curriculum was to find a way to instill in our students a greater capacity to critically evaluate a problem or dilemma, discern and weigh options, and make sound decisions. In other words, we needed to educate students to be "wiser."

GENESIS OF A CAPSTONE COURSE IN CROP MANAGEMENT

One of the college's learner outcomes statements, composed early in Project Sunrise, read: "Students graduating with a College of Agriculture degree should be proficient and competent in a major and capable of making sound professional analyses, judgments, and decisions." Another expected outcome was that students would be "able to discern relationships among current issues and be capable of participating constructively in discussion and resolution of these issues." The articulation of such outcomes as these set the stage for curricular and pedagogical changes that would achieve them.

At about this same time I encountered an obscure article whose title, "Because Wisdom Can't Be Told" (Gragg, 1940), revolutionized my views on the matter. If it is true that one of our goals in undergraduate education is to foster development of "wisdom" in our students, then some of us reasoned that our approaches to education, especially at the upper division, were wrong. The old "professor talks, students listen" approach to education, while very effective for imparting more knowledge to students, totally missed the mark when it came to instilling in them the capability "of making sound professional analyses, judgments, and decisions." Even if the professor utilizes "problem sets" in upper division courses to enhance problem solving skills, the skills exercised are usually prescribed and predictable and require the application of defined procedures that will lead to elucidation of the "correct" answer. Such exercises do not address the issue of wisdom.

It was in this climate of questioning the very essence of upper division undergraduate education that several of us began to consider jointly developing a capstone course for crop management majors in the College of Agriculture.[1]

GOALS FOR THE CAPSTONE COURSE

In spring of 1989, the capstone course development team began meeting to define course objectives and instructional approaches for a capstone course. We met with department heads and others interested and expert in the subject of crop management and interdisciplinary education. We were assured of departmental support and provided with good guidance about topics of importance to a senior-level "put it all together" course.

We identified five course objectives for students:

1. Improved competence and confidence in problem identification and in using technically sound, analytical approaches to problem solving

2. Improved ability to exercise judgment and assess options in crop management

3. Improved ability to use team approaches to problem solving and decision-making

4. Improved ability to describe and defend problem analyses and management decisions both orally and in writing

5. Greater understanding of principal management considerations involved in a wide array of agronomic and horticultural cropping systems

As the course outcomes took shape, it became evident that most related to objectives other than the attainment of new knowledge. It was clear from the beginning that this course would emphasize problem analysis, application of technical knowledge, and the student's capacity to make sound decisions. We determined that students in this capstone course should have a decidedly interdisciplinary experience and engage management problems encompassing a wide array of agronomic and horticultural cropping systems. With support of college and departmental administrators, it was agreed that the multidepartmental faculty responsible for the course would jointly instruct it. Thus the course was to feature a truly integrated, interdisciplinary approach rather than the "tag team" or "parade of stars" strategy that is often character-istic of multi-departmental course offerings.

EDUCATIONAL STRATEGY

Once the course objectives had been established, the course develop-ment team set about defining the pedagogical approach that would be used. Several faculty members on the team had participated in the Project Sunrise faculty development effort regarding use of case studies. Thus the option of utilizing cases in the course was imprinted before the course development process began. In fact, Charles Gragg's article, which had so greatly influ-enced my thinking about wisdom and education, had been originally writ-ten to highlight the importance of case education to the highly successful Harvard Business School. Within a short time we had concluded that case studies, or decision cases as we called them, would become the principal method of instruction in our capstone course.

THE DECISION CASE

A decision case is a special kind of case study that focuses on real dilem-mas viewed from the perspective of persons or organizations who must make decisions related to those dilemmas. A decision case is developed in such a way that the actual resolution of the case is not revealed, permitting students to formulate their own responses to the dilemma. The power of a decision case rests in how it engages the students and causes them to look at the problem from the perspective of the decision-maker, not merely to act as a critic of a decision-maker's actions.

Such "decision-forcing" cases have been used often and successfully in schools of business, medicine, and law, but not in the disciplines of food, agriculture, natural resources, and environmental studies. Experience at the University of Minnesota and elsewhere over the past six years has shown the value of decision cases as educational tools in the context of a College of Agri-culture. At Minnesota, decision cases are used at all levels of undergraduate education and in a variety of ways within a number of courses in the college. They may serve as enriching examples in conventional, lecture-focused cours-es, or comprise the framework of the entire course, as in our capstone course in crop management. In our course, students encounter from 12 to 14 cases during a ten-week term. The cases included in recent offerings of the course have ranged from producer-level decisions involving an array of agronomic and horticultural cropping systems to the decision-making role of agricultur-al industry and service professionals (see Table 13-1).

TABLE 13-1

Decision cases and descriptions included in recent offerings of the capstone course in cropping systems management

Case title	Description
Bobby's Broken Barley (introductory/non-graded)	Decisions are faced following the sudden collapse of a barley crop canopy during grain filling
Heavy Metal Veggies (introductory/non-graded)	A farmer considers the prospect that his garden produce has been contaminated by heavy metal-contaminated solid waste compost
Carpenter Orchard	An orchard producer weighs ethical, business and public opinion considerations in deciding whether to use a growth regulator on apples
Agricultural Manager's Dilemma	Problem analysis and decision-making by an agricultural manager responsible for harvesting perishable products from contract acreage
Linderman Farm	A producer of fresh vegetables and herbs considers options for marketing and small business development
Mueller Farm	A dairy farmer considers the option of producing lupines as an on-farm protein supplement for his herd
Norm Peters at a Crossroads	A small dairy farmer faces the necessity of transitioning from dairy to another kind of farming enterprise
Manomen Corporation	A strategy is developed for wild rice production in the face of diminishing pest management options
Red River Valley Crop Consultant (A-C)	A sequence of cases concerning a crop consultant's relationship with a small grain/sugarbeet farmer in the Red River Valley
Red River Valley Crop Consultant II	A consultant must advise a client producer regarding a chlorotic and stunted wheat crop
Kalmes Farm	Decisions are made regarding shifts to lower chemical use in an area with concerns about groundwater pollution
Peterson Farms	Crop management strategies are devised for a diversified farm in an urban-rural interface area

Most of the decision cases used in the capstone course have been developed by the faculty in the course. Unfortunately, very few cases suitable for this course are available from other case clearinghouses. One of the challenges of maintaining a course such as this is developing a new supply of cases to keep the course fresh from year to year. As a rule we try to introduce two new cases each year. We expect that, in the future, cases will become increasingly available from other sources as case development in agriculture continues to expand at Minnesota and other universities.

COURSE STRUCTURE

As noted earlier, the capstone course in cropping systems management is formatted entirely around decision cases. There are no lectures. The course meets officially twice per week (Mondays and Wednesdays) for 100 minutes each day. All of the core faculty participate in these sessions. A class period also is set aside each week (on Fridays) to allow students to work informally on their case deliberations in preparation for the other class meetings. One of the core faculty members is available at these sessions to answer questions and assist the students with their case deliberations.

During the initial class of the term, an ungraded introductory case is assigned and discussed. This case is relatively short and simple and can be assigned and discussed within a single class period. Through this case, students are introduced to decision cases, which is important since some have not encountered them before. This case discussion also provides an opportunity to acquaint the students with a simple model for problem analysis and decision-making that they can use in future case deliberations. The introductory case is followed by assignment of another ungraded case, somewhat more complex than the first. The students are given a two-day preparation period for this second case prior to discussing it during the second meeting of the class.

The third case of the term is assigned at the end of the second class period and has a five-day turnaround period. This case is more complex than the introductory ones but is still relatively simple compared with some of the cases that the students will encounter later in the term. We usually use a case here that addresses a dilemma with broad appeal and engagement. The students work on this case individually and are required to prepare a two-page written response stating their decision response to the dilemma and their rationale. This written response is graded.

The fourth case of the term is assigned at the end of the third class period and students are provided a week's deliberation time to prepare for the case discussion. This case approaches the level of complexity similar to that in later cases in the course; students work on it in groups of three to four students. The student response to this case is usually a graded oral presentation of the decision and rationale.

Throughout the term, students progress through the sequence of decision cases, responding either as individuals or in small groups through either written or oral reports. Students are provided a detailed schedule at the initial class period to help them keep track of the case assignments and discussion dates. On the date a case response is due, a group discussion of the case is also scheduled, led by one of the core faculty in the course or by a guest teacher. The leader for a particular case discussion is usually the person who researched and developed the case. Other core faculty members participate in the case discussion to help stimulate a lively and informative discussion.

A popular and effective feature of the course is the informal interview with case decision-makers after discussion of their cases. The entire class usually meets in a special room equipped with telephone conferencing equipment and a pre-arranged call is made to the decision-maker featured in a recent case discussion. Students have the opportunity to discuss their questions about the case or other related issues. We have found that students appreciate hearing the actual decision-maker confirm and reinforce some of the points made in the case discussion. Of course, these enrichments in the course help also to impress upon students the reality of the cases they have been considering.

Student grades are determined almost entirely on the basis of the written and oral case responses. Written case responses are evaluated by at least two of the core faculty. Oral responses are evaluated by one to four of the core faculty depending on the reporting mode used. A small percentage of the grade is determined by qualitative evaluation of each student's level of participation and contribution to the class discussions of the cases during the term.

Oral reports are a realistic and valuable response approach for some cases. For example, the Red River Valley Crop Consultant cases used in the capstone course require oral responses. We feel that this is appropriate since the actual decision-maker (an agricultural consultant) most often delivers decision recommendations to his client farmers orally. However, oral reports are difficult to administer since we desire to conduct the class group discussion of the case free of bias that would be introduced by the oral reports. Thus we have approached these reports in two ways. The first is to have the oral reports presented to the core instructors before the start of the class discussion, in break-out rooms where the rest of the students cannot hear them. This approach is cumbersome and time-consuming. In another approach, each student team prepares and records its oral report on a video sometime before the class. These videos are then reviewed by all of the instructors at a later time for evaluation. Some of the better video reports are played at an appropriate time after the whole-class discussion for the benefit of the other students. This approach, used in more recent offerings of the capstone course, seems to work reasonably well.

STUDENT RESPONSE TO THE CAPSTONE COURSE

Student evaluation of the capstone course in cropping systems management has been very gratifying. Most students rate the course experience as very good to excellent. A comment from one recent evaluation typifies the student response: "I think rather than teaching concepts and principles of a subject, this course taught how to approach problems and how to analyze them. Although I learned much about specific crop principles, I learned much more about how to thoroughly analyze problems."

The most frequent criticisms of the course from the students relate to structural and administrative issues—time given to analyze each case, difficulty of meeting in groups outside of class, confusion over the class schedule, etc. Students also frequently comment on the large amount of effort required to prepare the oral and written case responses and to prepare for the case discussions. In reality, I don't think the course requires an inordinate amount of time, but the type of effort students must expend is very different. There are no conventional exams in the course.

WHAT HAVE WE LEARNED?

Following are some conclusions that we can make to date based on the experience that we have gained thus far with our capstone course.

Team teaching is more difficult than teaching alone. Although the richness and benefits of an interdisciplinary course where all faculty are present at each class are very great, the approach does require considerably more coordination and lead time. All faculty differ to some degree in their teaching priorities and emphasis. Team teaching requires understanding those differences among the members of the team and learning to capitalize on them.

Faculty and administrators are sometimes unfamiliar with or unsupportive of true team teaching. Although the principle and value of team teaching has now been well-established with our capstone course, some faculty still questioned the commitment of four faculty to a single course. My response has been that if we want to provide a truly interdisciplinary experience for our students within the curriculum, involving more than one faculty member at a time is the minimal commitment that must be made. A number of students have commented about how unique and valuable an experience this course is within their overall university experience. I maintain that for undergraduate students to receive such concentrated faculty attention and effort once during their undergraduate careers is not asking too much. A capstone course, with its emphasis on integration and synthesis, seems to be a logical place for such an approach to be used.

Decision cases are an excellent tool for structuring a capstone course. Our core instruction team has no regrets about formatting our capstone course entirely around decision cases. Although cases are relatively new to us, and we have learned a lot through trial and error, both students and the core faculty are united in their belief that decision cases provide an exceptional means to accomplish the outcomes established for a capstone course such as ours. One difficulty is the need to be continually developing new case material for the course. This is not very different from the need to be continually bringing fresh material into any other course, but "stale" cases may be more readily apparent to students than "stale" lectures.

A Concluding Thought

Participation in the development and instruction of the integrated cropping systems management capstone course has been one of the most enriching teaching experiences of my career. Most students have responded enthusiastically to the course and the case approach used in it and have shown significant improvement in their confidence and ability to confront problems and to make sound decisions. If one's goal in higher education is, as Charles Gragg contended so many years ago, to help people become wiser decision-makers, capstone course efforts are a step in the right direction.

Note

[1] Faculty, in addition to the author, who are responsible for developing and instructing the capstone course in cropping systems management are Dave Davis, Department of Horticultural Science, Gary Malzer, Department of Soil Science, and James Percich, Department of Plant Pathology.

Steve R. Simmons is Professor of Agronomy and Plant Genetics, University of Minnesota.

REFERENCES

Association of American Colleges. (1985). *Integrity in the college curriculum: A report to the academic community.* Washington, DC: Association of American Colleges.

Gragg, C. (October, 1940). Because wisdom can't be told. Cambridge, MA: *Harvard Alumni Bulletin.*

14

SENIOR THESIS IN
LANDSCAPE ARCHITECTURE

Fahriye Sancar
University of Wisconsin-Madison

EDITOR'S NOTE

F. H. Buelow

One of the goals included in the University of Wisconsin-Madison's (UW-Madison) College of Agricultural and Life Sciences (CALS) Mission Statement for Undergraduate Instruction is: "Within at least one academic area of the college, students should understand and appreciate the current theories, principles, issues, and problems, and know where to find current information. All students should know how knowledge is generated, be able to critically evaluate data, and understand the contributions research can make to the solutions of problems."

The Mission Statement also indicates that undergraduate instruction in the college will result in the following educational outcomes for students:

- Ability to think critically and creatively, to synthesize, analyze, and integrate ideas for decision-making and problem solving

- Ability to work with others, in small or large groups, to recognize civic and social responsibilities, and to appreciate the uses of public policy in a democracy

- Respect for truth, tolerance for diverse views, and a sense of personal and professional ethics

- Ability to communicate effectively through writing and speaking, by

133

observing, reading, and listening, and in using appropriate technology for information management

In order to implement the stated goal and outcomes, the UW-Madison Curricular Revitalization Project appointed a Capstone Committee to help develop guidelines and approaches for integrative learning experiences. The committee suggested that a capstone course be defined as "a course or courses in which the student is called upon to integrate diverse bodies of knowledge to solve a problem(s) or formulate a policy(s) of societal importance."

To ensure that capstone courses provided good integrative learning experiences, the committee also suggested that each topic or problem addressed in capstone courses should:

1. Develop problem solving skills

2. Expose students to a multidisciplinary approach either within the department or among departments

3. Develop teamwork and interpersonal skills

4. Develop informational sources as appropriate for the professional solution of the problem

5. Consider societal, economic, ethical, scientific, and professional aspects in solving problem(s)

6. Require written, visual, and/or oral report(s) from each student

7. Have a course prerequisite of senior standing or consent of instructor

8. Require a minimum of two semester credits

The following essay by Fahriye Sancar illustrates the application of these criteria in a capstone experience in landscape architecture.

THE GOAL OF THE SENIOR THESIS

The main goal of the Senior Thesis is to give students the opportunity to find, define, resolve, and document the solution to a real-life landscape problem. In many ways this experience differs from previous studio exercises in that the boundaries of the project, the type of relevant information, and the criteria for judging success of proposals are all identified by the student rather than the instructor.

Like all real-life problems, the nature of the project will be ambiguous at the start and will unfold as the student interacts with the client on the one hand, and discovers relevant technical and theoretical information on the other. The scope of the project also will change as the student develops and negotiates innovative proposals with the client. Furthermore, in many instances the number and type of potential clients or users may increase as the student discovers more information about the problem context.

COURSE DESCRIPTION AND PROJECT ACTIVITIES

The completed thesis should represent the culmination of knowledge and skills acquired throughout the student's previous experience in landscape architecture courses and should reflect a professional image. We make two assumptions: 1) the students have all the basic knowledge and skills required of a professional, such as site analysis, construction, and planting design; and 2) they can efficiently create design solutions at regional, urban, historic, and open space contexts and scales. However, the thesis project presents several new challenges to students as they learn to:

1. Interact with clients in a timely, professional, and efficient manner

2. Decide on the types of contextual information (e.g., site characteristics, legal constraints, and other planning-related issues) and substantive information (e.g., knowledge about natural and human aspects) needed to resolve the problems in the project

3. Obtain, summarize, present, and interpret the relevant information to support design decisions

4. Organize all the above activities professionally to use available resources such as time and money, as well as advice from experts

5. Prepare a professional document that contains:

    a. A description of the nature of the design issue, including identification of the users, the context, main concern

    b. A site inventory, contextual analysis, and user inputs, as well as a description of research procedures, data, results, and interpretation

    c. The project program, including a detailed description of the activities and experiences to be provided

    d. A critical assessment of precedents referred to in the design literature, providing surveys and evaluations of other landscape projects similar to the one assigned

    e. The design concept presented as a formal statement or configuration which identifies the spatial experience in the proposal

f.   A detailed design proposal, including a master plan, detailed site plan, main activity settings, typical site features, and construction details

COURSE TOPICS

To help meet the challenges of the project, the following topics are reviewed as a part of this course:

1. Overview of design theory and methodology

2. Fundamental concepts of environment and behavior

3. The site analysis process: Natural and social determinants of design (contemporary landscapes and issues are discussed with specific reference to the nature of human interactions with the designed environment, activity patterns, aesthetic values, and issues of equity; and the nature of human impact on the environment and issues of sustainability)

4. Four programming areas:

   Housing: Issues and new concepts in neighborhood planning

   Wilderness recreation: Recreational opportunity spectrum, carrying capacity

   Public open space: User needs, social issues, and new esthetics; urban parks, plazas, and streets

   Community development: Economics, aesthetics, public participation

REQUIREMENTS AND RELATIVE WEIGHTS

First presentation: Problem statement and site inventory. Description of the nature of the design issue, the client, users, the issue context, and main concern; site inventory; and contextual analysis	10%
Second presentation: Precedents and design program	10%
Third presentation: Site analysis and design concept	10%
Final jury presentation: Summary of the thesis report (see below)	20%
Preliminary thesis report (in 8.5 x 11 report format): Site analysis; research data and interpretation Critical discussion of precedents Preliminary program and its justification Preliminary design configuration	40%
Class participation, individual/group consultations	10%

CLASS FORMAT

Students are expected to read the assigned literature and contribute to the class discussions at all times. During the group discussions in presentations and group consultations, all students are expected to take an active part in relating the particular research strategies to their own projects and to discuss how they plan to apply them. During the presentation weeks, class time is extended to two hours to accommodate presentations from all students.

CRITERIA FOR EVALUATION

Senior Thesis and Jury Presentations

The main objective of any presentation is clearly expressing the intended content matter. Presentation in design fields requires a combination of written, oral, and visual strategies. Both the oral presentation, which contains original visuals, and the thesis text, which explains the student's in-depth analysis and reasoning for the recommendations, are important and required. People may be stronger in one presentation mode than another. (Weaknesses in the oral presentation may be offset by excellence in graphics and by strength of the thesis document. It may be harder to compensate for weaknesses in the presentation of the thesis document, since the oral presentation will in all likelihood take place before the final draft of the thesis is finished.)

Presentations are evaluated based on the following criteria:

- Orderly format or structure
- Good verbal articulation
- Self-guiding text
- Visual display of information
- Appropriateness of the graphics
- Adequacy of the number of displays
- Clarity of delineation in graphics

Design Quality

Good design emerges from a central concern or focus, which is reflected in a solution concept commonly referred as the "design concept." The design concept helps the designer make the necessary trade-offs among the following criteria, which often conflict. Designers are expected to give a full account of how they define these criteria and why. These definitions can be challenged and/or enhanced by the group. Designers are then free to accept or reject these suggestions at their own risk. The design must:

1. Meet the functional needs:

   In general, the plan must:

   - be socially and politically acceptable and address equity concerns
   - address the client's goals
   - meet the users' cognitive needs, reflected in appropriate levels of complexity, order or legibility, "surprisingness," novelty or ambiguity, and contextual fit
   - meet the users' social interaction needs, based on who the users are, what the activity patterns ought to be, and distinctions between the public and private realms

   The site analysis must:

   - describe the social context
   - define the user types and issues

   The design statement must:

   - explain expected space performance in terms of behavioral outcomes
   - include an appropriate behavioral argument for the problem and context

   The design concept must:

   - include layout/zoning of the site appropriate for the behavioral justification
   - include an appropriate spatial organization

2. Support experiential quality by:

   - creating a sense of place
   - achieving a higher level of integration of the functional requirements

3. Promote environmental stewardship by:

   - creating a sustainable landscape that preserves and enhances the natural, regenerative processes

- including in the site analysis a description of the natural/ecological site features

- including in the design statement a definition of the environmental issues

- demonstrating in the design concept an appropriate environmental response in the layout/zoning of the site

4. Clarify the design concept by:

- including in the design statement a coherent story line and a logically consistent explanation of why the concept was chosen

- demonstrating an understanding of main issues or design challenges with respect to behavioral needs and environmental concerns

- reflecting an overall perspective and insight to organize design decisions

- indicating in the design concept the spatial/conceptual hierarchy of overall organization, parsimony, and elegance of the concept

5. Demonstrate design process considerations by:

- presenting and critiquing precedents

- describing a research plan to further assess the functional and experiential needs of the users

Fahriye Sancar is Professor of Landscape Architecture, University of Wisconsin-Madison.

15

CAPSTONE DESIGN COURSE FOR BIOLOGICAL SYSTEMS ENGINEERING

Glenn J. Hoffman
University of Nebraska-Lincoln

In 1990, the Agricultural Engineering Department at the University of Nebraska-Lincoln changed its name to Biological Systems Engineering. At the same time, an undergraduate engineering curriculum in Biological Systems Engineering, separate from the Agricultural Engineering program, was approved and initiated. One of the more important criteria for accreditation of an undergraduate engineering program is inclusion of an appropriate capstone design course. This senior-level course must provide an integrative experience in design that draws upon a substantial amount of knowledge gained in previous courses to solve an actual engineering problem.

The primary goal of our NUPAGE (New Partnerships in Agriculture and Education) project was the development of a capstone design experience for our new engineering curriculum. A second project goal was to assess the possibility of an interdisciplinary and intercollegial capstone experience.

Because several new majors as well as a number of existing programs address inherently complex issues of natural resources management and the productivity of biological systems, we envisioned an opportunity to provide an integrative, multi-major capstone course that would enrich the educational experience of students from several programs. Our approach to the capstone experience fit well with the mandate of the Chancellor's Commission for General Liberal Education at the University of Nebraska-Lincoln that colleges provide integrative senior experiences for all students. We seized the chance not only to provide the integrative experience needed by students but also to add to the quality of the curricula which nurture them and the co-curricular opportunities which expand their leadership skills.

The primary purpose of this report is to document how the faculty gained support for an integrative capstone course for Biological Systems Engineering seniors through:

1. Fostering direct and sustained interactions between students and industry, government, and faculty partners

2. Obtaining undergraduate student input in the planning and evaluation processes

3. Gathering information and support for the outcome at national accreditation and educational levels

4. Presenting the planning process results to the campus-level and national committees

BACKGROUND AND TRENDS

Presently in colleges of agriculture, natural resources, and engineering across the country, educational experiences of students are discipline-specific, especially in upper division courses and most certainly in the area of design. Unfortunately, the conventional wisdom in engineering is that because engineering majors have received in-depth training in mathematics, physics, chemistry, and engineering sciences, the engineer's capstone design experience should not be integrated with that of non-engineering students with less technical training. Similar philosophies exist in other disciplines.

The trend in industry and government, however, is quite the opposite. In the work place, people from all disciplines join together in teams, from product conception through sales. In engineering education circles, failure to recognize this reality has led to increasing criticism of the Accreditation Board for Engineering and Technology's (ABET) evaluation of design experiences. This can be especially true for new programs, such as Biological Systems Engineering, where creative interactions with biological sciences and natural resources are expected.

DESCRIPTION OF CAPSTONE EXPERIENCE DEVELOPMENT

Although we have not been able to develop a cross-discipline capstone design course, we have been successful in forming industrial partnerships for our course that include many disciplines in addition to engineering. Through a series of workshops, we also have actively invited input about the course from all departmental faculty as well as external partners and faculty from other disciplines. The course itself has been offered for two semesters, and we are using our planning and implementation experiences as a basis for sharing information about the course with others in the Biological Systems Engineering disciplines.

Partnerships

During the spring and summer of 1991, teams of three to four faculty consulted with key industry and government personnel in Lincoln, Omaha, Minneapolis, St. Louis, Kansas City, and Decatur. These visits effectively initiated industry and government partnerships appropriate for this project. They exposed faculty to various management styles for product development that they otherwise might not have known about. The time spent with these contacts provided at least ten design case studies for the capstone course. The personal contacts also will enhance the reputation of the university and establish job opportunities for our students. Additional benefits will be co-op and internship opportunities, protégé programs, and other co-curricular opportunities. Figure 15-1 identifies the firms contacted and their locations.

FIGURE 15-1

Identity and location of potential partners visited in 1991

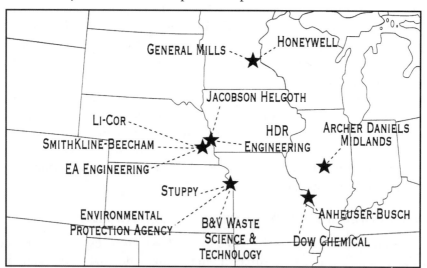

Capstone Design Workshop

In October 1991, a day-long workshop was held at UNL with departmental faculty, representatives from the companies and agencies visited, and faculty from other UNL departments. Representatives from 8 of the 13 partner industries attended the workshop. Some industries sent as many as four representatives, but most sent only one. Twelve faculty, all with teaching appointments, attended, as did both the acting associate dean of the College of Engineering and the chair of the Civil Engineering Department. The workshop was led by two facilitators from UNL. The workshop had two primary objectives: to identify essential knowledge and skills students should master and to design curriculum alternatives.

The participants were divided into three industrial teams and three faculty teams to identify the knowledge and skills competency areas required by students. The competencies identified by the three teams were strikingly similar:

- Problem solving (identification of problem, alternate solutions, social awareness, tedious work)

- Technical skills (facts, engineering knowledge, design limitations, legal issues, environmental concerns, analytical ability, sensitivity of systems)

- Communication (written, oral, computer, graphics, listening)

- Project management (scheduling, budget, awareness of client's position, quality product, closure, time and resource management, personnel)

- Team dynamics (leadership, team player, self-esteem, community awareness, conflict resolution, acceptance of criticism, delegation, understanding of the firm)

- Research (library use, data base awareness, contacts)

In summarizing the skills and knowledge required, the facilitators highlighted the major differences in perspectives among the teams. The industry teams were cognizant of the need to adapt the engineering process to the needs of the client. They all focused on the expectations of the clients. The faculty teams were concerned foremost with a logical, step-by-step analysis that would lead to the best solution.

The second workshop objective of identifying potential design experiences was addressed by the same teams. The following are examples of the possible design problems the teams identified for use in the capstone class:

- Design a wetland to meet wetland mitigation and use requirements for Hastings, Nebraska

- Design a composting facility and identify potential sites for Grand Island, Nebraska

- Describe for a food-processing plant in Nebraska City the impact of changing regulations on disposal and treatment of wastes

- Design an aseptic containment system for a potato chip manufacturer in Lincoln

- Find the most economic means to identify an antigen for a drug company in Lincoln

- Recommend the sensors and controls required for separating yolks in an egg processing plant

- Identify potential industrial products that could be made from wastes currently produced by a meat processing facility in Lexington, Nebraska

Workshop Follow-Up Session

In November 1991, seven faculty met to incorporate ideas developed at the workshop into the capstone design course. The following are abbreviated statements of intent agreed upon at the follow-up session:

- The capstone course should not be used to teach technical or communication skills. Students should have obtained these skills throughout the curriculum prior to this course.

- The course should be critically evaluated as it is taught by gathering student, faculty, and industry feedback, and opportunities for revisions based upon feedback should be scheduled.

- Functional teams should consist of four students or fewer.

- Student teams should meet and interact with a faculty coordinator and industry liaison frequently during the course, perhaps as often as weekly.

- Students should be asked to evaluate themselves, their team members, and members of the other teams taking the course.

- A prerequisite for entry into the course should be established.

- Students should identify and select their capstone design problem.

- Faculty should have collective responsibility for the course.

- At least one faculty coordinator is needed for the course.

The department's curriculum committee was asked to consider these recommendations or statements in developing the capstone design course.

Course Development

The department's curriculum committee acted upon the recommendations from the workshop and the follow-up session during 1992. The course was developed, approved, and offered for the first time in the spring of 1993. The syllabus for the course is included in an appendix at the end of this essay.

Currently (spring semester of 1994), eight engineering students are enrolled. Table 15-1 lists the design projects and industry and faculty partners. Prior to this semester, six students have completed the course.

TABLE 15-1

Design projects for capstone course

Design Project	Industry Partner	Faculty Partner
Spray Boom	Broyhill Manufacturing	Michael Kocher
Waste Management	UNL Animal Science Dept.	Dennis Schulte
Dam Design	Upper Big Blue Natural Resources District	Dean Eisenhauer
Seed Corn Dryer	Asgrow Seed Co.	David Jones

Sharing Results

One of the primary objectives of this project was to share our experiences with others, particularly those making similar changes in their programs throughout the world. A number of papers have been presented at regional and national meetings of the American Society for Engineering Education and ASAE-the Society for Engineering Agricultural, Food, and Biological Systems. As an example of the impact of new programs in biological and biological systems engineering, the name of our professional society was changed in 1993 from the American Society of Agricultural Engineers to ASAE-the Society for Engineering Agricultural, Food, and Biological Systems. The reference section of this article lists all papers sharing our experiences to date.

In addition to these papers, representatives of the department have been invited to share our progress with other universities: University of Missouri-Columbia, Texas A&M University, Florida A&M University, University of Wisconsin, and Michigan State University.

Extended telephone conversations and discussions at professional meetings have been held with colleagues at Oklahoma State University, Virginia Polytechnical Institute and State University, University of Arizona, Utah State University, and the University of Idaho.

Through international visitations, our program changes have impacted programs at the University of Concepcion, Chile; the Agricultural Engineering Research Institute in Cairo, Egypt; the Technical Services in Agro Business at Moscow University; and Shenyang University in China.

Student Evaluation

A sufficient number of students will have completed the course after this semester to warrant solicitation of their comments and recommendations. Several students have entered graduate school, and several have taken engineering jobs. We will solicit their views as well as those of students currently completing the course.

SUMMARY

This project has resulted in a new 3-credit senior-level capstone design course. The objective of the course is to expose students to actual engineering design problems. In collaboration with industry and faculty partners, teams of two to four students resolve engineering problems and propose design solutions.

A capstone design course, such as this, is a requirement for accreditation in all undergraduate engineering programs. The NUPAGE project enhanced greatly the probability of a far more meaningful and realistic capstone design experience for the students.

Glenn J. Hoffman is Head and Professor of Biological Systems Engineering, University of Nebraska-Lincoln.

REFERENCES

Hoffman, G.J., DeShazer, J.A., Hanna, M.A., & Schulte, D.D. (1990, June). *Biological systems engineering: Future directions in Nebraska.* Paper presented at the meeting of the American Society of Engineering Education, Toronto, Canada.

Hoffman, G.J., DeShazer, J.A., Hanna, M.A., & Schulte, D.D. (1990, December). *Biological systems engineering vs. agricultural engineering: A curriculum with a difference.* ASAE Paper #90-5517 presented at the meeting of the American Society of Agricultural Engineers, Chicago, IL.

Hoffman, G.J. (1991, December). *Undergraduate programs in the department of biological systems engineering, Nebraska.* One-on-one poster session presented at the meeting of the American Society of Agricultural Engineers, Chicago, IL.

Hoffman, G.J., Jones, D.D., & Kocher, M.F. (1993, September). Are perceptions reality? *Agricultural Engineering,* 14–17.

Hoffman, G.J., Jones, D.D., & Martin, D. (1993, December). *Incorporating design into biological systems engineering.* Paper presented at ASAE Winter Meeting, Chicago, IL.

Jones, D.D., Kocher, M.F., & Hoffman, G.J. (1992, June). *Experience with a new biological systems engineering curriculum.* Paper presented at the meeting of the American Society of Engineers in Education, Toledo, OH.

Jones, D.D., Kocher, M.F., & Hoffman, G.J. (1993). Experience with a new biological systems engineering curriculum. *Proceedings, Midwest Section, American Society of Engineering Education,* 3B 1–14.

APPENDIX A

SYLLABUS FOR CAPSTONE DESIGN COURSE

Ag Engr/BioSysE 480 — Design in Agricultural
and Biological Systems Engineering
Fall/Spring Semesters 1992–93

1993–94 Catalog Data	AgEngr/BioSysE 480: Design in Agricultural and Biological Systems Engineering (3cr I, II, III) Lab 3. Prereq: Senior standing in Agricultural or Biological Systems Engineering and permission of instructor. Definition, scope, analysis, and synthesis of a comprehensive engineering problem in an engineering area of emphasis within the Biological Systems Engineering Department. This is a full semester design activity using the team approach to develop a solution.
Textbook	None required.
Coordinator	L.L. Bashford, Professor of BioSysE.
Goals	This course is designed to give seniors in agricultural engineering and biological systems engineering a capstone design experience that is comprehensive in utilizing engineering principles.
Prerequisites by Topic	A senior-level design course in biological systems engineering.
Topics	This course is intended to be an extension of a senior-level design course offered in the department. Students work in teams of two or more depending on the objectives and degree of difficulty. The objective is to take a paper design project from one of the senior level design classes and further develop the design to the prototype including testing, evaluation, and redesign as necessary. The topics are selected in connection with a faculty advisor.
Computer Usage	The student is fully expected to use the computer including word processing, graphics, and spreadsheet software.
Laboratory Projects	The class is offered as a semester-long laboratory project. A comprehensive written report is required from all student design teams.

ABET category content as estimated by faculty member who prepared this course description:

Engineering design: 3 credits or 100%

SECTION 5

WRITING IN THE CURRICULUM

Edited and with an introduction by
Laurie Schultz Hayes
University of Minnesota

In this next section of essays, readers will note three different phrases: *writing within the disciplines, writing across the disciplines,* and *writing across the curriculum.* While the individual phrases may have special meanings for the authors of the essays, the conceptual framework that underlies all of them is roughly the same: college and university faculty are asking students to write and think about writing in classes other than the stereotypical freshman composition class. The essays offer helpful ideas for faculty and administrators who are considering new ways to use writing to improve their students' communication competence.

Lloyd Bostian's essay ("Writing Emphasis Courses: Objectives, Strategies, Techniques, and Results") introduces the topic by summarizing how the University of Wisconsin's College of Agricultural and Life Sciences initiated "Writing Emphasis" courses across the college. Ultimately, more than 70 faculty members, in disciplines other than writing, were encouraged to help students learn by having them write more in class. If faculty are going to participate successfully, Bostian asserts, the writing activities have to be easy to implement and manage. So, in a series of short lists, Bostian suggests writing activities that students can perform and several ways that instructors can evaluate these activities.

Project: CLASS was an effort by a team of faculty at the University of Nebraska-Lincoln to increase writing activities in a single department—the Department of Animal Science. In their essay ("Lessons Learned from Project: CLASS"), Elizabeth Banset, Virginia Book, Dennis Brink, and Mary Beck detail their short-term objectives and long-term goals. Readers looking for ways to motivate and sustain an academic department's ability to increase the communication competence of students will find several workable ideas in this discussion. The Project: CLASS team also learned valuable lessons about working with faculty, students, and industry and community partners. These lessons are shared with readers. The team also learned an unanticipated lesson about how to work as a team—in hindsight they were quite compatible, and in the essay they speculate on why that might have been the case.

Ann Hill Duin's essay ("Shaping Curricula through Writing, Collaboration, and Telecommunications") is a report by a single faculty member from the University of Minnesota's College of Agriculture on her multifaceted effort to affect student communication competence. For those looking for ways to structure seminars on writing for faculty, Duin outlines the content of her four workshops. As a reminder for many of us that students haven't always been connected on and by computers, Duin summarizes some of her early ground-breaking work in helping students use computer networks to experience real-world collaborative writing. Duin also describes her unsuccessful efforts to connect students at the University of Wisconsin-Madison with students at the University of Minnesota. The lessons she learned in that project highlight many of the dilemmas that still confront distance educators.

Two of the essays contain valuable reference lists. Three recent books, not included by any of the authors, also merit attention:

Fulwiler, T., & Young, A. (Eds.). (1990). *Programs that work: Models and methods for writing across the curriculum.* Portsmouth, NH: Boynton/Cook Publishers.

McLeod, S.H., & Soven, M. (Eds.). (1992). *Writing across the curriculum: A guide to developing programs.* Newbury Park, CA: Sage.

Gere, A.R. (Ed.). (1985). *Roots in the sawdust: Writing to learn across the disciplines.* Urbana, IL: NCTE.

Laurie Schultz Hayes is Associate Professor of Rhetoric and Associate Dean, Curricular and Student Affairs, College of Agriculture (now College of Agricultural, Food, and Environmental Sciences), University of Minnesota.

16

WRITING EMPHASIS COURSES: OBJECTIVES, STRATEGIES, TECHNIQUES, AND RESULTS

Lloyd Bostian
University of Wisconsin-Madison

The Curricular Revitalization Project at the University of Wisconsin-Madison included a number of educational outcomes in its Mission Statement for Undergraduate Education in the College of Agricultural and Life Sciences (CALS). One of those outcomes for students was the "ability to communicate effectively through writing and speaking, by observing, reading and listening, and in using appropriate technology for information management."

The Communication Arts and Foreign Language Core Task Force developed recommendations to implement this educational outcome. It reaffirmed the requirement of one speaking and one writing course in addition to English 101, but viewed these as entry level requirements the students should meet within their freshman and sophomore years. The task force encouraged departments to require upper division communication experiences for the students, including senior seminars, capstone experiences, and more availability of agricultural journalism upper division courses.

With respect to foreign language, the task force recommended that all CALS students be required to receive some basic foreign language training and skills before completing the undergraduate degree. A similar requirement has since been instituted for all undergraduate students at UW-Madison.

Although advisors and departments endorsed the concept of increased communication experiences, many instructors were reluctant to emphasize writing in their courses because: 1) more time would be required for evaluation; 2) they did not feel comfortable enough with their own language skills to try to teach them; and 3) they believed that grades given in a course should be based only on knowledge of the subject matter.

THE WRITING EMPHASIS PROGRAM: OBJECTIVES AND STRATEGIES

Some faculty and department chairpersons believed that additional writing opportunities should come from additional courses and experiences provided by the English Department, Journalism Departments, or the Writing Laboratory. Further, disparate views prevailed at the campus level regarding the type and amount of additional writing experiences needed, who should provide them, and how to fund them. After studying alternatives, the college chose to implement the task force's recommendations, through a "Writing Within Disciplines" program involving Writing Emphasis (WE) courses. The program has been directed by a volunteer faculty coordinator in the Agricultural Journalism department. The major objective of WE courses is to help students learn; a secondary objective is to help students improve their writing.

This program is based on the assumption that students learn to write best when that writing is an integral part of their coursework. They learn writing best when they have knowledge with which to practice writing, and so writing is most appropriate in upper division courses. A second major assumption is rooted in the nature of writing: writing is an excellent way to learn. Because knowledge is embodied only in language, writing becomes an avenue to better thinking and to knowledge. Writing aids creative discourse; it helps students learn to compare, evaluate, analyze, and synthesize. Writing aids research.

WE courses, then, use writing to achieve teaching objectives; writing becomes an integral part of the course and the learning experience. Writing experiences are designed to help students learn the subject matter of the course, not necessarily to report what they learn. They are designed to teach, but not usually to test what students learn.

All teaching faculty received an explanation of the writing emphasis program, plus suggestions for providing writing experience to students. All were encouraged to expand the amount and type of writing in their courses, to seek advice and help from the program coordinator, and to report their experience involving writing in their courses.

SELECTING WRITING EXPERIENCES

The writing experiences faculty choose to offer students depend on the course objectives, as well as both the extent to which improving student writing is an objective and the amount of time the instructor wishes to apply. Experiences, therefore, range from writing that is unevaluated, unrevised, uncorrected, and ungraded, to writing that is evaluated and revised several times, corrected for writing errors, and graded.

The program stresses that writing assignments need a realistic basis—a setting, hypothetical or real. The student always should know how the assignment ties into course objectives, what its purpose is, who the readers will be, and how the information will be used. Similarly, students gain more from writing when they receive explicit instructions on the why and how of the assignment and when they have models to follow—specific examples derived from the instructor's resources or from previous students' work.

TYPES OF WRITING

Writing ranges from a paragraph in immediate response to an instructor's question in class to a term paper or take-home exam. Instructors who prefer short writing products may provide as many as 15 to 30 writing opportunities a semester. Faculty preferring term papers help students construct them in stages, with multiple review and revision opportunities.

Common types of writing include:

- 1–2-paragraph responses to questions posed in class about a reading, a lecture point just made, or an instructor's next topic. Such assignments define or explain, evaluate or criticize, propose or recommend

- 1–3-page papers synthesizing or analyzing readings, reviewing articles or book chapters, class notes, or other material

- 1–3-page benchmark papers showing knowledge students have about a course topic before instruction begins

- 2–5-page research papers, position papers, or reports

- laboratory reports

- journals or logs containing the students' own observations and thinking about the course and material presented

- term papers or final reports

- essay examinations, in-class or take-home

EVALUATING STUDENTS' WRITING

Both peer-review and instructor-review help students learn and improve their writing. Just as writing assignments involve explicit instructions, so do evaluations. When students review other students' work, they receive models of critiques and specific instructions.

Peer review techniques include:

- Two students exchange papers in class and evaluate
- Students in small groups pass papers, each commenting on others' work
- Students read their writing and the group discusses
- A student takes home another student's work, returning the evaluation the next class

Instructor review can involve:

- Reading student papers without comment
- Commenting only on the paper's content in light of the assignment purpose and setting
- Commenting on the writing style
- Correcting errors in language use

IMPROVING WRITING SKILLS

Instructors who use writing experiences to help students improve their writing often do so both by instructing students in good writing principles and by commenting on and correcting their writing. Although writing without evaluation may help students learn, it provides little improvement in students' writing abilities. Faculty are using the following strategies to improve skills:

- Inviting writing experts to present an early lecture on good writing, provide handouts of writing principles and techniques, or comment on students' papers
- Keeping notes on each student's writing performance as well as their strengths, weaknesses, progress, and needs
- Commenting on writing and marking errors and shortcomings
- Referring students with serious problems to the Writing Laboratory for special help

PROGRAM RESULTS

Although the choices of type of writing, amount of writing, extent of revision, and evaluation vary tremendously from one instructor to the next, more than 70 faculty members have reported improvement in writing opportunities in their courses. Many departments have held meetings to plan how to expand writing opportunities for their students. Faculty members have attended college and campus seminars on how to develop WE courses and increasingly are seeking help from the Agricultural Journalism Department and the Writing Laboratory. Approximately 20 courses involve writing opportunities sufficient to be designated as WE courses.

Because the program requires faculty to change the way they teach, its success varies considerably among faculty and departments. Despite lack of program institutionalization, students do have more writing experiences available, and the long-run key to program success is that both faculty and students recognize how writing can help them professionally and how it can help them understand what they are learning.

Lloyd Bostian is Professor Emeritus of Agricultural Journalism, University of Wisconsin-Madison.

17

LESSONS LEARNED FROM PROJECT: CLASS

Elizabeth Banset, Virginia Book, Mary Beck, and Dennis Brink
University of Nebraska-Lincoln

Project: CLASS (Communication Literacy in the Animal Sciences) began during a comprehensive restructuring of the animal science curriculum at the University of Nebraska-Lincoln (UNL). Development of students' communication competence emerged as one of the highest priorities of the new curriculum. The need for improved communication skills—both oral and written—among students was recognized by faculty consensus and reinforced when employers of the Animal Science Department's graduates were polled and agreed that while most animal science graduates were technically competent, some lacked essential communication skills.

The department agreed to take collective responsibility for pursuing solutions to the problem. With funding from the Kellogg Foundation through New Partnerships in Agriculture and Education (NUPAGE) at UNL, a cooperative partnership was formed among faculty members from animal science and technical communication to address students' communication deficiencies. Support from the grant provided time and resources for the team to identify solutions and carry out ideas.

This essay reflects on the objectives and activities of the project and identifies key lessons we learned. We hope others who undertake similar projects can benefit from our experience. Our project taught us a great deal about working with faculty and with students, about the value of creating strong ties with industry and the community to create credibility and support for academic projects, and about the value of building rapport within a project team.

PROJECT OBJECTIVES

Our objectives were primarily student-focused. We hoped to change student attitudes about writing and speaking, as well as improve their performance in those areas. Our long-range goals were:

- to improve the communication competence of animal science graduates by providing opportunities to practice effective communication in the context of discipline-specific courses. The research component of the project was related specifically to this goal and designed to explore the effects of a communication-intensive curriculum on the development of communication competence in students.

- to create an adaptable model for writing-across-the-disciplines that could be used by others in CASNR, as well as other colleges and universities.

We established five short-term objectives to support our long-range goals:

1. to introduce writing components into all animal science courses
2. to provide a support system for students and faculty
3. to emphasize for students the importance of communication competence in their careers
4. to create closer relationships between the academy and industry
5. to disseminate information about the project

Expected correlated outcomes for students included increased competence in the animal sciences, stronger problem solving skills, and greater awareness of social issues related to animal agriculture.

HISTORICAL OVERVIEW

Fundamental to all writing across the curriculum (WAC) programs is the emphasis on the central role of language in learning (Fillion, 1979). This focus has helped create a climate more conducive to encouraging cooperation among communication instructors and other discipline specialists, and has helped faculty and students to better understand the value of interdisciplinary relationships (Young and Fulwiler, 1986).

Fulwiler (1984) suggests that writing across the curriculum projects require an extraordinary level of collegiality, primarily because faculty must collaborate in ways they ordinarily do not. They must work hard, tolerate occasional disagreements, and eventually trust one another so they may function as a community. Our Project: CLASS team did, in fact, experience these indices of adaptation in our work together and with various partners. The team itself became a microcosmic representation of the broader discourse community.

While WAC programs usually involve entire colleges and universities, writing across disciplines programs are generally narrower, more selective. Project: CLASS was further defined to apply only to writing in the animal sciences. Nevertheless, the lessons learned by those who have pioneered and tracked writing across the curriculum and writing across disciplines programs proved to be invaluable. The same general principles, questions, and problems applied to our specific instance as to the more inclusive programs.

For example, to develop realistic objectives and strategies we needed to reconsider our assumptions about the meaning of *good writing*, especially as they applied to the conventions of the animal science discipline. Odell (1986) suggests a series of questions that need to be addressed in planning writing in the disciplines activities: Are there characteristics of good writing that pervade academic contexts? Are there specific conventions of style and editing that change from discipline to discipline? What types of writing tasks are most appropriate for different disciplines? Are inquiry strategies and rules of evidence different in different disciplines? These and similar questions that have been asked and, in some cases, tested and answered, helped us formulate goals, objectives, and strategies in the context of animal science faculty expectations.

In addition to reviewing the literature on the theoretical underpinnings for WAC programs, we turned to research studies for guidance on developing evaluation and assessment tools and techniques (Beach and Bridwell, 1984; Cooper, Cherry, Copley, Fleischer, Pollard and Sartisky, 1984; Fulwiler, and Gorman, 1986; White, 1985; Huot, 1990). These and other sources provided valuable information about different types of assessment for different types of assignments, scoring techniques developed and tested in major programs (such as the one in the California university system), and various ways of responding to students' writing.

While planning workshops designed to help animal science faculty develop writing assignments for their classes, handle the paper load, and learn about assessment techniques, we relied on some of the sources mentioned earlier, especially White (1985), plus some additional sources that focus specifically on types of writing assignments faculty might wish to try (Stanford, 1984; Cross and Angelo, 1988; Lunsford, 1989).

A prerequisite for funding from the NUPAGE project was to form new partnerships. The Project: CLASS team itself is a new partnership between disciplines. In addition, we formed partnerships with the animal science faculty, with selected groups of undergraduate and graduate students, and with representatives from industry. The advantages of forming collaborative partnerships within and beyond academic boundaries are well documented in Reddish (1983), Odell and Goswami (1984), and Tchudi (1986), among others. The benefits derived from the exchange of ideas, the practical advice, the degree of support, and the quality of regard and trust that developed among the individuals within and between the various partnerships attests to the value of establishing these kinds of relationships in the educational system.

PROJECT COMPONENTS AND OUTCOMES

Based on our assessment of the needs of both faculty and students and in the context of ongoing work in writing in the disciplines, we developed several project components in support of individual objectives. This section describes the project components and explains the outcomes of each, beginning with components related to short-term objectives, followed by discussion of components related to long-term objectives and the research activities of the project.

Short-Term Objectives

Writing in Animal Science Courses. All animal science teaching faculty were asked to include writing activities in their courses, at either a baseline or an intensive level. Through a series of initial workshops, the project team worked with faculty to help them: a) determine both practical and pedagogical objectives for using writing as a teaching tool, b) design writing assignments consistent with those objectives, and c) develop an efficient and effective system for responding to student writing. Seventy percent of all courses in the animal science curriculum now include a writing component.

Support Systems for Faculty and Students. Although Project: CLASS was strongly endorsed by animal science faculty, implementation was not without challenges. Many faculty members were reluctant to venture into less familiar territory by adding writing components to their courses. In addition, some already felt overwhelmed by workloads. Students, too, who were not accustomed to extensive writing in their major courses, needed support to help them manage the writing that instructors were asking them to do. We developed several strategies to meet these challenges:

- Designation of one member of the project team to serve as a part-time, on-site communication coordinator who spent time each week in the Animal Science Department to consult with faculty and students and manage other support functions. The coordinator was responsible for organizing the faculty workshops and discussions and for consulting with faculty who needed advice or assistance developing writing assignments.

- Extensive handouts and resource material about writing-in-the-disciplines for faculty and student reference

- Periodic informal breakfast or lunchtime gatherings of faculty to discuss and critique the effectiveness of writing activities, to talk about writing in the disciplines, and to explore successful writing activities developed by faculty

- Establishment of a writing resource room for faculty and students that housed a small library of print, visual, and computer resources related to writing and served as an office for the communication coordinator and graduate student assistants

- Trained graduate teaching assistants available to consult with students and to help faculty read and respond to writing assignments

Emphasis on the Importance of Communication Competence in Students' Future Careers. Ultimately, the project's efforts have focused on students, to help them change their attitudes about writing and see the value of learning to communicate clearly about scientific ideas. A significant evaluative component of the project was a longitudinal study of student writing, to help us assess the impact of a communication-intensive curriculum on communication competence. (See later section on Assessment.) All students who provided writing samples for assessment received a report of the results, along with an analysis of areas that needed improvement. Instructors encouraged students to visit the writing resource room for help with writing projects or answers to questions about effective writing. Faculty also occasionally invited the communication coordinator to come to classes to discuss writing with students.

In addition, we sponsored "Communicating With the Pros Day," an event which brought industry representatives to campus to talk to students about the importance of effective communication in animal science careers.

Relationship Between the Department of Animal Science and the Animal Science Industry. We met with our external partners regularly to inform them of the project's progress and to elicit ideas and suggestions for improvement. The external partners were actively involved in the project, especially through their participation in "Communicating With the Pros Day." Their encouragement helped to validate the project in the eyes of both faculty and students, and their involvement led to increased visibility of the University of Nebraska and the Animal Science Department in the industry sector.

Dissemination of Information about Project: CLASS and its Results. Team members have made presentations about the project at meetings of various professional organizations and have authored several project-related articles. (See the section of this article, Products of the Project, for a complete listing.)

We also have described the project and offered project-related workshops within the college on occasions ranging from informal "brown bag" noon hour discussions to a day-long winter interim workshop on writing in the disciplines.

Long-Term Goals

Some long-range goals have been met; others are likely to be achieved soon.

Improvement of the Communication Competence of Animal Science Graduates. We are completing a longitudinal study of writing competency among animal science undergraduates, beginning with those who entered the curriculum in fall 1990. Since that time, animal science majors have been, and will be, exposed to a variety of discipline-specific writing activities throughout their academic careers. The research component of Project: CLASS was designed to track the development of students' communication skills through four years.

At the beginning of the project, control groups of students were identified (control groups consisted of animal science seniors graduating before the curriculum included a significant writing component; finishing first-year students; and entering first-year students). Each student was asked to write a response to one of three questions developed by the project team. Questions were general enough that students' backgrounds did not introduce inherent bias in their responses, but specific enough that students could write their responses in 30 minutes. The three writing prompts became the basis for our ongoing assessment of student writing.

Students received a handout describing the writing task one week before the writing took place. They were told to think about which question they wanted to answer. If they wished, they could research the question and plan how they would respond. They wrote their responses in a controlled 30-minute period in selected classes. (First-year students were assessed in Animal Science 100, a large lecture class required of all entering animal science majors; seniors were assessed in Animal Science 490, a required senior seminar.)

We gathered data from first-year students for four semesters (fall 1990 through spring 1992) and from graduating seniors for eight semesters (fall 1990 through spring 1994). Writing samples were evaluated and scored on a numerical scale by the same panel of evaluators, using the same evaluation criteria. Additional evaluative instruments, such as case studies, writing portfolios, and attitudinal studies, will be used to validate and interpret the results of the longitudinal research. Research will be completed this year. Once all data are collected, we will compare the scores of students who have completed a four-year, writing-intensive curriculum with the scores of those who graduated before the writing-intensive curriculum was instituted, and draw conclusions about their competence as writers.

To facilitate rating a large number of student writing samples, we developed a modified holistic scoring sheet, based on a scoring instrument devised at the University of California. The scoring sheet was designed to allow raters to assign a single score (from 1 to 5, representing qualitative assessment from unacceptable to excellent) to each writing sample for easy comparison. In addition, the scoring sheet provided room to respond to individual features of the writing sample, thus allowing useful feedback to students. The scoring sheet also proved valuable to individual faculty members who modified it and used it to respond to course-related student writing.

Adaptable Model for Other Writing-in-the-Disciplines Projects

The success of the Project: CLASS model has been demonstrated not only by its effective implementation in the Animal Science Department, but by the recent addition to the CASNR curriculum the requirement that all departments in the college offer at least two communication-intensive courses at the junior/senior-level. A group of faculty from several disciplines has come together as a teaching community to foster a better understanding of and dedication to development of communication competence as an essential component of the well-educated student.

Lessons Learned about Working with Faculty

The primary lesson we learned was that any project designed to change student attitudes and behaviors must first focus on changing the behavior and attitudes of faculty. Further, writing-in-the-disciplines projects may reach untimely ends if the only impetus for implementing them comes from outside the discipline in which they function. In the case of Project: CLASS, almost all the successes we experienced were due to early involvement of faculty and responses to their concerns. The project developed from the inside out, not from the outside in. It was an idea that emerged among animal science faculty who called upon the communication experts for assistance, not an idea imposed by communication experts on animal science faculty. The sense of ownership created an environment that encouraged experimentation and supported risk-taking. That environment allowed individuals to discover for themselves the benefits of emphasizing written and oral communication in regular course work and went a long way to sustain the project, even when supporting funds were no longer available.

Changes Faculty Have Made in Approaches to Teaching

The strength of faculty commitment to the principles of Project: CLASS is apparent in the number of courses that now emphasize communication-related learning activities. At least 70% of all animal science courses now include some type of writing/speaking component. Further, most of those courses can be described as communication-intensive because they include more than one communication activity. The range of assignments has been impressive, too, from 5-minute in-class writing exercises, to journals, to correspondence, to comprehensive analytical reports.

At a Project: CLASS reunion of faculty and industry partners in the fall of 1993, faculty reflected on the lessons they learned from the project. All agreed that their teaching has improved since they started using writing as a learning tool, because asking students to write forces instructors to think about a course's objectives and methods. Further, instructors who expect effective communication skills from students must work to hone their own communication competence, to set an example for students. Faculty also have found that student writing is a valuable assessment tool to determine how well students have grasped the concepts and ideas of the discipline. Especially gratifying to the faculty has been the discovery that writing assignments do not have to be long and laborious, in either scope or assessment, to be effective.

Support Systems to Help Faculty

The support systems offered by the project made a significant difference in overall faculty response to the project. Workshops and discussion sessions for faculty were always well-attended (especially when they included a meal or refreshments). Among the most useful of these opportunities for faculty interaction were informal end-of-semester breakfasts that took place on three days during exam week. We invited faculty to drop in to the departmental conference room from 8 to 10 a.m. for coffee, croissants, and conversation. The discussions followed no agenda, but were lively, informative, and invigorating.

The role played by the communication coordinator as an on-site consultant contributed significantly to the success of the project, mainly because she had an office in the Animal Science Department and kept regular office hours. Her presence in the department made it easy for faculty to stop in and ask questions, for the consultant to engage in informal conversations with faculty about communication activities in classes, and for students to visit the consultant when necessary. If she had remained across campus in her own office, faculty would not have taken the trouble to seek her out for assistance and she would not have been able to maintain informal contact with faculty.

Faculty also appreciated and used the services of animal science graduate students who were specially trained as reading assistants for instructors who taught large classes or needed help evaluating extensive student writing. We learned several things through our association with the graduate assistants.

First, they were able to give us sound advice about the needs and expectations of the undergraduate students, from the vantage point of having been, in the not too distant past, undergraduates themselves. Second, the undergraduate students seemed to respond more readily to the advice and support of the graduate assistants than they did to the communication coordinator or some faculty. We attribute this response to the nature of the student-to-student relationship and the fact that students felt apparently less threatened having another student evaluate their writing. Third, the graduate students appreciated the opportunity to develop skills in reading and assessing student writing, especially those who expected to someday be teaching in the discipline.

The practical nature of the project's support systems also contributed greatly to positive faculty response. We developed and gave to faculty practical tools they could use directly—not merely theory and thoughtful discourse. Faculty left our workshops with adaptable examples of writing assignments culled from the many we had gathered in our research into writing in the disciplines; worksheets to help plan writing assignments; templates for creating writing assignment sheets for students; checklists and criteria sheets to use in assessing student writing; and a promise to provide one-on-one feedback to individuals who developed writing assignments and wanted help polishing and refining them. In short, we offered a workable process for planning, developing, and assessing student writing—complete with tangible, visible tools for doing what we all agreed should be done.

Extending the Project Model to Other Faculty

Our ambition to create an adaptable model for use by other departments in the college reached mixed success. While no other department has developed as extensive a model as Project: CLASS, the new college curriculum will emphasize communication-related instruction. All departments, starting in fall 1994, will be required to offer at least two communication-intensive (CI) courses for students at the junior and senior levels. Members of the Project: CLASS team were involved in drafting guidelines for developing communication-intensive courses, and three members of the team are now part of a teaching community interest group working on managing CI courses.

We also learned that other faculty at other institutions are happy to hear about the success of our project and to share ideas and concerns about writing in the disciplines. We have disseminated information about the project in a number of forums, both written and oral, at several levels—local, regional, national, and international—and in disciplines related both to food science/animal science and to communication.

LESSONS LEARNED ABOUT WORKING WITH AND FOR STUDENTS

Student Involvement

Unlike faculty, students were less receptive to offers of support. They seldom visited the writing resource library, did not often consult the communication coordinator or graduate assistants, and responded only in a limited way to activities designed to interest them in writing and speaking as components of their careers. Still, we believe providing these resources for students served a vital function. The atmosphere of support was, we found, more important than the support itself. The mere fact that we would offer assistance to student writers lent credibility to the project and to the increasing number of communication assignments required in animal science courses. It also is possible that we introduced our entire arsenal of student support too soon. Perhaps it would have been better to wait a year or two, until faculty had developed a better sense of how to help students use the project's support services most effectively, but funding and time limitations kept us from exploring this option.

We did, however, involve students in the project in a number of ways and are beginning to see positive responses from them in forms we hadn't anticipated. Early in the project, we relied on a team of student partners to tell us what students needed and wanted from their instructors to help them manage writing projects. We learned that students know themselves pretty well, and their direct input helped us define the project's direction. We also brought together student discussion groups from time to time to get input and feedback from students involved in various parts of the project. We specifically enlisted the help of the student organization, Block and Bridle, to help plan and host "Communicating With the Pros Day."

Direct student involvement with this event both increased student interest and commitment and impressed our industry guests with the quality of student leadership.

Development of Student Communication Competence

While we believe we have helped change student attitudes about writing, we cannot yet say with scientific certainty that the project has made students better communicators, because our analysis of the data from our longitudinal study is incomplete. However, anecdotal evidence supports the view that our goal has been accomplished. Instructors in animal science, especially the leader of the senior seminar, have observed that students seem to be writing better as a result of the practice they have gotten in their previous animal science courses. In addition, the department has received some feedback from supporters and scholarship sponsors, indicating that student correspondence seems to have improved in quality over the past three years. While we are pleased to hear such positive news about the communication competence of animal science students, we must still consider other variables which may have contributed to higher quality communication skills in graduating students, such as maturation and preparation in secondary schools.

Student Views of Their Own Writing

Our hope that students would take the first-year writing skills assessment more seriously was somewhat misguided. Our primary purpose for collecting a writing sample from all students was to gather data for our longitudinal study of the effects of a strong communication-based curriculum. But we also tried to use the sample as a tool to call students' attention to the importance of effective writing. We reported scores to the students, along with an explanation of the strengths and weaknesses we found in the writing sample, and encouraged them to speak with their instructors, advisors, or the communication coordinator for further feedback. They didn't. The lesson here is not easy to pinpoint, but we suspect a "Missourian" attitude: students saying "show me the benefits" and expecting to be shown before jumping on the bandwagon.

What we may have seen here, too, is a corollary to our earlier observation that success for writing programs depends on the degree to which participants buy into them. In the case of Project: CLASS, the instructors of the introductory course (in which we collected the initial writing sample) offered only a lukewarm accommodation for this component of our project. They did not reinforce for students our conviction that the writing sample would serve as a useful snapshot of their writing skills. If we had it to do over again, we would work harder at getting those introductory course instructors on the bandwagon early; they might have carried a few more students aboard with them. Still, students are slow to embrace change, especially if the impetus for change comes from someone else, so we might never have seen an immediate positive response from students. Their understanding of the benefits of mastering communication skills would have to come, as indeed it did, gradually, after they began to see the positive consequences of their own good writing.

Additional Discoveries About Student Writing in Animal Science Courses

We did learn what we had suspected all along: connecting writing to the discipline has made it easier for students to learn to write—or at least has made writing seem more relevant. Students write not "papers" or "essays" but "proposals" and "abstracts" and "lab reports"—the stuff of their future professions. Moving writing into the discipline's classroom makes it a clear mode of articulation for demonstrating mastery of subject matter. Additionally, when professors expect students to produce clear and complete writing, and make their expectations known, students usually prove capable of meeting the expectations; not always right away and not always well, but they get the idea. Writing for consequences, both immediate (the "grade") and long-term (future employability), has a profound effect on student performance.

We also were surprised to learn the degree or extent to which the quality of student writing is related to what and why they are writing. Our initial attempts to design an instrument for assessing writing skills of first-year students taught us this lesson well. Thinking that students could better demonstrate mastery of higher order thinking skills by writing about topics that required them to take and defend a stand on a relevant but controversial issue, we asked questions that apparently rubbed hard against their collective cultural bias. For example, we asked one group of students to address the question of whether the world would be better off if the grain used to feed livestock were used instead to feed hungry people. The question elicited remarkably emotional responses coupled with remarkably poor writing, characterized by fragmentation, frenetic pace, offensive tone, and (in some cases) surprising vulgarity. Many student writers (most of them from agricultural communities with strong ties to animal agriculture) perceived the question as a threat to their very livelihoods and responded out of anger or fear, paying little attention to the qualities of effective persuasive writing that we thought our questions would inspire. Consequently, we dropped the more controversial questions and asked questions that demanded less emotional responses.

LESSONS LEARNED ABOUT WORKING WITH INDUSTRY AND COMMUNITY PARTNERS

We benefitted a great deal from the involvement of external partners from the community and are especially grateful to the contributions of the NUPAGE outreach coordinator, who helped us establish strong ties with several community partners who stayed with the project from its beginning.

We relied heavily on our external partners for advice about what aspects of communication to stress with our students; for helping us cement faculty commitment to the project; and for their tenacity in holding us accountable for our work. This component of the project worked for us because we made our community and industry partners active players in the project's development and assessment. The animal science faculty quickly developed a rapport with the external partner team, and the cooperative arrangement soon took on the look of a friendship rather than a mere business relationship. The commitment of our partners to the project was evidenced in their willingness to give us valuable time for meetings, brainstorming sessions, and interaction with students. In addition, the partners took information about the project outside the university community and added credibility to both the project and the Animal Science Department through their enthusiastic association with us.

LESSONS LEARNED ABOUT TEAM DYNAMICS

When we began this project, we did not specifically discuss team membership, group dynamics, relationships, possible conflicts, or conflict resolution. Remarkably, we did not have any conflicts, nor did we experience the tensions so often associated with team projects.

We are convinced the attribute that contributed most to the success of this project was the deeply-held commitment of the team members to the goal of the project: to help improve students' communication competence. Without the strength of that commitment, the demands on time and the extensive planning, implementation, and ongoing assessment required could not have been sustained. The project was a high priority, which translated into equal dedication of team members to all aspects, phases, and activities for the duration of the study. A strong sense of responsibility to the team developed, to the extent that members rarely missed meetings or deadlines, which continued year-round. If someone could not participate in a meeting or activity because of an unavoidable conflict, that person found other ways to lend special expertise.

To develop team rapport and ensure balance, we learned both leader and team members needed to understand the personalities and learning/work styles of the others. While we proved to be an extremely compatible team, that doesn't mean we were mirror images of one another, nor would we promote compatibility as the sole basis for team formation. We believe the interdisciplinary nature of the team continuously revitalized our efforts and created an important balance of perspectives. At the same time, we knew our strong commitment to this project came from some similar experiences and backgrounds. One of the animal scientists has an undergraduate degree in English; another had participated in a semester-long course designed specifically to encourage and help faculty integrate writing in their disciplines. The communication specialists teach writing in the College of Agricultural Sciences and Natural Resources. The team members were selected because of these qualities and interests; they became important ingredients.

Much of the ease with which our team functioned is attributable to the project initiator/leader whose low-key management style was well-suited to the personalities of the team members. His excellent organizational skills, ability to keep the team on task, patience, and clear vision combined to create an environment in which cooperation, civility, and productivity flourished. Everyone was comfortable expressing ideas and exploring issues and possibilities. We focused on the process: how to accomplish goals, how to move forward. As a group, we planned and agreed on all actions, including deadlines and how to meet them. The team was consistently task- and process-oriented.

We learned we could relieve stress and still accomplish our goals if we did not take ourselves too seriously. We had a good time; we liked each other's company; we enjoyed solving problems together; we looked forward to planning activities and working together.

Finally, we learned that appreciation and respect for one another's professional abilities and commitment, both to the educational process and to students and faculty, enriched our collective psyche. We learned that, as a team, we could come close to achieving our goal, something we could not have done individually.

CONCLUSIONS—FOR THE TIME BEING

We have gathered information about the writing of animal science students for almost four years. This spring we will collect writing samples from our last group of graduating seniors (students who have experienced the communication-intensive curriculum in animal science for a full four years) and careful analysis may show that students in 1994 are more competent writers than were students in 1991. Yet, despite what the numbers will show us, we do know that students' attitudes about the value of communication competence have changed over four years, as have the attitudes of the faculty who influence students.

We speak of our project in the past tense, but that is a matter only of grammar and style, indicating that what *we* did as a project team was somehow finite. But we do not wish to give the impression that the project started, bloomed beautifully but briefly, and then somehow died on the vine. The spirit of the project continues still, and those faculty who accepted the responsibility for helping students become better communicators about animal science will not soon abandon that commitment. Indeed, animal science faculty themselves have become proponents of writing in the disciplines and are now serving as resource people to other faculty in the college who want to know how to make communication activities work in their classrooms.

ACKNOWLEDGEMENTS

The success of our project depended on a number of people who became part of our team in some way or another. One key lesson we learned is that if you let people know you appreciate them, they will come back again and again to encourage, to support, and to praise your efforts. These are the people we appreciate:

Our external partners: Willard Waldo, Carolyn Johnsen, Paul Clark, Mark Dana, Dave Howe, Larry Himmelberg, and Chuck Ball; our dean and department heads: Don Edwards, Elton Aberle, Gary Vacin, and Allen Blezek; our graduate assistants: Keith Darnell, Glenda Borcher, Karla Hollingsworth, Eric Larsen, Deb Padilla, and Doreen Blackmer; our NUPAGE coordinators: Joyce Lunde and Maurice Baker; our NUPAGE outreach coordinator: Becky Thomas; the entire animal science faculty, especially Keith Gilster; the students in the College of Agricultural Sciences and Natural Resources.

PRODUCTS OF THE PROJECT

Presentations

Nebraska Teachers Improvement Council (Lincoln, NE, May 1990 and Wayne, NE, May 1991)

National Testing Network in Writing (New York, Nov. 1990)

Midwest Modern Language Association (Kansas City, Nov. 1990)

Conference on College Composition and Communication (Boston, March 1991)

International Communication Association (Chicago, May 1991)

American Society of Animal Science (Laramie, WY, Aug. 1991)

Poultry Science Association (College Station, TX, Aug. 1991)

American Meat Science Association (Fort Collins, June 1992)

National Association of Colleges and Teachers of Agriculture (River Falls, WI, June 1992)

Society for Teaching and Learning in Higher Education (Toronto, June 1992 and Winnipeg, June 1993)

Conference on Writing in Engineering Design (Houghton, MI, June 1992)

Publications

Brink, D.M., Banset, E.A., Beck, M.A., Book, V.A., & Gilster, K. (1991). Developing competence in written communication in an animal science curriculum. *Journal of Animal Science,* 69 (suppl.): 566.

Beck, M.A., Brink, D.M., Banset, E.A., Book, V.A., & Gilster, K. (1991). Writing in an animal science curriculum: A model for agriculture. *Poultry Science,* 70 (suppl.): 12.

Brink, D.M., Banset, E.A., Beck, M.A., Book, V.A., & Gilster, K. (1992). Partnerships to enhance communication competence of animal science graduates. *NACTA Journal,* 36 (September, 1992): 18–19.

Banset, E.A., & Brink, D.M. (1993). Communication literacy across the sciences: Designing and evaluating writing assignments. *Proceedings, 45th Annual Reciprocal Meats Conference, American Meat Science Association,* 45: 27–35.

Elizabeth Banset is Assistant Professor of Agricultural Leadership, Education and Communication, University of Nebraska-Lincoln.

Virginia Book is Professor Emerita of Agricultural Leadership, Education and Communication, University of Nebraska-Lincoln.

Mary Beck is Associate Professor of Animal Science, University of Nebraska-Lincoln.

Dennis Brink is Professor of Animal Science, University of Nebraska-Lincoln.

REFERENCES

Beach, R., & Bridwell, L.S. (Eds.). (1984). *New directions in composition research.* New York, NY: The Guilford Press.

Carroll, J.A. (1984). Process into product: Teacher awareness of the writing process affects students' written products. In R. Beach & L.S. Bridwell (Eds.), *New directions in composition research.* (pp. 315–333). New York, NY: The Guilford Press.

Clegg, S., & Wheeler, M.M. (1991). *Students writing across the disciplines.* Orlando, FL: Holt, Rinehart and Winston.

Cooper, C.R., Cherry, R., Copley, B., Fleischer, S., Pollard, R., & Sartisky, M. (1984). Studying the writing abilities of a university freshman class: Strategies from a case study. In R. Beach & L.S. Bridwell (Eds.), *New directions in composition research.* (pp. 19-52). New York, NY: The Guilford Press.

Cross, K.P., & Angelo, T.A. (1988). *Classroom assessment techniques: A handbook for faculty.* (Tech. Rep. No. 88-A-004.0). Ann Arbor, MI: University of Michigan, National Center for Research to Improve Postsecondary Teaching and Learning.

Fillion, B. (1979). Language across the curriculum: Examining the place of language in our schools. *McGill Journal of Education,* 14, 47–60.

Freedman, S.W. (1984). The registers of student and professional expository writing: Influences on teachers' responses. In R. Beach & L. S. Bridwell (Eds.), *New directions in composition research.* (pp. 334-347). New York, NY: The Guilford Press.

Fulwiler, T. (1984). How well does writing across the curriculum work? *College English,* 46, 113–125.

Fulwiler, T., & Gorman, M.E. (1986). Changing faculty attitudes toward writing. In A. Young & T. Fulwiler (Eds.), *Writing across the disciplines: Research into practice.* (pp. 53–66). Montclair, NJ: Boynton/Cook.

Gere, A.R., Schuessler, B.F., & Abbott, R.D. (1984). Measuring teachers' attitudes toward writing instruction. In R. Beach & L. S. Bridwell (Eds.), *New directions in composition research.* (pp. 348–361). New York, NY: The Guilford Press.

Huot, B. (1990). Reliability, validity, and holistic scoring: What we know and what we need to know. *College Composition and Communication,* 41, 201–213.

Hult, C.A. (1990). *Researching and writing across the curriculum.* (2nd ed.). Belmont, CA: Wadsworth.

Lunsford, A. (1989, April). *Short and sweet assignments that combine writing, reading, speaking, and thinking.* Paper presented at the National Testing Network on Writing Assessment, Montreal, Canada.

Odell, L. (1986). Foreword. In A. Young & T. Fulwiler (Eds.), *Writing across the disciplines.* Montclair, NJ: Boynton/Cook.

Odell, L., & Goswami, D. (1984). Writing in a nonacademic setting. In R. Beach & L. S. Bridwell (Eds.), *New directions in composition research.* (pp. 233–258).New York, NY: The Guilford Press.

Rabkin, E.S., & Smith, M. (1990). *Teaching writing that works.* Ann Arbor, MI: The University of Michigan Press.

Reddish, J.C. (1983). The language of the bureaucracy. In R.W. Bailey & R.M. Fosheim (Eds.), *Literacy for life: The demand for reading and writing.* (pp. 151–174). New York, NY: Modern Language Association.

Stanford, G. (1984). *Classroom practices in teaching English: How to handle the paper load.* Urbana, IL: National Council of Teachers of English.

Tchudi, S.N. (1986). *Teaching writing in the content areas: College level.* Washington, DC: National Education Association.

White, E.M. (1985). *Teaching and assessing writing.* San Francisco, CA: Jossey-Bass.

Young, A., & Fulwiler, T. (Eds.). (1986). *Writing across the disciplines.* Montclair, NJ: Boynton/Cook.

18

SHAPING CURRICULA THROUGH WRITING, COLLABORATION, AND TELECOMMUNICATIONS: LESSONS LEARNED AND LIMITS LESSENED

Ann Hill Duin
University of Minnesota

What happened between 1986 and 1988 when I led three Project Sunrise projects at the College of Agriculture, University of Minnesota? What is it about writing, collaboration, and telecommunications that had the capacity to change teaching and learning? How will this combination continue to enhance education as we look to the next century?

PROJECT SUNRISE PROJECTS

From 1986 through 1988, I proposed and implemented three Project Sunrise grants for the purpose of integrating writing, collaboration, and telecommunications throughout the College of Agriculture (COA) curriculum:

Project Writing Assist

I presented four writing-across-the-curriculum seminars in which COA faculty identified the purposes and goals for writing in their courses; determined how to structure and sequence their writing assignments; explored ways to help students plan, organize, draft, and revise their work; and practiced ways of conveying knowledge of good writing in their disciplines to their students. After the seminars, I continued to consult with faculty by attending their courses and reviewing their writing assignments and response strategies.

Courseware for Collaborative Writing

I led a team in the development of courseware that instructed students in the skills of working together to acquire information, research a topic, analyze potential audiences, and organize, revise, and package technical documents. Our team studied students' use of this courseware and compared learning styles to those of students who did not use the courseware (Duin, Jorn, & DeBower, 1991). When coupled with the AppleShare system for telecommunications, this project won the 1989 EDUCOM and NCRIP-TAL higher education software implementation award for the Best Curriculum Innovation in Writing.

Collaborative Writing Teams

We proposed to have University of Minnesota students collaborate with University of Wisconsin—Madison students and with people out in industry. The telecommunications system (electronic mail) we envisioned using for this project was not developed in time for this specific proposal. Instead, students from various sections of writing courses throughout our college collaborated through the use of the AppleShare telecommunications system. By 1991, this project evolved to include teams of university students mentoring high school students via additional telecommunications systems (Duin et al., 1994). By 1993, this project further evolved to allow university students to collaborate across distance with other students via a desktop videoconferencing system (Duin, Mason, and Jorn, 1994).

In the following sections I describe in retrospect the lessons learned and the limits lessened through each of these projects.

ASSISTING FACULTY WITH WRITING ACROSS THE CURRICULUM (WAC)

According to Russell (1987), "since the modern university first took shape toward the close of the nineteenth century, and the new elective curriculum relegated writing instruction to freshman courses in the English Department, hundreds of schools have tried to broaden responsibility for improving student writing" (p. 184). Most recently, McLeod (1989) sent surveys to all 2735 post-secondary institutions in the United States and Canada. From her 40% return, she found that all but five of the 695 respondents had WAC programs in place or had plans for such a program. In her words, "this seems a remarkable number, considering that just a decade ago only a handful of such programs existed" (p. 338). McLeod also noted that most programs progress in two stages: a developmental stage in which instructors need the basics about how to begin, and a second stage in which instructors need advice on how to continue.

Focus on Faculty

The purpose of Project Writing Assist was to help COA faculty with the first stage of writing across the curriculum: rethinking writing assignments through a process perspective. Specifically, I helped 14 faculty members review their context for developing and implementing writing assignments through a process perspective toward writing. That is, instead of assigning a paper due at the end of the term and graded at the last minute, we worked on the following:

Workplace Writing. During the first workshop we identified the characteristics of writing done in participants' respective fields and brainstormed multiple purposes for writing in their courses. For each instructor, we took one "typical" assignment and worked to give it a decent, realistic *name*, identify the *audience* and *purpose* for the assignment, determine the larger *context* surrounding the assignment, establish the *conventions* or specifications for the assignment in terms of the particular discipline, and come up with ideas for *integrating* the assignment more deeply into understanding the subject matter of the course.

Since the seminars took place at the beginning of a term, some faculty chose to implement their ideas immediately in the courses they were teaching. In one case, a professor who had previously simply required a final detailed paper, added short writing activities—note-taking, interviewing, summaries, drafts—to help his students explore their topics and get outside advice before developing a final "publishable" text.

Sequencing. During the second workshop we worked on sequencing assignments by dividing longer ones into segments and designing ways to get earlier feedback to students. We practiced the very strategies we developed, and participants wrote their comments about that day's workshop to me in the form of short notes. Most wrote that they now wanted to start working one-on-one on their developing ideas ("I got a great idea I want to explore and I need help!!!"). Others wrote that now that they would be assigning sequenced assignments, they would need help in giving feedback on students' early writing ("I need help on critiquing their earlier writing as well as helping students critique their own and others' efforts at writing.").

Coaching. During the third workshop we identified strategies for coaching students through the writing process. We tried out ways of analyzing assignments, finding information, generating ideas and focusing topics, drafting and revising, and then identifying the stylistic conventions appropriate to their different disciplines. By this point, participants who had assigned shorter writing activities that would lead to larger ones found themselves with mounds of papers. We discussed ways to involve peer review throughout the writing process and ways to group students for peer review.

Critiquing. Last, during the fourth workshop, we compared and struggled with the dual roles of writing coach and writing critic. Participants brought examples of good and poor student writing, and we discussed ways to help students with substantive matters (content, critical thinking through writing) as well as surface concerns (mechanics, organization, tone) in their writing.

Lessons Learned and Limits Lessened

Looking back through my Project Writing Assist folders, I have uncovered piles of assignments from COA courses; while the assignments were rethought, redesigned, and implemented in new ways, in some cases I do not know how a particular professor is doing with the writing tasks he or she has assigned in the years hence.

WAC programs are increasing, but according to Jones and Comprone (1993), their survival depends on effective coordination of administrative, pedagogical, and research components. In addition, according to Bazerman (1991), a WAC program must "attach itself to the lifeblood of communication by means of which disciplines and professions organize themselves" (p. 210). To ensure a WAC program's survival, one needs to study the writing pedagogy in disciplinary classrooms and the role of writing in the development of individual students (Jolliffe, 1988).

While Project Writing Assist's formal funding ended after these workshops, in some cases faculty have asked me to continue to work with them as they have implemented WAC in their courses. Over a three-year period, I team-taught a senior capstone course with an animal science professor. In a circle with his dozen students, we talked about designing reviews of literature for dairy science, and students witnessed and then entered a dialogue about what constituted "good" writing for dairy science publications. At an early meeting in the first semester we worked together, the animal science professor bluntly stated that students should never use "you" in their formal writing. That week I searched out dairy science publications from the past and the present and brought them to the next class to study. We discussed how language had changed (*I, you,* and *we* were clearly present in more recent publications), how language might change in the future, and how students could enter the discourse of their field.

The connections made through these workshops lessened the distance between our fields. Writing across the curriculum connected us. Our struggles with integrating writing into content areas were similar. Faculty continue to call me, and we have designed and implemented subsequent WAC projects. Most recently, Professor Steve Simmons and I led a project titled "Decision Cases for Writing Across the Curriculum," a project funded by the University of Minnesota's Center for Interdisciplinary Studies of Writing (see Duin, Simmons, & Lammers, 1994). In this project, students in an upper-level environmental science course used decision cases with WAC components. They then discussed the cases with high school students (who had also developed written arguments) via a desktop videoconferencing system.

Project Writing Assist and these later projects have continued the WAC movement throughout our College of Agriculture. We have learned that, in order to work, a WAC program must attach itself to the lifeblood of communication and to the projects and courses vital to faculty and students.

DESIGNING COURSEWARE FOR COLLABORATIVE WRITING

A vital skill in the workplace is collaboration. Workplace writing involves a great deal of collaboration: a supervisor may assign a document to be written by a staff member and later edited by the supervisor (Paradis et al., 1985); a group may plan a document that is then drafted and revised individually (Odell, 1985); individuals may plan and draft a document that is revised collaboratively (Doheny-Farina, 1986); peers may review co-workers' drafts (Anderson, 1985); two or more people may coauthor documents (Ede & Lunsford, 1986). Even though surveys indicate that about 75% of professionals write collaboratively on the job (Anderson, 1985), as was evidenced in Project Writing Assist, college instructors develop and assign primarily individually-authored documents.

Focus on Students

The purpose of the Courseware for Collaborative Writing project was to help students learn to collaborate or coauthor nonacademic documents, cooperate and give feedback on other students' documents, and use telecommunications as a means to collaborate and give and receive feedback. I led a collaborative team in the design, development, implementation, and evaluation of Collaborative Writer (CW) courseware, an interactive learning and productivity tool to enhance the process of collaborative writing (Duin, Jorn, & DeBower, 1991). Our design team included a content expert/instructional designer, a technical communicator, a graphic artist, and a programmer. In developing the tutorials, we incorporated open-ended writing prompts (Kemp, 1988), promoted a process orientation toward writing (Barbour, 1987; Trimbur, 1985), and strove to help students view writing as a social process (Bruffee, 1983; Wiener, 1986). Figure 18-1 shows how students could integrate information in tutorials with a word processing tool for practice and performance.

FIGURE 18-1

Tutorial Menu in Collaborative Writer

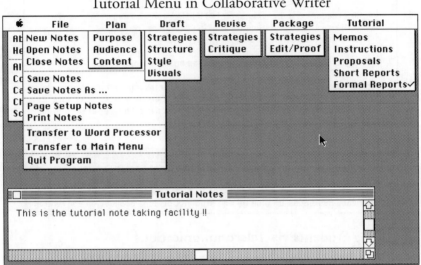

Using the menu labeled *Collab Info*, students accessed information on the differences between cooperation and collaboration (Hord, 1986), alternative strategies to follow when collaborating (Forman & Katsky, 1986), and variables that influence success and satisfaction in collaborative writing groups (Ede & Lunsford, 1986). The remaining tutorials contained information on how to plan, draft, revise, and package memos, proposals, instructions, short reports, and formal reports. For example, under the Plan menu, students analyzed their audiences, developed and refined purposes for writing, and generated content for the particular documents they were developing. Under the Draft menu, students organized and structured their planning notes into drafts; under the Revise menu, students critiqued their own and others' work; and under the Package menu, students edited and proofed their final documents. As Figure 18-2 shows, question prompts throughout these tutorials helped students generate ideas and compose drafts of the actual documents.

FIGURE 18-2

A Student's Notes While Using CW

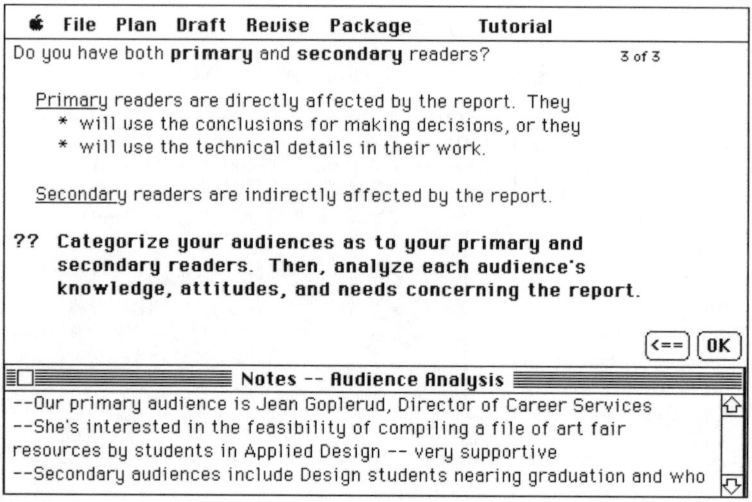

```
┌─────────────────────────────────────────────────────────────────────┐
│  🍎  File  Plan  Draft  Revise  Package        Tutorial              │
├─────────────────────────────────────────────────────────────────────┤
│ Do you have both primary and secondary readers?           3 of 3     │
│                                                                       │
│    Primary readers are directly affected by the report. They         │
│       * will use the conclusions for making decisions, or they        │
│       * will use the technical details in their work.                 │
│                                                                       │
│    Secondary readers are indirectly affected by the report.           │
│                                                                       │
│ ??  Categorize your audiences as to your primary and                  │
│     secondary readers. Then, analyze each audience's                  │
│     knowledge, attitudes, and needs concerning the report.            │
│                                                                       │
│                                                       ┌<==┐ ┌ OK ┐    │
├─────────────────────────────────────────────────────────────────────┤
│▤□══════════════ Notes -- Audience Analysis ══════════════            │
│ --Our primary audience is Jean Goplerud, Director of Career Services ⬆│
│ --She's interested in the feasibility of compiling a file of art fair │
│ resources by students in Applied Design -- very supportive            │
│ --Secondary audiences include Design students nearing graduation and who ⬇│
└─────────────────────────────────────────────────────────────────────┘
```

Connecting Students via Telecommunications

At the time of this project (1987–1988), few students were adept at using word processing programs, much less telecommunications. To connect students via telecommunications, we worked with our University's microcomputer group to become connected to our phone system's LAN-mark Ethernet service and to acquire AppleShare networking software that would allow students to collaborate across the distance of University of Minnesota campus computer labs.

In order to organize the flow of documents between the instructor and students, we created four types of folders on this network: group, private, instructor, and conferencing folders. We arranged group folders according to collaborative groups, and students' private folders were located inside their group folders. In an instructor folder, students could send documents to the instructor, but only the instructor could access documents in this folder. In a conferencing folder, students left messages and drafts for students in their particular group. Figure 18-3 shows part of what a student saw when accessing a group folder via this system.

FIGURE 18-3

A Student's Use of the Telecommunications System

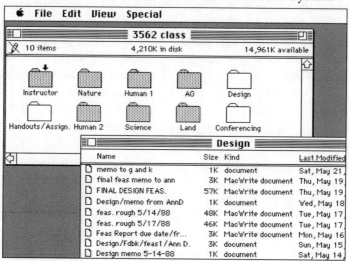

Lessons Learned and Limits Lessened

The technology in this project provided an integrated, unique collaborative tool. Students at the University of Minnesota often work 30–40 hours-per-week jobs, and rarely are able to schedule face-to-face meetings. Telecommunications made possible a significant increase in student-student and student-instructor collaboration. Students could access their instructor's knowledge at any time from (then) any of 70 lab locations (this system is still being used, and the labs now number in the hundreds). This project promoted significantly more interaction than typically would occur in traditional classrooms (see research studies reported in Duin et al., 1991 and Duin, 1990).

Even more important, the CW courseware made a unique contribution to learning and to the social context of the classroom. In traditional courses that involve writing groups, students often reiterate the instructor's comments, making little transfer of knowledge to their own writing processes (DiPardo & Freedman, 1988). Theorists such as Kuhn (1963) and Rorty (1979) argue that knowledge is not a static body of information but rather is "socially justified" and evolves as communities of "knowledgeable peers" interact, shape, extend, and reinforce each other's ideas. CW offered students the knowledge and vocabulary needed to write collaboratively and to conference with each other. Through this technology, students interacted, shaped, extended, and reinforced each other's ideas.

The information presented to students via the CW courseware has now been integrated into more powerful computing packages that evolve daily. With the exponential growth of computer packages, one might wonder why we delved into courseware development for collaborative writing purposes. At the time, no such packages existed; "collaboration" was not yet a buzz-word claimed by multiple industries; the society for Computer-Supported Cooperative Work (CSCW) was in its infancy; telecommunications was rarely used by a College of Agriculture professor, much less an undergraduate student.

Today, every faculty member and student at the University of Minnesota has an Internet electronic mail address. In every class that my colleagues and I teach, we "collaborate" daily with our students via Internet. As I write this document, my computer beeps; I know I have "mail waiting" from my students, I answer their queries, I "listen" to their discoveries. Collaboration—a concept that needed explanation and guidance in 1987—is slowly becoming more transparent as students interact via Internet with other students and with faculty from here and throughout the world.

Today, the Courseware for Collaborative Writing project has evolved further into telelearner systems that include interactive multimedia, desktop videoconferencing, and virtual reality components. However, our focus remains the same: to develop systems that connect learners for the purposes of collaborating, socially constructing knowledge, valuing diversity, and less-ening learning time and distance between learners.

Connecting Collaborative Writing Teams Across Universities

The purpose of the Collaborative Writing Teams project was to have students at the University of Minnesota collaborate with students at the University of Wisconsin-Madison via a telecommunications system. As stated at the beginning of this essay, the technology we envisioned using was not developed in time for this specific project, and students instead collaborated with students from other courses via our AppleShare telecommunications system. A second reason our universities did not connect was lack of knowledge about how to implement projects in which faculty and students collaborate across university boundaries. The boundaries that exist when professors at the same university wish to team teach only expand when one tries to move beyond the boundaries of a single university.

While the technological boundaries that existed in 1989 no longer exist today (i.e., faculty and students from around the world can communicate and collaborate via the Internet), other boundaries remain.

University Schedules

Recently, I wanted students in a course I was teaching to collaborate with students at another university. I sent queries out (via Internet) to numerous faculty from other universities. The problem? Our university schedule so conflicted with those of institutions on a semester schedule or on a schedule that began much earlier than ours (beginning in late August or early September versus late September) that faculty were reluctant to try to make our projects overlap for collaborative purposes between our students.

Student Credit Hours

Because of the Internet, I now receive multiple queries daily from students around the world. I reply and collaborate; these students are my future colleagues. However, the "credit hours" for this work go elsewhere. New systems must be envisioned for "credit" in our communication age.

Transfer of Technology

Those who search for ways to place technology's power in the hands of learners and to transfer this knowledge to learners, are few. Many professors opt to keep the latest technology in their hands alone, lecturing from fancy multimedia platforms. We must move beyond the boundary of professor as owner of technological as well as content area expertise; we must transfer this power, this ownership, to students in every possible course.

Inservice Training

To transfer this knowledge to students, faculty need training in how to do so. At the time of our courseware development efforts, several centers existed at the University of Minnesota for the sole purpose of helping faculty learn and develop new technologies to support teaching and learning. No such center or program exists today. This is a severe boundary to future innovative technological developments that focus on learners' needs.

Professional Support

When I began these Project Sunrise efforts, I was an assistant professor. Many national and international colleagues urged me to reconsider the path I had followed of assisting other faculty when I should assist myself alone, of developing courseware and designing technologies to support collaboration when I should author documents alone, of connecting learners when I should focus on theory or empirical research alone. Some colleagues said my college would not support such activity in promotion and tenure decisions (indeed, many professors have written about this dilemma at their institutions). Thus, I made sure to design and publish empirical studies related to these projects. We must increase our professional support for efforts related to innovative teaching and curricular development.

THE QUEST CONTINUES

How will this combination of writing, collaboration, and telecommunications continue to enhance education as we look to the next century? The answer is simple: it will continue as long as we focus on learners' needs and as long as there is support for innovation.

Support for innovation allows faculty to be innovative; it speaks to the need for more projects such as Project Sunrise. Assistant professors entering our college today have no Project Sunrise in place. Project Sunrise encouraged experimentation; colleagues across disciplines collaborated on common learner needs. Project Sunrise supported faculty and students in a quest toward innovation in both traditional and non-traditional settings. The seeds from these projects have led to further connections between learners of different ages and different backgrounds. Currently, mentoring projects are underway where university students help high school students in science, language, and social science courses. The university students mentor high school students via a state-of-the-art desktop videoconferencing (DTV) system (Duin, Mason, and Jorn, 1994). This term, university students will collaborate with people in industry using this same DTV system, and by the time this is published, that system will be replaced by one that is even more powerful.

The thing that will not change is the goal, the purpose, the reason for our teaching and learning. The focus throughout Project Sunrise was on teamwork, collaboration, leadership, problem solving, active learning methods, communication, and interdisciplinary work. This focus does not change; it bravely moves forward through people willing to support it.

Ann Hill Duin is Associate Professor of Rhetoric, University of Minnesota.

REFERENCES

Anderson, P. (1985). What survey research tells us about writing at work. In L. Odell & D. Goswami (Eds.), *Writing in nonacademic settings* (pp. 3–83). New York, NY: Guilford Press.

Barbour, D.H. (1987). Process in the business writing classroom: One teacher's approach. *The Journal of Business Communication, 24,* 61–64.

Bazerman, C. (1991). Review: The second stage in writing across the curriculum. *College English, 53(2),* 209–212.

Bruffee, K.A. (1983). Writing and reading as collaborative or social acts. In J. N. Hays, P.A. Roth, J.R. Ramsey, & R.D. Foulke (Eds.), *The writer's mind* (pp. 159–170). Urbana, IL: NCTE.

Dipardo, A., & Freedman, S.W. (1988). Peer response groups in the writing classroom: Theoretic foundations and new directions. *Review of Educational Research, 58,* 119–149.

Doheny-Farina, S. (1986). Writing in an emerging organization: An ethnographic study. *Written Communication, 3,* 158–184.

Duin, A.H. (1990). Terms and tools: A theory and research-based approach to collaborative writing. *Bulletin of the Association for Business Communication, 53(2),* 45–50.

Duin, A.H., Jorn, L., & DeBower, M. (1991). Collaborative writing: Courseware and telecommunications. In M.M. Lay & W. M. Karis (Eds.), *Collaborative writing in industry: Investigations in theory and practice.* Farmingdale, NY: Baywood Publishing Co.

Duin, A.H., Lammers, E., Mason, L., & Graves, M.F. (1994). Responding to ninth-grade students via telecommunications: College mentor strategies and development over time. *Research in the Teaching of English.*

Duin, A.H., Mason, L., & Jorn, L.A. (1994). Structuring distance-meeting environments. *Technical Communication, 41(4),* 695–708.

Duin, A.H., Simmons, S.R., & Lammers, E. (1994). *Decision cases for writing across the curriculum.* Minneapolis, MN: University of Minnesota. A monograph for the Center of Interdisciplinary Studies of Writing.

Ede, L., & Lunsford, A. (1986). Why write…together: A research update. *Rhetoric Review, 5,* 71–81.

Forman, J., & Katsky, P. (1986). The group report: A problem in small group or writing processes? *The Journal of Business Communication, 23,* 23–35.

Hord, S.M. (1986). A synthesis of research on collaboration. *Educational Leadership, 43,* 22–26.

Jolliffe, D.A. (1988). *Advances in writing research: Writing in academic disciplines.* Norwood, NJ: Ablex.

Jones, R., & Comprone, J.J. (1993). Where do we go next in writing across the curriculum? *College Composition and Communication, 44(1),* 59–68.

Kemp, F. (1988). *Stimulating creativity in the computer-based writing classroom.* Paper presented at the Computers in Writing and Language Instruction Conference, Duluth, MN, 1988.

Kuhn, T. (1963). *The structure of scientific revolutions.* Chicago, IL: University of Chicago Press.

McLeod, S.H. (1989). Writing across the curriculum: The second stage, and beyond. *College Composition and Communication, 40(3),* 337–343.

Odell, L. (1985). Beyond the text: Relations between writing and social context. In L. Odell & D. Goswami (Eds.), *Writing in nonacademic settings,* (pp. 249–280). New York, NY: The Guilford Press.

Paradis, J., Dobrin, D., & Miller, R. (1985). Writing at Exxon ITD. In L. Odell & D. Goswami (Eds.), *Writing in nonacademic settings,* (pp. 281–307). New York, NY: The Guilford Press.

Rorty, R. (1979). *Philosophy and the mirror of nature.* Princeton, NJ: Princeton University Press.

Russell, D.R. (1987). Writing across the curriculum and the communications movement: Some lessons from the past. *College Composition and Communication, 38(2),* 184–194.

Trimbur, J. (1985). Collaborative learning and teaching writing. In B.W. McClelland & T.R. Donovan (Eds.), *Perspectives on research and scholarship in composition.* New York, NY: MLA.

Wiener, H.S. (1986). Collaborative learning in the classroom. *College English, 48,* 52–61.

SECTION 6

ETHICS AND AGRICULTURE

Edited and with an introduction by
Maurice Baker
University of Nebraska-Lincoln

Ethical and value issues in agriculture are not new. My father and grand-father frequently discussed whether neighbors were treating their livestock, particularly draft horses, humanely. They attributed feelings and thought processes to those animals similar to those for humans. Over the years, issues of ethical personal behavior in business and professions have gained greater attention. These kinds of issues relate to the individual or personal moral issues and choices.

Development and adoption of technology have increased the complexity of the ethical and values issues surrounding agriculture. Spillover effects, such as odors from confined livestock feeding facilities, have increased, and the recognition of these effects has been more keenly developed over time. The vast majority of people in the United States have no direct or indirect contact with agriculture; therefore, they see issues such as confined livestock feeding in a different light from the operator of such facilities. People working within agriculture have become more specialized; therefore, they make decisions from a narrower viewpoint than did members of previous generations. Farm-ers no longer produce a wide variety of crops and livestock. Instead, we have specialized corn producers, wheat producers, cow/calf operators, feedlot operators, crop production economists, livestock production economists, weed specialists, wheat breeders, and others. All these changes have given rise to the development of more public policy with respect to decisions being made within agriculture, and these decisions involve ethical issues.

Student and faculty recognition of these evolutionary changes has given rise to the need to better understand how to deal with ethics and values.

Faculty have sensed something is lacking in the professional and scientific education curriculum. Students are socialized to their professions and taught to "think like professionals," but there is a need to have educated professionals. Thus, we should undercut the emphasis on professionalism by encouraging students to look at current practices from a different viewpoint. Out of these concerns for a better understanding, colleges of agriculture have devised a variety of approaches to address these needs.

Some colleges have hired philosophers as faculty members, either full-time or part-time. Others have found current faculty members who are interested in gaining expertise at analyzing ethical and value issues and in subsequently developing educational experiences for their students. In these cases, philosophers sometimes work directly with the college of agriculture faculty members in both a faculty development role and as a partner in developing student learning experiences. Some philosophers continue as members of a teaching team; others drop out once the college of agriculture faculty develop the needed abilities to adequately guide the learning experiences of students in this area.

The organization of the learning experience also differs from one campus to another. On some campuses, courses devoted specifically to analyzing agricultural ethical issues are developed and offered. In other instances, the learning of skills to deal with ethical and value issues is incorporated into existing disciplinary courses. Again, some of these courses incorporate analysis of ethical and value issues throughout the course, while others devote only a small portion of the course to these issues.

The essays in this section demonstrate alternative ways of approaching the introduction of ethics within the context of agriculture. They also identify the challenges inherent in introducing these topics into the college curriculum.

Maurice Baker is Professor of Agricultural Economics, University of Nebraska-Lincoln.

19

HUMAN/ANIMAL RELATIONSHIPS: BIOLOGICAL AND PHILOSOPHICAL ISSUES

Patricia B. McConnell
University of Wisconsin-Madison

"Human/Animal Relationships: Biological and Philosophical Issues" has become an established and popular course at UW-Madison, with a 1993 enrollment of over 180 students (at this point enrollment was capped, and it is safe to assume that more students would have taken the course if allowed to do so). The course is designed as an interdisciplinary approach to our complex and often contradictory relationship with animals. It emphasizes the obligations of professionals and citizens alike to make educated and carefully considered decisions regarding interactions with non-human animals.

PHILOSOPHICAL BASIS

The human/animal relationships course design is underscored by two beliefs: first, that a lack of biological knowledge can interfere with wise decision-making on issues of tremendous social and personal importance (from environmental concerns to the ethics of cross-species organ transplants); and second, a solid philosophical framework is believed to be just as important as biological knowledge in making meaningful decisions about our relationships with and obligations to other animals. Certainly the interest is not restricted to faculty; the impressive enrollment suggests that students share a deeply felt communal interest and concern regarding our place and duties in the natural world. The origin and history of the course is unique, and is briefly described here in hopes that it may provide information to others about the potential for similar courses elsewhere.

COURSE DEVELOPMENT PROCESS

The course originated when the Curricular Revitalization Project, supported by the Kellogg Foundation, put out a request for course proposals that could enhance the curricular offerings of the College of Agricultural and Life Sciences. Professor Robert Kauffman of the Meat and Animal Science Department had long been concerned about the lack of attention to ethical issues in agricultural education; his concerns matched the interests of the project's Agriculture, Technology, and Society Committee in "ethics in agriculture" courses. He was provided seed money to develop a course, and hired a coordinator and researcher (Nancy Paul) to organize an eclectic group of faculty and staff members from a variety of perspectives.

The experimental course was designed by an interdisciplinary committee assembled by Professor Kauffman. Disciplines represented were veterinary medicine, rural sociology, meat and animal science, zoology, environmental studies, psychology, veterinary science, and philosophy. The committee spent a year, meeting approximately monthly, designing a course that represented many different perspectives related to human/animal interactions. The following course description and request for input aptly summarized the state of the course at that point:

We are developing an experimental course (with support of the Kellogg Curricular Revitalization Project) for all University students to gain a greater intellectual understanding of how humans should relate to and think about other species of animal life that share their environment. The title is "Philosophical and biological foundations for animal use and well-being." The content will include basic physiological concepts, especially those related to stress, pain, and behavior. Historical, traditional, and current uses of animals will be reviewed, and other species will be compared to the humans as they relate to extinction, health, food, entertainment, research, companionship, sport, and humaneness. All of these subjects will be bolstered by and integrated around philosophical concepts that attempt to clarify the intellectual, moral, and humane understandings that underlie existing assumptions and relationships. The course has no prerequisites except junior standing, will provide 3 credits, and will include two lectures and several discussion sessions per week.

The committee communally designed the course syllabus, and revised the name listed above to "Human/Animal Relationships: Biological and Philosophical Issues." Designing a course, lecture by lecture, in a large committee format has its obvious drawbacks. Certainly fewer people might have gotten more done in less time. However, in spite of its somewhat unwieldy format, committee members agreed that the variety of perspectives expressed by such an eclectic committee were essential in creating a truly interdisciplinary course.

This philosophy continued in the design of the lectures, with seven different lecturers from the Departments of Zoology, Meat and Animal Science, Veterinary Science, Wildlife Ecology, and Philosophy. The course also was cross-listed in seven different departments to reflect its interdisciplinary perspective. It was taught in the fall of 1989, with an overwhelming student response of 140 class members enrolled. Student evaluations were favorable, with 93% stating that the course "was important and should be offered again." Upon reflection, the committee agreed that the course was a valuable addition to the curriculum, but no department was able, at the time, to fund the course.

McConnell later wrote a successful grant proposal to the Kemper K. Knapp Foundation (UW-Madison) which has an interest in supporting efforts to enhance students' awareness of social issues and social responsibilities. After receiving funding, McConnell became the coordinator and primary lecturer, and guest lecturers continued to provide an interdisciplinary approach. Subsequent to funding by the Knapp Foundation, the Departments of Zoology and Wildlife Ecology became the home departments (the course is now cross-listed in those two, and only those two, departments). The second year showed an increase in student enrollment, a trend which continues (1993 enrollment was capped at 185). Currently zoology provides a lecturer position, and wildlife ecology (as of 1994) provides a teaching assistant.

CURRENT COURSE OBJECTIVES

The course, as it now stands, is designed to:

1. introduce the breadth and depth of the issue of human/animal relationships

2. explain the biological relationships between human and non-human animals, including a comparative survey of our genetic, behavioral, cognitive, and physiological traits

3. introduce ethological principles necessary to evaluate an animal's internal state, species-specific needs, and cognitive ability

4. provide a philosophical framework on which to base ethical decisions about our relationships with other animals

5. objectively present a wide range of views on animal rights

6. relate all of the above to relevant issues in agricultural production, animal research, zoos, pet ownership, and the human impact on wild animals

In summary, the goal of the course is to provide students, whether they are majoring in veterinary medicine, meat production, psychology, or English literature, with the information they need to make educated and constructive decisions about society's attitude toward non-human animals and their own personal interactions with non-human animals.

STUDENT RESPONSES

For two years (1992 and 1993) students completed a survey that addressed some of their attitudes about societal interactions with animals, from using cats in bio-medical research to eating meat. The same survey is administered the first day of class and the last. Some questions are designed primarily to get students thinking about difficult issues on the first class day (Example: 1. Would you support research that required killing domestic dogs if you knew that some human lives would be saved? 2. If it took 100 dogs to save your life, would you sacrifice the dogs? 3. What if it just took one dog? Yours?) Other questions are designed to look for attitude changes (Example: Agricultural animals suffer a great part of their lives before they are killed for consumption. Do you totally agree, somewhat agree, somewhat disagree, totally disagree or don't know?). The data from these surveys are currently being analyzed and should provide some interesting insights into attitude and attitude changes.

Student evaluations have provided a great deal of information about the value of this course and provide perhaps the most important lessons in this process. First, student interest has always been, and continues to be, extremely high. This issue clearly touches many people from different perspectives. Animals themselves have always been of tremendous interest to a wide variety of people, illustrated by the high ratings of TV nature shows, the constant attraction of live animals in classroom settings, the "recession proof" nature of pet economy—even advertisers know that animals help sell products, because they get people's attention. But beyond a simple interest in animals, I suggest that many people are not clear what guidelines or foundations to look toward to help guide them in a changing and confusing society. As our technology increases, we have the capability of treating animals more and more like machines, and tend to live increasing distances from animals, but at the same time our growing knowledge of animal psychology and ethology suggests that we are not alone in experiencing emotions and complex thoughts. Thus what is right and what is wrong in relation to us and other animals is unclear, and students clearly stated how important they felt the course was in helping them sort out their own feelings about these difficult issues.

LESSONS LEARNED

The course has made it clear that this is an excellent vehicle to educate students in two "difficult" topics—biology and philosophy. The students are mainly comprised of zoology, wildlife ecology, psychology and humanities majors. Most of the biology majors have not and will not take any other courses in ethics or philosophy, and many of the humanities majors stated that they were looking for a science class that was not "too intimidating" and was also interesting. Students may be surprised initially to learn (although the word, by now, is out) that the course is actually very demanding, but they are willing to take the challenge and pay the price to learn something important.

Student evaluations have made it clear what they feel is valuable about the course: they prize its interdisciplinary nature and eclectic atmosphere. For example, all lecturers are asked to begin by explaining to the students who they are and how they relate to animals in a personal and professional way. The course takes the attitude that no person is truly objective, and that we all come with our own biases and perspectives. Thus students listen to lectures, debates, and presentations from livestock producers, bio-medical researchers, humane society workers, and radical animal rights activists, to name a few. All are received with respectful, but critically analytical, attention. Experience has shown, however, that it is critical to have one primary person shape the course to insure that information is not presented in a disorganized fashion or that unsubstantiated claims or "facts" do not go unchallenged.

Another lesson of this course is how important it can become as a vehicle for teaching critical thinking, including basic concepts of ethical decision-making (instruction most students are not receiving any more in a college program), and good writing skills. Students are evaluated on two written essay exams, each of which demands that they put information learned together in a new way to answer many of the questions, and one term paper of the student's choice on one of five topics. (Topics have included: the biology and philosophy of re-introducing wolves into Yellowstone, BGH and genetic engineering, eating meat, using cats in bio-medical research, greyhound dog racing, etc.) Although most students say the course was much harder than they thought it would be, they also say they were still glad they took it, because it caused them to think carefully about so many things they had just taken for granted in the past. And teaching young people to think, to think critically, to challenge assumptions, to write lucidly and thoughtfully, and to ponder how they should fit into the society around them is perhaps the highest goal of education. A well-designed course on human/animal relationships provides the perfect vehicle to work toward those goals.

Patricia B. McConnell is Adjunct Assistant Professor of Zoology, University of Wisconsin-Madison.

20

ETHICS IN AGRICULTURE AND NATURAL RESOURCES

Laura Casari and Bruce Johnson
University of Nebraska-Lincoln

With funding from New Partnerships in Agriculture and Education (NUPAGE) at the University of Nebraska-Lincoln (UNL), we collaborated with student and professional partners to develop the best educational medium for working with ethical issues reflected in the value systems of individual students and the various disciplines represented in the College of Agricultural Sciences and Natural Resources (CASNR) at UNL. The result was "Ethics in Agriculture and Natural Resources," a three-hour course piloted in Spring 1990 with an enrollment of 25 students.

We have taught this course five semesters with varying enrollments; it is open to all students at UNL, but most students who enroll are typically from CASNR. During one semester, the first author (Casari) experimented by incorporating an AGSAT (the national agricultural satellite transmission service) course, "Ethics in Agriculture," which was networked to six universities and taught by Paul Thompson, Texas A & M (Thompson, 1991). Presently, our course fulfills a humanities option for juniors and seniors in CASNR.

PROJECT'S GENESIS

Both of us had recognized through our regular teaching assignments (in technical communication and agricultural economics, respectively) a need for education in ethics even before NUPAGE afforded us the opportunity to address it. Students at all levels in agriculture economics had exhibited a diversity of views and values, while students from many majors who took technical communication courses often expressed quite different values, apparently dependent on their majors.

Students' Needs

Our individual experiences confirmed the need for analyzing varying value systems, as well as for developing students' reasoning capacities and their ability to deal with conflicts in values that anticipated professional conflicts. For example, students in conservation and water science might hold significantly different attitudes toward water use than would those planning to work in crop science. Students needed to learn that the ethos of individuals and individual majors is not always shared.

Even though we were aware that differences in majors did not automatically cause differences in values, we believed it essential for students to become aware that they held values; that values affect decision-making; and that it would be essential for them, as professionals, to recognize and take responsibility for the roles values and ethics play in negotiating and implementing policy, as well as individual decision-making. Here we trace our thinking and actions from our earlier intimations of need for attention to ethics to the ultimate development of a three-hour cross-discipline course in applied ethics.

Course Framework

As we communicated with external partners and others in the university community, we became aware that people are often unclear about what constitutes ethical reasoning and what skills might be employed to allow individuals to make ethical/moral choices. We assumed our students would know immediately how to go about making ethical choices. In fact, however, we discovered that, while our students were sensitive to and appreciative of the scientific method, they felt uncomfortable, if not ill at ease, with the less technical world of ethics and ethical decision-making. We believed that stressing the rigor of philosophical thinking and teaching the constructs of ethical reasoning would help our students understand that a sound and long-lived tradition functions in ethical decision-making, just as a long-lived scientific tradition functions in the technical arenas. We hoped to leave students with some sense of how to define ethical issues, make choices, state policy, and implement action determined by their combined scientific and ethical decision-making abilities.

After recognizing that we had to grapple with applied ethics in agriculture and natural resources and identify goals and environments for learning, we had to figure out how to fit a course in ethics into current graduation and accreditation requirements, and into our assigned professional loads in teaching and research. Modifying curriculum structure and existing teaching loads proved the hardest part of this project.

Goals and Objectives

We anticipated several outcomes for our project: students would discover the implied ethos of their intended professions, learn to identify the tools with which to analyze ethical issues, begin to understand how their professional and personal decisions affect the social order, and become more skilled at negotiating and implementing public policy. Dramatizing ethical differences would help students learn about the power of professional knowledge and the responsibility they, as professionals, bear in establishing and carrying out policy.

Rationale for Choosing the Classroom Arena

We chose the college classroom as our arena, to serve simultaneously as a stage for dramatizing professional ethics and conflicts and as a haven for practicing and enacting policy construction. But just because we chose a classroom arena did not mean we meant to conduct the course in a conventional lecture and recitation format. We decided that a three-credit-hour, cross-discipline course would best fit existing curricular requirements and demonstrate ethical differences among disciplines. The team-teaching approach allowed us to model team work and to stress that applied ethics functions across disciplines.

Creating a three-hour course reflected our awareness that change within institutions, though desirable, must occur in stages. It was more pragmatic to request approval of a three-hour course than to seek approval for several different, irregularly scheduled (depending on actual events in our area) theatrical enactments of agricultural and natural resource policy battles that would call for serious student reaction and analysis. We also believed we could better use our time designing an innovative course within traditional constraints than trying to change the institutional structure, however worthy such change could be.

COURSE DEVELOPMENT

Although designing a course may not appear to be highly experimental, we did not intend the course itself to be all that traditional. We wanted students to learn to define ethical issues, make conscious choices which reflected some school of philosophical thought, define or refine policy, and implement action when necessary.

Contributions of Student and Faculty Partners

At the design stage, we asked student partners for their responses to our planned content, reading assignments, exams, and oral and written projects. The students, selected by NUPAGE personnel, discussed proposed assignments with us, stated what they liked, and suggested changes in construction and time allowed for completion of assignments. We implemented their suggestion that we use take-home exams almost exclusively. After we developed our first syllabus, students reacted to it, making suggestions about timing of assignments and the amount of reading. We did make changes in due dates for projects based on student input, but we didn't cut down on reading assignments.

Because we ourselves needed to learn many basic philosophical concepts, we asked our team partner in philosophy, Professor Nelson Potter, Department of Philosophy, to help us identify concepts needed to teach applied ethics of any kind. Professor Potter's practical experience in developing and teaching applied ethics courses (such as medical ethics) helped us balance the practical and theoretical. Potter also suggested ways to combine speakers from outside the university with assigned reading in the required text.

Contributions of Outside Partners

The first semester we taught this course, Bill Lock, a legislative analyst, worked with the class. With his help, students studied corporate ownership of agricultural land and production in rural Nebraska, a topic enlivened by the question of legality of out-of-state ownership. He taught us how to work with legislative issues and explained procedures we could use to help students who may, in the future, wish to do projects on current legislative topics affecting farming and natural resources.

Other partners included speakers on biogenetics, NAFTA, bank regulations, and sustainable farming. These experts helped define issues for our students and offered to help as students continued their research for our course. Notable is the generosity with which partners performed; many of them returned long after money for small gratuities ran out. However small the gratuities were, they seemed a powerful gesture of good will, breeding, in turn, returned good will. We are personally grateful for the help of our partners and know students felt a sense of mature corroboration as these partners spoke to and worked with them.

Texts, Methods, and Content

The eminently practical text, Rachels' *The Elements of Moral Philosophy* (1986), provided limited but sufficient instruction on such philosophical concepts as utilitarianism and egoism. We also used a compilation of essays from Regan's *Earthbound* (1984). Mirroring the growth of interest in ethics in agriculture and natural resources, more sources have since become available. We now use Blatz's *Ethics and Agriculture* (1991), which includes essays on agricultural research, land and water use, and many other topics, including intellectual property.

We began the course by helping students develop analytical skills by working with policy and actions already part of history. Because students studied forces contributing to developing and developed policy, they began to see how individuals definitely influence political and social action. The texts helped students identify their own values and understand the roles values play in both policy formation and the larger social order. Working with speakers, partners, and cases made the course practical. Further, the course offered occasions to learn that working ethically in a community requires defining what a community is and identifying the individual's responsibilities to the community.

Student Teams and Typical Projects

To help students learn their ethical responsibilities as professionals, we asked them to work in teams on policy issues that required representatives of different majors to work together. After students began to recognize and trace the evolution of their own values, we introduced case studies, to be considered in a team setting. We began with cases designed to model value development and conflict, in order to teach the role of values as well as the modes of philosophical thought that could be applied in decision-making. A simple case, for example, asked students to model decision-making about irrigation when conflicting needs and uses perilously reduced amounts of available water. Though utilitarianism may be abstract, deciding who gets to use water at what point is not abstract; and the ethical issue may be framed by the conceptual notion of utilitarianism.

Later, students formed larger teams, working with issues currently before the Nebraska Legislature, such as the legality and desirability of non-family corporations owning land and other production means in rural Nebraska. Another issue tied to legislative action included the regulation of agricultural pesticides. These issues are still alive, and, in one form or another, still act as topics or conceptual resources for team work almost every semester.

We also divided students into groups based on similar career aspirations and assigned them the team task of developing a professional code of ethics for that particular career path. Here, as well, the philosophical abstractions suddenly became concrete when applied to the world of work students soon would face.

Our focus on the team project has proven successful for two reasons. First, students are able to deal with real professional and policy issues and seek those in the community who can provide expert experience and opinions. Second, working in teams simulates the dynamics of public policy-making as students themselves define issues, examine alternative positions, struggle with divergent values, and seek group consensus.

SUMMARY: LESSONS LEARNED

About Teaching

In retrospect, we believe the course has confirmed what we initially surmised: most students bring with them to college a diversity of value sets which they have not completely reasoned through. When challenged or confronted by opposing positions, they are ill-equipped to thoughtfully consider the issue at hand and make reasoned choices. A course in applied ethics related to their fields of study can be a revelation to them, demonstrating that the world is not comfortably "black and white," not offering only simplistic answers. The course makes students aware that others do not share similar values and that decisions to be made in the workplace, as well as the policy-making arena, are complex and difficult.

Simply put, the course has expanded students' modes of reasoning and thinking. One student summed it up well in a post-course survey: "This course has caused me to reflect more carefully on the decisions and choices I make. I will value this experience long after I am out of school."

Much of the richness of an ethics course is in the context of active student involvement. Presentation of abstract concepts and hypothetical applications, while at times useful, simply does not fully engage the student. Only in the face of a real world dilemma, involving personal value sets and other people, does the teachable moment really begin. We believe that by structuring the course pedagogy around student assignments and practical projects, we have been able to capture in the classroom the dynamics of today's world.

For many of our students, this type of classroom dynamic is unsettling. They have been conditioned by their educational experience to be mere observers in the classroom and to act independently of others in terms of educational performance. Even the most reserved students, however, seemed to rather quickly respond to the opportunity to reason and actively discuss with their peers relevant ethical issues. This experience, as well as the opportunity to develop skills in group work and collective decision-making, has been a positive spillover of the course.

About Course Development Processes

In addition to the lessons we learned about teaching, we also learned a great deal about the process of developing a course. While NUPAGE provided the funding for developing the ethics course, the ability to sustain such a course depends on the college's commitment of existing or new funds. Persons responsible for making decisions about resources must be convinced that a new activity (such as continuation of an ethics course) holds a higher priority for the faculty involved than other activities those faculty members may have previously been involved in.

If the course is taught from a team approach, the amount of effort required of the faculty team members may be viewed differently by faculty members and administrators. Consequently, there may be differences of opinion about the amount of credit a faculty member who teaches as part of a team should receive toward teaching load calculation. This is particularly true if unit administrators have no direct or indirect experience with the demands or requirements of team teaching.

We also learned that approval for a non-traditional course (such as ethics) in a college of agriculture may take some time, especially when the faculty members who have developed and wish to teach it do not hold formal academic credentials in philosophy.

Finally, any new learning experience must be carefully promoted to students and faculty. Unless the course becomes a requirement in the curriculum, there may be a continuing need to "market" the course to maintain sufficient enrollment to justify the resources expended to teach it. The issue of the formal academic credentials of the instructors also may cause other faculty members to hesitate in their endorsement of a non-traditional course such as ethics.

REWARDS

In spite of the "hard" lessons we learned, there have been rewards as well. Working with NUPAGE staff helped us increase our awareness of the need to involve teams, to modify old patterns of learning, and to reach out for the new. In our case, we were able to travel to meet others in similar cross-discipline studies, to present papers at two conferences, to publish a paper, to add a great number of new works and monthly publications to our lists of "have-to reads." Both of us sensed that we did our best to supply a solution to what we saw as an academic need: study in applied ethics in agriculture and natural resources to help the student become the complete professional.

Laura Casari is Associate Professor of Agricultural Leadership, Education and Communication, University of Nebraska-Lincoln.

Bruce Johnson is Professor of Agricultural Economics, University of Nebraska-Lincoln.

REFERENCES

Blatz, C.V. (1991). *Ethics and agriculture: An anthology on current issues in world context.* Moscow, ID: University of Idaho Press.

Rachels, J. (1986). *The elements of moral philosophy.* New York, NY: Random House.

Regan, T. (1984). *Earthbound.* New York, NY: Random House.

Thompson, P. (1991). *Ethics in agriculture* [AGSAT course]. College Station, TX: Texas A&M (Funded by Department of Agriculture, 1991–2).

21

ETHICS AND VALUES AS HUMANITIES EDUCATION

Tom Scanlan
University of Minnesota

My Sunrise projects, and my work in course and curriculum development over the past 15 years in the University of Minnesota's College of Agriculture (COA), suggest that when pedagogical talk turns to ethics and values in the curriculum, different meanings, with different emphases, are attached to these terms. While these various approaches to ethics and values aren't necessarily contradictory or mutually exclusive, the implications that emerge are distinctive. Keeping these differences in mind at the outset might be helpful to anyone thinking about including ethics and values in the goals of an agricultural curriculum.

THREE APPROACHES TO INCLUDING ETHICS AND VALUES IN A CURRICULUM

Differences in thinking about how to include ethics and values in a college curriculum can be summarized as three separate approaches. Each is briefly described here.

Emphasis on Moral Philosophy

One approach is that of the moral philosopher. Here ethics is seen as a particular branch of philosophy with a long tradition in the construction and critique of moral arguments concerning, say, the claims of justice. This approach to ethics is the most rigorous and professional, but (at least in my own case) it is also potentially the most frustrating for students and for faculty when it comes into the classroom. Very special skills are needed to move easily from the close analysis of abstract arguments to the concrete issues of farm production.

Perhaps I am simply being too autobiographical here: for several years an animal scientist and I together taught a course on issues of animal welfare. We both loved the idea of the course, worked hard on it, and learned a lot from doing so; in the end, however, we never felt we had found enough ways to bridge the gap between the methods of philosophical argument on the one hand and on-farm experiences and practices on the other. We simply became bogged down in dealing with such tangled concepts as intrinsic value, moral agent, moral object, utilitarian calculation, self-consciousness, and suffering (among others). In the end, distinctions we thought crucial seemed either confusing or fussy to most of the students. I trust there are courses and teachers elsewhere that take more successful approaches than we were able to find.

Emphasis on Public Policy

It is no accident that one of the learner outcomes in the COA advising portfolio is captioned "Ethics and Policy," since a second approach to ethics and values emphasizes public policy. This way of thinking about ethics and values leans toward the world of the social scientist, especially in the areas of economics, political science, and rural sociology. The main interest of this approach is examining, or at least introducing, the social implications of agricultural practices, especially in the context of government rules and/or the pressures exerted by economics, whether in production, processing, marketing, or nutrition.

This interest has two emphases: raising questions about the contemporary social norms and public agendas that agriculture operates within, and pointing out the social implications of present practices or of advocated changes. The great advantage of this approach is that it deals with contemporary issues that are practical in their implications and alive in the minds of students and faculty alike. In agriculture these days, such issues often are framed as questions relating to public policy and the environment.

Emphasis on the Humanities

In my experience, the third approach taken in incorporating ethics and values into the curriculum of COA is the broad one of the humanities. Here history, literature, art, and language are used, either separately or in an interdisciplinary structure, to examine the values we have inherited from the past, particularly those which are reflected (and refracted) in present day concerns. Such cultural and historical materials might focus specifically on agriculture, or more generally on its larger context, in such areas as the values inherent in capitalism, science, or our relation to nature. Courses taught in the Rhetoric Department have reflected the humanities approach: "Land in the American Experience" and "Agricultural Heritage" are more specific to the concerns of agriculture, while others, like "In Search of Nature," "Science, Religion and the Search for Human Nature," "The Industrial Revolution," and "Scientific Controversy," are more contextual.

INTEGRATION OF ETHICS AND VALUES INTO TECHNICAL AND PROFESSIONAL EDUCATION

Project Sunrise offered me an opportunity to continue and expand my work of integrating the humanities, with its emphasis on ethics and values, into technical and professional education in COA. Here I briefly describe the two projects I pursued.

Technology, Society, and Self

My first project led to the development of a new course entitled "Technology, Society, and Self," focusing on issues of technology aimed primarily, but not exclusively, at scientific and technical communication (STC) majors. The University of Minnesota already offers an excellent array of courses on the histories of science, technology, and medicine, but STC students found these rather too specialized for their needs as communicators. When they enter the work world, STC majors find that they are mediators between experts and the public. Their professional loyalties are divided between the creators of technology, whose work they must reflect accurately, and the users of technology, who need accessibility and demystification—in everything from computer manuals, to government regulations on the environment, to safety specifications. People in this profession especially need to understand the powerful role technology plays in our lives, both social and personal. They must then examine the values we associate with technology, the assumptions about technology we have inherited from the past, and the symbolic meanings technology holds for us today.

My proposal was to develop a course using interdisciplinary materials that would ask students to reflect on how technology influences us: How have people in the past thought about technology? Is there a technology mindset? Is there a technology aesthetic? How do particular technologies make us feel? How do they make us act? What sorts of systems are created? How do experts function in a democracy?

These questions, and others like them, were aimed at introducing (and reintroducing throughout the quarter) such value issues as our attitudes toward work, power, control, gender, nature, and wants vs. needs. In the course students are asked to write analytic papers on the assigned reading, to write reflective, personal commentaries on the felt experience of technology in their lives, and to submit a creative project which embodies at least one of the themes of the course (common examples to date are short stories, collages, sculptures, and videos). By the way, the creative project is not graded on artistic skill but on effort and on relevance to the course topics.

I titled the course "Technology, Society, and Self" to stress that technology is a powerful mediator between our inner and outer lives. I use materials from literature, art, agriculture, organizational theory, computer designing, and the history of technology, although the materials change somewhat each time I teach the course. If the course begins by asking what technology means to us, it ends by asking whether technological change is a matter of choice or, rather, something we are not able to resist.

The course varies from year to year in the technologies studied, but the three most common have been mass production, agriculture, and computers. For example, in one section of the course last year we read materials that described the coming of mass production in the 19th century and the resulting large-scale corporate systems of management so typical of 20th century life. Next we looked at slides of paintings that presented technology (e.g., steamboats, railroads, dynamos, factories) as heroic; we discussed the power of these paintings in terms of the concept of the technological sublime and the assumptions of progress they depended on. Finally we concluded this section by reading Mark Twain's critique of 19th century technological values, *A Connecticut Yankee in King Arthur's Court*, with its layers of ambiguity.

A later section of the course took up the similarities and differences between factory mass production and the changes in farm production, using Mark Kramer's *Three Farms: Making Milk, Meat, and Money from the American Soil* (1980) in order to see the connections between the personal, social, and historical changes in American agriculture. This, in turn, led to a reprise of themes in a third section of the course using Jayne Anne Phillips' novel, *Machine Dreams* (1984), slides of the architectural revolution of the Bauhaus and the International Style, and Tracy Kidder's examination of the computer culture in *The Soul of a New Machine* (1981).

The course was designed for and is required of the undergraduate STC majors. I limited the course to juniors and seniors for two reasons: 1) in my experience, the reflective, personal assignments work better with older students; and 2) these students have some familiarity with the work of their major field. (The graduate STC program has asked that I allow graduate students into the course and upgrade work requirements for them. This request is currently under discussion.) The course has not yet been widely publicized outside the department, because it works well with an enrollment of about 20 students, and I am reluctant to add 10-15 more for fear of changing the chemistry of class discussion. So far I have been able to maintain this luxury.

The course could easily be of interest to other students, in both COA as well as other colleges of the university. However, recent changes in university-wide general education requirements would mean that the course would have to be redesigned to fulfill distribution requirements according to the new criteria.

Consultations with Other Faculty to Add Ethical Dimensions to Existing Courses

In a second Project Sunrise undertaking, I offered to consult with agricultural science faculty who wished to add an ethics and values approach to their classes. Professor Art Walzer and I took the lead in this effort. We had two such requests from faculty, but one—to work with Plant Pathology on its capstone senior seminar—never went beyond the exploratory stage. The other, from Professor Steve Simmons of the Agronomy Department, was completed with moderate success. Professor Simmons was preparing to teach an agronomy course, in which teams of students would examine a series of cases, requiring them to consider a range of issues before they could make a recommendation. I developed a bibliography of readings for Simmons and met with him several times as he planned his syllabus for the next quarter. Walzer and I attended the class periodically and raised questions and made suggestions about future assignments. For example, one of the cases required students to determine which crop should be grown in a particular area that did not have much water. Irrigation was one of the options, and I was able to provide Simmons with materials on the problems irrigation had caused to wildlife refuges in California.

In retrospect, I would say that my work on Simmons' course is a good example of what I spoke about initially: the need to be clear as to what is meant by ethics and values in the curriculum. I approached the course thinking as a cultural historian. The bibliography I gave Simmons— whatever the worth of the readings as, say, general background in Jeffersonian thought, historical geography, the philosophical issues underpinning the conservation movement, and so forth—was too general a context for Simmons' pedagogy. Such historical and cultural approaches cannot be added to a course, but must be central to its construction. The impulse of the class was toward issues of contemporary policy, an approach that required not just different materials but a different way of thinking.

OTHER POSSIBILITIES

My work with Simmons led me to a basic question that might be usefully applied in developing either introductory or capstone courses in the agricultural sciences. One might design a course in part or in toto around the question: what is the ethos of this discipline? In other words, what fundamental attitudes and values underlie agronomy (or animal science or soil science or agricultural economics, etc.)? There are a number of ways to approach materials that might be revealing for students and faculty alike: statements in popular introductory texts, keynote speeches at professional associations, editorials in the journals, departmental mission statements, personal interviews.

A course designed around such a basic question will eventually explore the history and development of the discipline which, in turn, might reveal changing values, hidden ambiguities, and shifting constituencies. Perhaps there are implicit conflicts between some of the disciplines. At any rate, examining the values that underpin a discipline could be a useful way to introduce ethics into the agricultural curriculum. In effect, the agricultural sciences could be seen for a moment as a way of thinking, a liberal art.

Tom Scanlan is Associate Professor of Rhetoric, University of Minnesota.

22

PRODUCT SAFETY AND LIABILITY AS THE FOCUS OF A SENIOR SEMINAR

Arthur E. Walzer
University of Minnesota

A small grant from Project Sunrise, the curriculum revitalization effort of the University of Minnesota's College of Agriculture, supported my attendance at a day-long workshop entitled "Product Safety and Liability Prevention: the Role of Warnings and Instructions," sponsored by the Department of Engineering Professional Development at the University of Wisconsin-Madison. I intended to use what I learned at this workshop to create and teach an experimental version of our department's senior seminar for majors in scientific and technical communication.

It seems to me that senior seminars are expected to respond to several, often competing, purposes: to present a final and rigorous intellectual challenge, to polish skills in preparation for the first job, and to raise questions of ethics and values that may not have found their way into the curriculum earlier. Perhaps the question of the technical communicator's role in product safety and liability could meet these purposes simultaneously. Questions of law and liability both provide intellectual challenge and raise issues of ethics; the creation of warnings involves both written and visual communication; a simulation in which students would define and complete tasks in response to a realistic case would give them practice in group decision-making and communication. It was worth a try.

The Course Foundation: Safety and Liability Issues in Parks vs. Allis-Chalmers

I wanted a real case on which to base my simulation, and, after spending a day in the law library, I settled on *Dwight Parks vs Allis-Chalmers Corporation*, a case tried in Beltrami County, Minnesota in 1977. Plaintiff Parks lost a portion of his right arm when, while attempting to unclog corn stuck in the rollers of a forage harvester, his arm was drawn into the whirling knives. Because Parks' attorney successfully argued that the inadequacy of the warnings on the harvester and in the manual was one source of Allis-Chalmers' negligence, the case seemed relevant to the concerns of technical communicators. Although a sign on the machine did instruct operators to "Keep away from rollers unless power is off," Parks' attorney, with the help of testimony from safety experts, persuaded a jury that the warnings were inadequate to alert users to the dangers inherent in attempting to free corn stuck in the rollers, as Parks had attempted to do.

My course established an imaginary division, the Safety and Liability subgroup, of a fictitious communication firm, Contract Writers Associates (CWA). In the case I created for the course, CWA had contracted with an imaginary Johnson Brothers Equipment (JBE) to review and, if necessary, revise the safety system for its forage harvester, a machine identical to the Allis-Chalmers machine found lacking in the *Parks vs Allis-Chalmers* case.

Course Management

Classes were run as student-led meetings of the Safety and Liability subgroups. (Because the class consisted of sixteen students, I divided them into two separate sections, each working on the same problem but meeting at different times. Within each section of eight, students worked on different aspects of the project in subgroups of four each). I attended the meetings as a silent manager, participating only to answer questions in that role. Students reviewed the relevant laws, regulations, and conventions that influence determinations of legal liability; they examined the forage harvester from pictures and explanations provided by our technical expert, Cletus Schertz of Agricultural Engineering, a colleague whom I pressed into service. Students created a proposal to Johnson Brothers, pointing out the inadequacy of the current safety and warning system in the manual and on the harvester, and recommending specific changes. After the acceptance of the proposal, they attempted to create a safety system consistent with the recommendations of the American Society for Agricultural Engineers (ASAE), the American National Standards Institute (ANSI), and the

"Product Safety Sign and Label System," a widely-used system of signage created by the FMC corporation.

Students were not told of the case on which the class experiment was based until after they created their systems. Only then did I introduce *Parks vs Allis-Chalmers*. The systems the students created were at that point held up to the criticisms the plaintiff leveled against the signage on the Allis-Chalmers forage harvester and against the warnings in the manual. Would the students' systems have met the criticisms that plaintiff's attorney success-fully leveled against the signage and manual of the original equipment? The adequacy of their safety systems to meet the objections of the plaintiff Parks was my measure of the success of the systems the students created.

ETHICAL ISSUES

Product safety is obviously not necessarily a question of ethics. In trying to ensure that their products are safe, manufacturers often are as motivated by fear of lawsuits as they are by a desire to satisfy customers, meet their obligations to others, or serve the public good; in other words, concern with safety is often motivated by self-interest and prudence. In my view, genuine ethical pressures are felt when doing what's right is incompatible with self-interest or a narrowly-conceived prudence. I wanted to introduce an element into the senior seminar that would pose a genuine question of ethics and give students an opportunity to test their courage.

I created this ethical problem about halfway through the course. The first formal assignment the Safety and Liability subgroup had to produce was a proposal to JBE, in which CWA proposed to improve the manual and the signage on the harvester. Since one of the purposes of the proposal was to win the contract to create a new safety system, students naturally empha-sized the inadequacy of the current system in the problem section of their proposals. The current system, they proved, did not meet current ANSI or ASAE standards; JBE might well be liable if an accident occurred.

After they completed their proposal, I attempted to create the ethical problem. Playing my role as general manager of CWA, I wrote a memo informing the Safety and Liability subgroup that JBE was not pleased with all aspects of what JBE called the "draft" of the proposal CWA had submit-ted; JBE had returned the "draft" for our "revision." While JBE was impressed with the system CWA proposed, it wanted significant changes in the problem section of the proposal, my memo said. JBE did not want on the record evidence that the current warnings on the harvester and in the manual were inadequate or any mention that users were at risk, since the changes were to be introduced on new harvesters and in new manuals only. In the event that a user of an existing machine were injured, the CWA proposal would be part of the "safety documentation" and would, therefore, necessarily become an issue in a court case.

As their manager, I asked the group to re-write the problem section of the proposal. The revised version could state that the current system might be improved in light of changes in standards since the harvester and manual were first produced, but it should not state that the existing system was inadequate. The goal in revising the system must be expressed as an effort to make a good system better, not to correct a deficient one.

At the next meeting of the Safety and Liability subgroup, students discussed how to respond to the request to remove or at least soften their criticism of JBE's existing safety system. They offered a number of reasons for acquiescing to the request.

The most persuasive seemed to be the argument that the legal requirement to save all documentation pertaining to safety made it imprudent for JBE to acknowledge the inadequacy of the manual and of the signage on existing harvesters. The law puts JBE in a bind, one student insisted, that makes it all but impossible for JBE to acknowledge the problem. We should acquiesce to JBE's request and soften the criticism. A second argument that seemed to carry weight was a pragmatic one: the most important thing was that the signage and the manual be improved (and that CWA get the contract to do so); in accepting the proposal, JBE was, in effect, acknowledging the cogency of CWA's criticisms. What material difference did it make if the problem section of the proposal were changed? A third argument was that this decision was "management's call," not one for writers of the subgroup: the writers are in no position to decide what CWA should do.

A minority of students rejected these arguments: the current system was inadequate; we wrote that it was, they said; we cannot deny that now. One student threatened not to go along with the majority, even if it meant quitting the group. But those who favored acquiescing to their manager's request carried the day.

After the groups reached their decision, I intervened (for the only time in the course) and we discussed the issues that the ethical problem raised: how the law, which frequently evolves from ethical imperatives, sometimes promotes unethical actions; how they might have adopted a third alternative, perhaps by proposing to JBE that CWA create stickers that could be mailed to owners of older machines who would put them on their harvesters and in their manuals; about whether it is possible to resolve disagreements that pit utilitarian arguments (those that judge actions by their effects) against deontological ones (those that judge actions in and of themselves). We talked about whether students really did see technical communicators as "user advocates," a view that many students casually espouse, as distinguished from viewing technical communicators as "mouthpieces" for their employers. If technical communicators are "user advocates," shouldn't improving the signage on existing machines have occurred to them?

DEFENSE OF STUDENT-DEVELOPED SYSTEMS

During the last week of the course, students were to imagine that two years had passed since their new safety system had been accepted and deployed. A letter from JBE described a lawsuit brought against JBE by a farmer who had lost part of his arm as a result of an accident with the forage harvester. The accident I described was identical to Dwight Parks', and JBE's counsel had sent briefs from that case for our review.

Members of the Safety and Liability subgroup were to examine these briefs to see if their systems held up to the criticisms of Parks's attorney in the earlier case; then, they were to write a memo to JBE assessing whether the CWA systems were adequate in light of the criticisms in *Parks vs Allis-Chalmers*. JBE would decide whether to litigate or settle on the basis of CWA's judgment of the adequacy of the revised signage on the harvester and warnings in the manual. (One group's signage and manual met the test of Parks' attorney; the other did not).

ASSESSMENT OF THE COURSE

In response to the question, "What was the most important thing you learned in the course?" most students expressed appreciation of the knowledge they gained about manufacturers' responsibility for product safety, about liability law, and about systems of signage. Five of the sixteen students singled out the session on ethics in response to this question. One student wrote, "What was the most important thing I learned? Not to change my opinion because I'm threatened in a memo! Can't believe I fell for that. But it's a lesson I won't forget." Most students liked the simulation, judging it most appropriate for a senior seminar.

The most frequent student complaint was about my "hands off" role. Although many acknowledged that the simulation required me to let them flounder and thanked me for detailed comments on their work, many expressed frustration about the lack of direction at meetings and at not knowing what was expected of their final papers. Two students, perhaps with my "observer" role in mind, complained that they felt, in the words of one, "a bit like a subject in an experiment." And members of one group complained about the dynamics of the group—that work was not fairly shared; some people dominated; others made hurtful remarks. (The other group praised the way it had come together to cooperate to complete the tasks.)

This version of the course did all that I hoped it would do: it put into practice most of the skills and knowledge that our program is intended to teach, challenged the students intellectually, and raised questions of ethics and law. Also, I was impressed by the quality of the work students produced in the course, as was Cletus Schertz. Yet despite this success and although I (and other senior seminar instructors) use the materials on safety product liability I brought back from the workshop, I did not use the simulation again in senior seminar.

I abandoned the model described here because I felt it would be artificial to use it again. During the simulation version of the course, I silently worked with the students, examining the harvester and the manual, thinking about where warnings might go, etc. In a sense, I shared in their inspirations and frustrations. While there is some artificiality in all teaching, the degree is crucial to me; to do the same case again seemed false. What would I be learning? What would I be contributing? Students really would be rats in an experiment.

The solution to the problem of artificiality may be to find more cases, but finding a case that is actually litigated, in which signage and warnings are crucial, and in which actual documents are retrievable is not easy—at least not for me. If I were to do this simulation again, I would work with a law student or a law librarian, who could both help me find more cases and serve as a legal consultant in the course to complement Cletus Schertz, the technical expert. Unfortunately, both the complications of arranging a collaboration and the expense (probably $1000 for a law student to help select cases and to be available for consultation with the student groups) makes it unlikely that this version of the course will become a permanent model for our department's senior seminar.

Arthur E. Walzer is Associate Professor of Rhetoric, University of Minnesota.

SUGGESTED READING

On Safety and Liability

A good introduction to the role the technical communicator plays in safety and liability is the special issue of IEEE *Transactions of Professional Communication,* 30 (September 1987), which was devoted to this question. These essays appear alphabetically in the list below.

Beford, M.S., & Stearns, F.C. (1987). The technical writer's responsibility for safety. *IEEE Transactions of Professional Communication,* 30, 127–32.

Clement, D.E. (1987). Human factors, instructions and warnings, and products' liability. *IEEE Transactions of Professional Communication,* 30, 149–56.

Conrads, J.A. (1987). "Illustruction": Increasing safety and reducing liability exposure. *IEEE Transactions of Professional Communication,* 30, 133–5.

Driver, R.W. (1987). A communication model for determining the appropriateness of on-product warnings. *IEEE Transactions of Professional Communication,* 30, 157–63.

Paradis, J. (1991). Text and action: The operator's manual in context and in court. In C. Bazerman and J. Paradis, (Eds.), *Textual dynamics and the professions.* (pp 256–278). Madison, WI: University of Wisconsin Press.

Strate, L., & Swerdlow, S. (1987). The maze of law: How technical writers can research and understand legal matters. *IEEE Transactions of Professional Communication,* 30, 136–48.

Verlotta, C. (1987). Safety labels: What to put in them, how to write them, and where to place them. *IEEE Transactions of Professional Communication,* 30, 121–26.

Walter, C., & Marstellar, T.F. (1987). Liability for the dissemination of defective information. *IEEE Transactions of Professional Communication,* 30, 164–71.

Ethics

Richard L. Johannesen's *Ethics in Human Communication,* 3rd ed. (Prospect Heights, IL: Waveland Press, 1990) is the best general bibliography for work done in ethics and communication. For ethics and technical communication, see *Technical Communication and Ethics,* R. John Brockmann and Fern Rook, (Eds.), (Washington, DC: Society for Technical Communication, 1989).

SECTION 7

COMPUTERS AND THE
CURRICULUM

Edited and with an introduction by
Laurie Schultz Hayes
University of Minnesota

The use of computer-aided delivery systems is a radical development in the history of education, representing the first qualitative change in delivery-system technology since the printing press. Although other technological innovations, such as the tape recorder, motion-picture projector, and television, have contributed to the refinement of the traditional teacher- and textbook-based delivery system, theirs were contributions of degree and not of kind. The computer offers something qualitatively different, that is, a way of replicating intelligent interactions with the learner, thereby changing not only the kind of delivery but also the meaning and roles of the other part of the educational system.[1]

Each of the three curricular revitalization projects had a computer component, but the focus of each was different. An explicit goal of the University of Minnesota's project was to "make good progress in incorporating modern computer and telecommunications uses into our classrooms." Designers of the University of Wisconsin's project wanted students and faculty to acquire information management and communication skills, to "gain experiences with word-processing, data base management, and spreadsheets, and gain an awareness of expert systems." The University of Nebraska's NUPAGE objectives did not mention computers specifically as a part of designing new education experiences for students, but computers were not excluded as possible elements in "opportunities for active learning" and "problem solving in experiential settings."

This diverse focus is reflected in the next three essays. "Managing A Strawberry Farm: A Computer Simulation," by Emily E. Hoover and Albert H. Markhart, is an example of the University of Minnesota's efforts to integrate the use of computers into the classroom. Minnesota's College of Agriculture funded several curriculum projects using computers in communication, (see Duin, this volume) food science, nutrition, and horticultural science. Each of these employed instructional techniques ranging from tutorials to expert systems. In "Managing A Strawberry Farm," Hoover and Markhart describe how they, as two horticulture faculty members, worked with software and programming consultants to complete 95% of an expert system designed for undergraduate students or extension service clientele. While their simulation is still not ready to use, Hoover and Markhart admit that the project helped them learn even more about strawberry production and forced them to struggle with the dilemma that the "easiest" choices to program for students in the simulation were those that are "unreal" or "unethical."

F. H. Buelow's "Improving Computer Use in Undergraduate Instruction," offers a brief summary of the nine different projects funded by the University of Wisconsin's College of Agricultural and Life Sciences in an effort to improve the information management and communication skills of faculty and students. Buelow notes that during the time of the project, faculty interest in improving their own computer skill level was especially high.

The last essay in this section is the most elaborate. In "Agribusiness Learning Experience (ABLE)," Dennis M. Conley outlines how he used a computer simulation developed at Purdue University to revise his course in agribusiness management at the University of Nebraska. Conley was looking for a way to involve his students more actively in real problem solving situations and had hoped to design and construct a new computer simulation; but like Hoover and Markhart at Minnesota, he discovered how much time that project would consume, so he postponed it. Instead, he developed a pedagogical model for instruction (ABLE) using the Purdue Farm Supply Management Game as the core. In his essay, Conley describes the ABLE model, explains how he has implemented it in his class, and closes by discussing some other active learning techniques he has used successfully while moving away from lecture-dominated teaching.

In the time since these projects were funded, there have been many additional advances in the capabilities of computers and people who use them. But the authors of these essays are not raising "dated" questions or offering unusable models. Computer-aided or computer-based instruction is attractive for its ability to adapt to the needs and locations of various learners, but investment in it requires careful deliberation. Computers still aren't perfect and, for sure, they are not yet cheap. The advantage of the projects outlined in the following pages is that they represent modest efforts by faculty that can still be emulated.

A good resource book that offers teachers and administrators valuable lists of advantages and disadvantages for various instructional media, including computers, is: Ronald H. Anderson, *Selecting and Developing Media for Instruction, second edition,* New York, NY: Van Nostrand Reinhold Company, 1983.

NOTE

[1]Bunderson, C.V., & Inouye, D.K. (1987). The evolution of computer-aided educational delivery systems, in *Instructional technology: Foundations,* R. M. Gagne, (Ed.), Hillsdale, NJ: Erlbaum, p. 283.

Laurie Schultz Hayes is Associate Professor of Rhetoric and Associate Dean, Curricular and Student Affairs, College of Agriculture (now College of Agricultural, Food, and Environmental Sciences), University of Minnesota.

23

MANAGING A STRAWBERRY FARM: A COMPUTER SIMULATION

Emily E. Hoover and Albert H. Markhart
University of Minnesota

Our motivations for creating a computer simulation of a strawberry operation were direct. We wanted students to integrate economic and cultural knowledge from a variety of sources to "produce" a profitable crop. The computer simulation we designed synthesizes information students have had in a variety of courses together in one experience. We chose strawberries because, of all the perennial fruit crops, strawberries need limited cultural manipulations to be successfully grown. We were curious about using simulations in teaching and looked upon it as a challenge.

PROJECT BACKGROUND

We began working together because we had complementary skills. One of us (Hoover) was the strawberry expert and the other (Markhart) bridged the gap between Mark DeBower, the computer programmer, and the strawberry expert. We initiated this project when the University of Minnesota was selected as one of 19 sites for a grant from IBM. The grant stipulated that software be developed for educational use, using IBM equipment. Thus, we began the simulation with equipment support from IBM.[1]

We soon realized we needed to hire a programmer since neither of us felt competent to learn the Turbo Pascal programming language. We obtained $2000 from the University of Minnesota's Educational Development Grant Program (sponsored by the Northwest Area Foundation) to hire a programmer, who worked with a shell we developed using our own time and resources. We then obtained funds to finish the programming for the

simulation from Project Sunrise, the College of Agriculture project supported by a grant from the W.K. Kellogg Foundation.

DESCRIPTION OF THE SIMULATION

The strawberry computer simulation was designed for upper division
undergraduate students and extension clients interested in becoming strawberry producers. The overall objective of the computer simulation is to have
students perform cultural practices and make management decisions at the
proper time in the development of the crop, to maximize profit. Before the
simulation begins, the computer randomly selects one of three possible
weather scenarios and one of three possible soil types. The simulation begins
in April, just prior to growth of the crop. Each week during the growing season (35 weeks) the computer tells students the weather forecast for the
upcoming week, and the current status of the crop. Students then make
management decisions for the week.

To make the weather in the simulation realistic, we obtained actual
weather data from different years, representing a variety of temperature and
rainfall. The growth of the crop is modeled on heat units (sum of the aver-
age daily temperature minus 50°F), which were calculated from actual
weather records.

The management options are broken down into eight categories:
mulch, irrigation, pest control, fertilization, renovation, personnel, adver-
tisement, and harvest. The effect on crop yield of the student's decision in a
particular management area is evaluated based on the crop's current stage of
development, the current weather, and the water status of the soil. For
example, mulching is done in late fall to protect plants from cold winter
temperatures. Mulch must be removed in the spring to allow plants to grow.
Therefore, the date a student removes the mulch in the spring is a critical
factor. If mulch is removed too early, the plants may still be damaged by cold
weather; if it is removed too late, most of the plants will die from heat build-
up and lack of light. If mulch is removed at the proper time, no yield loss
occurs; removal of mulch either too early or too late results in considerable
yield loss.

The cost of a selected management practice is calculated from estimates
of labor and material costs. A running total of expenses is always displayed
on the screen. As students progress through the simulation, they decide how
to advertise and sell the crop. Depending on crop yield, the student receives
a gross income, which is then adjusted for the expenses during the season
and a net profit is determined. At the end of the "season," students can

review all decisions they made during the season and compare them with recommended practices.

ADVANTAGES OF THE COMPUTER SIMULATION AND RELATED ISSUES

An important aspect of the simulation is flexibility. We wanted to create a number of different weather scenarios and soil types, all interacting with all possible management decisions. To accomplish this, we incorporated empirical models that enable the computer to determine for each week the plant's stage of development and the soil's water content. With this information and current weather data, the computer program evaluates the consequences of any management decision. We made substantial assumptions, but the flexibility gained with this approach is tremendous. Each time a student runs the simulation, the potential exists for conditions to be different, therefore allowing the student to experience different seasons as growers do.

We hoped the simulation would increase discussion about cultural systems for growing strawberries as well as require students to think about how the system needs to be integrated to successfully grow this and other crops. We ourselves learned a great deal about strawberry production, as well as what we do not know about the crop.

One of the major issues we struggled with in the design of the simulation was how to deal with important ethical issues. For example, the application of pesticides to food crops is tightly regulated. Regulations specify which chemicals can be used and when they can be applied. However, following regulations does not necessarily produce maximum profit. We debated several alternative approaches to deal with this issue in the simulation: 1) not allow any practice that was against the law; 2) allow the illegal practice, coupled with discovery and imposition of fines; and 3) allow the illegal practice, with only a chance of discovery determined by a function in the program. Option 3 best represents what happens in the "real" world; option 2 offers the best opportunity to teach ethics; option 1 is the easiest to program.

CURRENT STATUS OF THE PROJECT

The computer program is 95% completed. Even with a variety of sources for funding, we ran out of money to pay the programmer who was writing the code. We underestimated the time it took to teach the programmer enough about the project so he could write the code without having to modify it extensively. Since neither of us is (or was) fluent enough in Turbo Pascal to complete the code, the program is still only 95% complete. The idea is excellent, but the project was seriously flawed when we decided to use a computer language we could not write.

A variety of authoring systems are currently available that would be useful for this type of simulation. We feel the project has great potential merit in small fruit production courses and can serve as a model for other production simulations.

NOTE

[1]On August 1, 1985, IBM Corporation announced its intent to provide $7.5 million in hardware, software, and other support over three years to help faculty plan innovative projects in computer-based instruction. The University of Minnesota was one of 19 sites participating in the Advanced Education Project (AEP) with IBM's Academic Information Systems (ACIS) division.

Emily E. Hoover is Associate Professor of Horticultural Science, University of Minnesota.
Albert H. Markhart is Associate Professor of Horticultural Science, University of Minnesota.

REFERENCES

Hoover, E., Markhart, A., & Nassauer, J. (1989). IBM computers for innovative teaching in horticulture and landscape architecture: Project AG01. In *Project Woksape Final Report.* (p. 27). Minneapolis, MN: University of Minnesota.

Hoover, E.E., & Markhart, A.H. (1987). Horticulture—Managing a strawberry farm: A computer simulation. *Academic Computing, 2(2),* 32–33, 52.

24

AN AGRIBUSINESS
LEARNING EXPERIENCE (ABLE)

Dennis M. Conley
University of Nebraska-Lincoln

T he original intention of the Agribusiness Learning Experience (ABLE) project at the University of Nebraska-Lincoln (UNL) was to change from a classroom environment where students practice "school skills" to a situation replicating an agribusiness experience where students are expected to practice "workplace skills." Skills taught at school are many times not the same as those required at work. School skills involve taking notes, reading assignments, and doing textbook problems to answer teacher's questions, if asked, and to pass exams. In the workplace environment, employees read, write, compute, and communicate orally to perform tasks and solve problems.

The challenge for educators is: can and should we go beyond teaching school skills to help develop workplace skills as we lead students through a course? Cognitive and learning theories can help answer the question. Words, symbols, and concepts only go so far. Students need experience in applying the disciplinary knowledge they are learning. Through use of simulations, students are physically in a classroom but the simulated "workplace" environment will require them to critically read, transform data into information, analyze it, make business decisions, monitor performance, and communicate by listening, speaking, and writing.

ABLE PROJECT BACKGROUND

The ABLE project was designed for junior and senior students majoring in agribusiness and for other disciplinary majors in the College of

Agricultural Sciences and Natural Resources (CASNR) who have an agribusiness option. (From the beginning of the project, however, we also perceived that a broader set of learners was possible, including managerial employees in industry.) The agribusiness major has the largest enrollment in the college (over 300 students), and the course in which the ABLE project is applied, Agribusiness Management (Agricultural Economics 316), has one of the larger enrollments for an upper level course.

The course has been offered for over ten years, and for most of those years some form of an agribusiness simulation game was used to facilitate the learning experience. However, a review of the literature on business simulation and experiential learning led to an important insight. Teachers and researchers on teaching found that in a number of cases, course simulation games were simply filling classroom time. The simulation was not being exploited to facilitate and reinforce disciplinary knowledge, nor to enhance the learning experience. Instead, students were going through exercises that made little or no connections with course content, did not show cause and effect relationships, and still maintained a passive learning environment.

This insight had considerable influence on the design and purpose of the ABLE project, and on the structure and conduct of the Agribusiness Management course. I wanted to minimize the practice of lecture-dominated presentations with no student-teacher and student-student interaction. I was going to make sure the learning experience for students was active rather than passive.

One important source of ideas that helped establish the context for the ABLE project was my own five years of business experience. After teaching for eight years, I left academia and worked in industry; upon returning, I initiated the ABLE project.

The industry experience led me to recognize that the teaching approach of transferring as much disciplinary knowledge as possible in a semester-long course excluded valuable learning experiences. These experiences center on understanding and practicing advanced forms of communication and interpersonal skills. For example, well-developed communication skills involving oral expression and written correspondence can sustain win-win outcomes. Interpersonal skills involve learning cooperatively from each other and working together as a team.

My experience in business, combined with disciplinary knowledge acquired from prior years of teaching, gave me the confidence and motivation to try different approaches in teaching. The opportunity offered by the

Kellogg Foundation through a NUPAGE grant to develop ABLE was time-ly, and the community of NUPAGE partners was encouraging.

WHAT IS ABLE?

The vehicle for creating the overall "workplace" environment is the ABLE model which illustrates the objectives of the project. It is composed of five parts as shown in the following figure. At the center is a computer simulation and surrounding this core are four pedagogical components.

FIGURE 24-1

ABLE Model

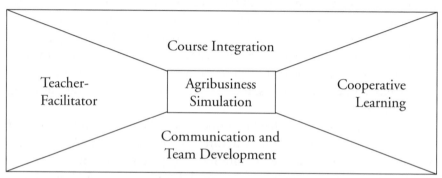

The core *Agribusiness Simulation* includes financial statements and operating information for a firm competing in an oligopolistic market area. Students are required to make a number of price and operating decisions. They encounter and must deal with competition from other firms in the market area and external shocks, such as drought, higher interest rates, and foreign competition. Fidelity of cause and effect should be evident.

Surrounding the core simulation are the pedagogical parts which complete the ABLE model. Borrowing the concept of "high tech-high touch" from computer terminology, the core simulation is the "high tech" part, and the three components of teacher-facilitator, communication and team development, and cooperative learning are the "high touch" parts. The *Teacher-Facilitator* part involves the interaction of the teacher as both an instructor and facilitator with the student. *Communication and Team Development* requires interaction of students among themselves and as a team with the teacher. The third pedagogical part is to make use of *Cooperative Learning* concepts. The combination of "high tech" and "high touch" is expected to give the learning experience its robustness.

The final pedagogical part of the ABLE model is the integration of disciplinary course material (*Course Integration*). The sub-disciplines integrated within agricultural economics include agricultural policy, agricultural marketing, farm management, and production. Within business they are micro and macro economics, management, finance, marketing, and personnel.

WHAT HAPPENED

Once the ABLE project was accepted, a number of activities ensued. A reinforcing element was that the agribusiness management course already existed and provided the classroom laboratory where the ABLE project could be tried and tested. The agribusiness simulation, which was the initial focal point in the ABLE Model, ran on a mainframe computer and was refined for use on a personal computer. The simulation was made more challenging by allowing the teacher to influence the agribusiness environment.

Classroom Experiences

The simulation game used in the course was the Purdue Farm Supply Management Game (Babb and Bohl, 1969), in which student teams of three members role play as managers. The farm supply centers compete in an oligopolistic market area with the student teams deciding selling prices for fertilizer, feed, and related services, and buying prices for grain and contracting activity. Students must make non-price decisions about advertising expenditure, personnel, fixed-asset purchases, borrowing, investments, credit policy, and ordering for inventory. The agribusiness is managed for 12 one-year decision periods during the semester. Student interest is maintained for 12 decisions based on the expectation that they not only manage the internal aspects, which they usually master in six to eight decisions, but also cope with significant external conditions.

The components of the ABLE model surrounding the simulation game were also implemented during the semester. From the beginning, *course integration* occurred by covering material relevant to the most important and most frequent decisions. For example, pricing methods were covered first, followed by inventory management decisions, and then the reading and analysis of financial statements.

Combining course content with the role as a team member led to *cooperative learning*. Course content accumulated and became more complicated as the semester progressed. The team situation encouraged members to rely more on each other to assure understanding of content and to make valid decisions as managers.

While this cooperative learning led to some aspects of *team development*, the required oral reports bonded individual students into a team. Each management team had to present a six-year progress report on its agribusiness, and each student had to participate. No free-riders, or social loafers. The presentations were videotaped and subsequently reviewed and critiqued by the team. A second oral report was given at the end of the semester.

Completing the ABLE Model is the *teacher as a facilitator*. Some course content was delivered as lecture, but sufficient classroom time was scheduled to allow a student team to work together. As the teacher, I made myself available to each team for answering questions, and, in some cases, directed questions at a team. I moved from behind the podium or overhead projector, and physically placed myself in close proximity to a team when there was dialog. More recently I have created an alternate role model for myself as the owner and general manager of the agribusiness to which each of the three-student team members report. Sometimes the owner is pleasant, and sometimes he is terse in telling the student-managers they need to think more carefully about how they manage the owner's business. The owner suggests from time-to-time that perhaps reading and listening, and even asking questions of the professor, may be of some benefit to them as managers.

This combination of a refined simulation game, complemented by the surrounding components, yielded good educational experiences for the students. They were responsive, active, and to a degree enthused. However, the design and construction of a new computer simulation game as originally envisioned was postponed. Building a new simulation game was more work than expected—by triple. After learning more about teaching methods and personality types and having a somewhat better feel for how students learn, I realized the prototype game probably put too much emphasis on numerical and analytical abilities similar to my own. It did not sufficiently emphasize dealing with ill-defined situations and problems, true decision-making, and inter-personal skills, all of which require higher order skills of analysis, synthesis, and evaluation.

New Paths

Other significant lessons I learned from the ABLE project came mostly from unanticipated diversions and exploration of new paths for learning through experimentation in the classroom. I wanted to see how students responded, either positively or negatively, to a more active teaching approach.

I conducted one experiment to evaluate development of students' cognitive skills from Bloom's taxonomy through active and intense use of the

ABLE model during the semester-long course. A longitudinal survey was taken during the semester to identify students' responses to stimuli coming from the simulated environment. The experiment revealed that students moved to higher order learning skills when confronted with unexpected situations (Conley, 1991).

Another experiment identified the cross-sectional profile of Myers-Briggs personality types in the classroom, and then tested for personality bias in evaluating student performance on exams and oral reports (Conley and Simon, 1993). Some of the material for the exams came from the *Agribusiness Simulation* component of the ABLE model, and the oral reports were required assignments in the *Communication and Team Development* component. Students' personality types were compared to each other and to mine to see if the exams and oral reports favored one personality type over another. The results showed no biases.

Another classroom experiment monitored the stages of group development to see if team formation actually occurred as students managed a simulated agribusiness (Conley and Simon, August 1993).

Exploration of how students learn and of the teacher-student relationship made me realize how difficult it is to really achieve teaching objectives prescribed by education theory. The teacher who wants to develop the higher order learning skills in students faces a difficult and challenging task. It is easy to regress back to lecture-dominated, passive learning which develops only the lower level skills.

Outcomes

Four specific outcomes resulted from the ABLE Project:

1. Based on both formal and informal feedback from students, the objectives outlined and methods for attaining those objectives will continue to be implemented in the course. It is clear that most students value experiential learning, and they recognize the value of reinforcement and integration of key concepts from the business discipline. They are mostly silent on the interpersonal and team aspects of the learning experience, but seem to appreciate the opportunity to test their own abilities in this area before entering the workforce. They also appreciate the opportunity to practice their oral communication skills and build their confidence in preparation for future job expectations. The ABLE project will not remain static, but will be a continuing effort of experimentation and evolution to achieve meaningful learning experiences for students.

2. The project has enhanced my own understanding of how students behave in a learning environment, and how each student is a unique, complex person trying to assimilate information, knowledge, and experiences. This understanding has led me to a long-term exploration of methods for teaching students and has given me the courage to experiment with my own ideas on methods.

3. The project has enlightened me about how much more can still be done to enrich the learning environment for students and to heighten the motivation for learning. The ABLE approach will not only help students learn more and be better learners, but will also cause them to take more responsibility for learning.

4. Some of the ABLE project objectives that were planned were realized, but some unplanned, coincidental opportunities presented themselves, as well. These opportunities allowed for improvements in the educational function that extended beyond the ABLE project at both the departmental and college level.

STATUS OF THE PROJECT

The ABLE project as defined was implemented into the course Agricultural Economics 316, "Agribusiness Management," over the past four years. The project gave order to and formalized the method for teaching the course. Student feedback has been very encouraging and positive. But, in a sense, the ABLE project probably will never be finished. I still want to create and implement a new version of the simulation game. The possibility also exists to formalize this course and teaching approach so it will be available to other academic institutions and even for education programs in industry. But the main reason the ABLE project will never be finished is because it encouraged further experimentation with the learning experiences of both students and teachers.

Dennis M. Conley is Associate Professor of Agricultural Economics, University of Nebraska-Lincoln.

REFERENCES

Babb, E.M., & Bohl, L.P. (1969, May). *Manual for Purdue farm supply center management game.* EC-321. Lafayette, IN: Purdue University, Cooperative Extension Service.

Conley, D.M. (1991). Student perceptions of cognitive skill achievement in agribusiness management. *Agribusiness: An International Journal. 7(2),* 135–141.

Conley, D.M., & Simon, D. (1993). Testing for personality bias in evaluating agribusiness students. *Agribusiness: An International Journal, 9(2),* 119–127.

Conley, D.M., & Simon, D. (1993, August). *The management challenge of team formation in an agribusiness.* Selected paper for the annual meeting of the American Agricultural Economics Association, Orlando, FL.

25

IMPROVING COMPUTER USE IN UNDERGRADUATE INSTRUCTION

F. H. Buelow
University of Wisconsin-Madison

For a curricular revitalization project to succeed, it must be given a high level of visibility among administrators, faculty, students, and alumni. Faculty must become interested in and enthusiastic about changing their curricula. One of the ways that the University of Wisconsin project built this interest was to make available seed money for curricular improvement projects. This program showed the faculty that curricular revitalization of undergraduate programs was an important activity, and the selection of projects to be funded gave significant direction toward accomplishment of the project mission.

Of the 48 curricular improvement projects funded at the University of Wisconsin, nine were directed at improving computer use in undergraduate instruction. None of the projects included the purchase of computers. The descriptions of the projects below illustrate the range of applications that faculty proposed and that were funded.

- B. Bavister, Veterinary Science Department, developed a semi-interactive software program to replace the use of live animals in the blood pressure control lab. Because of this program, the "experiments" are no longer subject to unanticipated reactions in test animals that could lead the students to incorrect conclusions. The learning is thus better controlled and easier to carry out.

- J. Harrington, Landscape Architecture Department, attended a five-day seminar on the use of computer-aided design and drafting using

AutoCAD and LANDCADD, a system developed for land planners and designers. He also used this system to develop instructional materials for two undergraduate courses, and assisted other faculty in the development of materials for six other courses.

- J. Griffith, Agricultural Journalism Department, attended a conference on computer graphics to gather information for revising the curriculum and developing a computer graphics laboratory for agricultural journalism courses. Because many ag journalism graduates are employed by organizations that have very few communications people, they need to understand and operate desk top publishing and computer graphics equipment as a part of their jobs. Currently the students, faculty, and staff routinely make use of computer graphics software and techniques to do their agricultural journalism work.

- R. Jeanne and colleagues, Entomology Department, refined and embellished simulation software used in undergraduate courses for teaching insect population ecology, insects and disease in forest management, and insect behavior. The programs are being used to help students understand insect responses to various inputs. The students are taught the use of the program in workshops, and then they "play" with the software to develop their understanding of insect behavior.

- R. Harris, Soil Science Department, developed a range of software programs for instructional use in soil science courses. The department already used computer models and graphics in the instructional areas of soil morphology, classification and mapping, advanced soil physics, and microclimatology; the new programs were additions to these. They are enhancing several of the soil science courses by giving the faculty and students access to more effective software.

- Denise Ney and colleagues, Nutritional Sciences Department, assessed and developed the undergraduate dietetics curriculum in order to teach students how basic computer skills can be applied to clinical dietetic practice. These efforts resulted in very effective training for faculty in the use of computers for instruction, and most are using it now. Instruction, as a result, is more efficient and effective. The computer skills of students have been enhanced, and as a result, more assignments are now being done on the computer. Students' improved computer skills have had a positive effect on their placement and employment.

- J. Coors and J. Staub, Agronomy and Horticulture Departments, developed computer-aided instruction for plant breeding and genetics courses by integrating a statistical package with instructional software. They prepared five program modules, each of which helps students understand a basic tenet of quantitative genetics. The program is called "Artificial Selection," and the five modules are: 1) the prediction equation for selection; 2) the genetic basis of quantitative traits; 3) changes in gene frequency; 4) changes in mean phenotype; and 5) the number of genes affecting quantitative traits.

- J. Buongiorno, Forestry Department, modernized existing software and developed new software to teach decision-making methods in natural resources management. As a result, students find the spreadsheet easier to use for optimization problems and do not need to be concerned as much with the technicalities of the software. The software currently is in use, resulting in more efficient and effective instruction.

- W. Kenealy, Biochemistry Department, set up a computer-guided tutorial which instructs students in the theory of operation, equipment handling and use, and practical aspects of mass culture of microorganisms. Kenealy learned that it took more time to set up the tutorial than to give the lectures it was to replace. Therefore the payoff would come only if it were used often. The tutorial was set up so that it could be kept up to date easily, and thus remain usable over a long period of time. The Hypercard system could be an effective approach for teaching the development of pilot plants for the mass culture of microorganisms.

Computer courses for faculty in the College of Agricultural and Life Sciences were set up by the curricular revitalization project. After the courses were completed, the former participants were surveyed and asked to characterize their computer use during their most recent semester of teaching. The most often used function was word processing, which led all other functions by quite a margin. Other functions were cited in the following order:

- communicating with other faculty

- graphics

- communicating with students

- grading and/or student records

- programs, data bases, or spreadsheets for students

- programming assignments for students.

Since the project components described above were completed in 1989, the use of computers as instructional aids and enhancements has continued to grow rapidly. The growth is being nurtured by the availability of more and better computer hardware and software at lower cost, but also by more computer-literate faculty and students. Both faculty and students have realized that computer technology makes possible more in-depth instruction in less time and at less cost. The result is that computers are being used extensively to achieve teaching objectives, and therefore have become an integral part of the learning experience.

F. H. Buelow is Professor Emeritus of Agricultural Engineering, University of Wisconsin-Madison.

CONCLUSION

OUTCOMES AND LESSONS LEARNED

Joyce Povlacs Lunde
University of Nebraska-Lincoln

The curriculum projects described in the foregoing chapters provide a sampling of the process of course and curriculum revitalization on each of our campuses.[1] While individual projects on each campus were unique, innovative, and often creative in themselves, similarities in programs, results, and structures extend across our three campuses. This concluding chapter briefly summarizes the outcomes for each project—the results of the "revitalization."

The reader is invited to reflect with us on the lessons we have learned in the process. Large amounts of time, energy, and resources were directed toward curriculum revitalization by faculty, administrators, and students on our three campuses, as well as by the Kellogg Foundation. One major lesson we learned again is that work on the academic programs is never done; teaching, learning, and the curriculum are never fixed for all time. Therefore, lessons we learned in this experience should make us better prepared to improve the process and the product of academic innovation that will take us far into the twenty-first century.

MINNESOTA OUTCOMES

According to the Project Sunrise Third Annual Report (June 1990), the College of Agriculture had achieved all the goals set forth in the original proposal to Kellogg. The accomplishments were:

- An updated curriculum guide, specifying learner outcomes for all college graduates

- Implementation of new and collegiate and intercollegiate majors
- Design and implementation of an outcomes-based advising system, utilizing the portfolio concept
- Revision of the College Curriculum Committee, to reflect the majors and advising system
- Intensive faculty development for use of alternative learning strategies, including:

    writing across the curriculum

    computer-assisted instruction

    cooperative learning

- Strategies implemented for teaching critical thinking, problem solving, and decision-making
- Integrated orientation courses developed for new majors
- Establishment of undergraduate projects and theses
- Improvement of pre-registration advising procedures

The ten new collegiate and intercollegiate majors, which reduced the number of majors on the books and gave focus to undergraduate education across departments, include:

- Agribusiness Management
- Agricultural Education
- Agricultural Industries and Marketing
- Animal and Plant Systems
- Applied Economics
- Food Science
- Natural Resources and Environmental Studies
- Nutrition
- Science in Agriculture
- Scientific and Technical Communications

Even with the new curricula and advising procedures in place, there are continued needs or "growing points." The new organization of majors is accompanied by a need to retain the vision that infused Project Sunrise. It is also important to build a sense of community for students and faculty in the collegiate majors put in place as a result of Sunrise. Faculty interest and commitment to undergraduate concerns need to be maintained, and departments must take collective ownership for undergraduate majors. The reorganization of the curriculum, new contents, and new methods of learning were major parts of the innovation, but work will continue to maintain and build on the gains.

NEBRASKA OUTCOMES

The New Partnerships in Agriculture and Education (NUPAGE) project at Nebraska resulted in the development of 18 individual design projects. These ranged in size and scope from revitalizing an established course, designing a new learning experience, and developing a new program of study, to putting in place an entirely new curriculum (Natural Resources Majors) in the college, as well as changing the College of Agriculture's name to the College of Agricultural Sciences and Natural Resources (CASNR).

During the second year of the grant program, NUPAGE objectives were incorporated into *Project Scholar* (1990), CASNR's three-year action plan. This action helped assure that NUPAGE outcomes would be disseminated throughout the college curriculum. In addition, the Curriculum Revitalization Task Force, as described earlier in Chapter Six, led a process which put in place the new general education requirements for the college, including new requirements for writing and communication and an integrative capstone experience. The new general education requirements, developed before the university finalized its plans for basic and integrative studies, proved to be a good fit with the university-wide requirements.

The NUPAGE Project therefore led to a number of outcomes. Some of these are:

Inclusion of new teaching and learning strategies in current courses:

- Case studies
- Computer simulation
- Dual path for mechanized systems management
- Critical thinking
- Communication literacy

Establishment of new courses:

- Ethics in Agriculture and Natural Resources

- Science of Food
- Biological Systems Engineering Capstone Course
- Quality of the Environment

Facilitation of new programs of study:

- Environmental Studies
- Natural Resources majors
- Landscape Architecture (minor)

Revitalization of the general education (core) requirements.

With NUPAGE's focus on involvement of faculty, interdisciplinary teams, and external partners, curriculum revitalization moved more inductively than deductively. Hence, we had some projects that did not become permanent parts of the curriculum, or perhaps had minimal impact. However, by leaving the outcomes relatively open, we did achieve a number of goals in curricular revitalization.

WISCONSIN OUTCOMES

The Curricular Revitalization Project at the University of Wisconsin-Madison had three general components: assessing the curriculum, developing new programs, and supporting faculty. Outcomes occurred in each area, with the consensus rewriting of a Mission Statement being essential to the success of the project as a whole. Accomplishments in component areas include:

Curriculum Assessment

- produced a mission statement for undergraduate instruction
- awarded mini-grants to revitalize courses and introduce new teaching strategies in courses
- stimulated the review of degree and major requirements across the college
- led to adoption of a flexible set of college core curriculum and degree-based advanced skills requirements, replacing a system that had been in place since 1961
- recommended a capstone requirement for all undergraduates in the college

Agriculture, Technology, and Society

- developed 11 new courses and revitalized two existing courses
- identified 25 existing courses with content relevant to this area
- introduced a new certificate program giving students opportunity to explore critical linkages between agriculture, technology, and society

Information Management and Communication Skills

- supported faculty in improving computer skills
- developed and distributed five audiotapes on the learning styles of non-traditional students
- sponsored development of four videotapes on "Coping with Academic Stress"

Quest Fellowship Program

- promoted the importance of students' developing perspectives on the university and acquiring a peer group
- developed and offered "An Orientation to the College of Agricultural and Life Sciences," a permanent interdisciplinary course for incoming beginning students
- demonstrated to faculty the possibilities for increased use of hands-on experience in the undergraduate curricula

In addition, two significant unanticipated outcomes can be identified:

- encouraged efforts to computerize and individualize undergraduate advising system
- proposed writing across the curriculum program

The faculty's experience with the project suggests that their original expectation of achieving comprehensive curricular revitalization and faculty development was realistic, with one important qualification. Faculty and project leaders, first of all, had decided to avoid making piecemeal education reform proposals through the formal governance structure of the college. At the same time they rejected a "top down" reform strategy that would have given project leaders the authority to impose changes by administrative fiat. This proved to be a realistic choice—indeed, one that was essential to achieving the project objectives. However, the time needed to establish and start up the project's staff and the decentralized style of decision-making prevalent in CALS meant that the work took longer than anticipated.

LESSONS LEARNED

At a meeting hosted by the Kellogg Foundation in November 1992, project leaders from Minnesota, Nebraska, and Wisconsin gathered in Battle Creek, Michigan, to discuss results of the projects with Kellogg program officers and to look toward the future. At that time, common themes emerged from the "lessons learned." Some themes were broad in scope. For example, faculty involvement and faculty development were deemed necessities in making curricular change happen. Other themes had to do with maintaining innovations introduced, such as writing across the curriculum and use of decision cases in learning. Some of the lessons learned had to do with organizational and administrative structure. For example, the role of project directors and the infra-structure each managed were critical to success.

Faculty Involvement

One common element in all three projects was the recognized need for faculty involvement. While faculty participation was inherent in the projects funded by Kellogg, the concept was tested, proved, and extended throughout the activities of the grant. Lessons learned can be stated as what to do. For example:

- Convince faculty that change is essential. No real curricular change is possible if faculty are not enthusiastic participants in the process.

- Involve both teaching and research faculty members who should together own the process and the product.

- Involve faculty on many different levels in many different ways (task forces, seminars, workshops, retreats, money to support autonomous activities, money for teaching replacement and/or release time). Involving faculty on different levels leads to changes from both bottom up and top down.

Lessons learned about faculty involvement also include these reflections:

- A variety of ways to involve faculty will require more time than originally anticipated.

- The original assumption that effective curricular change can best be achieved by helping change faculty members proved valid, particularly for an institution where faculty governance is strong.

- Build slowly and consistently. Have people with you throughout the process. Final voting and approval should be sought only when over-whelming support and implementation are assured.

Faculty Development

In addition to the imperative to involve faculty in the change effort, faculty development was recognized by project leaders on the three campuses as an integral part of the change process. Lessons learned included:

- Make professional development of faculty members an integral part of major change in academic programs.

- Encourage faculty to work in teams or with external partners. Faculty are reluctant to expose their ideas and thought processes to scrutiny until they have a nearly completed product, but once the ice is broken, faculty grow from fresh insights.

- Work with teams as they conceptualize and develop learning experiences so that their work will be less bound by past practice and thus more creative.

- Provide resources, recognition, and rewards for faculty participants.

Organizational Relationships

One major lesson learned was the awareness that the externally-funded grant project had to become integrated in the structure and governance of the colleges and institutions of the three projects. At the same time, changes in the contents of curricula and the form of the organization itself constituted an ultimate outcome. Many of the lessons learned, including those which were raised at the 1992 Battle Creek meeting, focus on issues of change. Some reflections include:

- Changes in the curriculum can bring about change in the organizational structure and vice-versa.

- Faculty ownership of courses is fiercely protected, and departments feel a real sense of loss when their names are no longer associated with a major.

- A system must be in place to assure faculty members that taking risks will be rewarded.

- Faculty are creative and willing to work hard at changing the learning outcomes for students when a little recognition and funding are made available to undertake changes.

- Faculty can and will work together in developing multi-disciplinary learning experiences if the activities are recognized as important through making resources available to teams.

Project Administration

Comparisons of the administrative structure of each project reveal similarities in intentions, personnel, and lessons learned. Some of these, as stated at the 1992 meeting, are:

- Keep the project's mission in focus for participants and define its expected results. On the other hand, don't over-control the project's direction. Design simultaneous activities and allow for serendipitous outcomes.

- Set short-term goals, the accomplishment of which can act as motivational benchmarks.

- Don't hide project outcomes. Communicate frequently to keep the project visible, both to inside and outside audiences. Awareness by an external audience helps to increase the commitment of participants. Businesses and agency people are willing and enthusiastic partners in developing, designing, selling, supporting, and legitimizing new learning experiences.

- Maintain flexibility in curricular designs and methods of operation so that adjustments can be made and tested easily.

- In judging progress, do not focus exclusively on concrete products. Building relationships and networking are less tangible but significant outcomes.

- View problems as opportunities. Project leaders should be imaginative optimists who point to and help participants look for silver linings in the clouds.

Some further observations and reflections on managing change and project operations include:

- Orchestration of a multi-faceted approach to curricular revitalization is the most difficult: as, for example, multiple disciplines, partners from private sectors, and new learning experiences that do not fit easily into established curricula or programs of study.

- Seed money given to curricular improvement projects in departments shows the faculty that curricular revitalization of undergraduate programs was an important activity, and the selection of projects to be funded gives significant direction toward accomplishment of the project mission.

- Curricular revitalization projects have a better chance of success if they have a leadership team or project directors consisting of an academic dean, faculty leaders, and an instructional consultant. In addition, a variety of committed faculty and community partners should be included.

- Having a director of curricular revitalization is essential for success. If the director leaves and no one fills the void, momentum will be lost.

- Faculty are more likely to use external or student partners if an active outreach coordinator is available to perform a number of functions, including identifying and contacting partners; arranging meeting places, dates, and agendas; facilitating meetings; and providing feedback to teams.

If projects are to succeed, they have to find their way into the mainstream of the curriculum through established processes. Some observations regarding efforts to sustain projects beyond the life of the grant include:

- Pilot programming is an effective method for getting faculty, students, and administrators to try new activities. It serves as an effective process to help institutionalize successful program thrusts and is equally effective for allowing phase-out of programs not judged successful.

- Innovations are fragile. In hard times, when budgets are being cut, innovations and innovators can be lost. Goals, mission statements, and strategic planning help to bolster new courses and curricula as they are taking root.

- Advisory groups serve two valuable functions: They can learn about and support the project, and can serve as a vital testing ground for curricular revitalization concepts.

- Documentation of learner outcomes, difficult as valid assessments are, should be part of curriculum revitalization.

A FINAL WORD

The experiences reflected in accounts of curricular revitalization as described in this volume have something to say to those engaged in evaluating and reshaping land grant and higher education today. The need not only to respond to change but also to lead change in programs of study is never stilled. As we address current issues, we need to ask questions about the nature of knowledge, its discovery, and its dissemination. We need to take a critical look at who we are, the clients and students we serve, and the problems in the world which we should be addressing. We need to unfreeze categories and include others in envisioning, designing, and implementing new curricula. Resources are needed not merely to maintain current academic structures, but to discover or invent new perspectives and direction. The accomplishments as well as the shortcomings of the projects described here, therefore, might best be studied for the interactive and sometimes transforming processes which should inform all academic work.

NOTE

[1] The sources for this section include the writings of the contributors, personal communication with project leaders, observations made by editors and the author of this chapter, other informal notes, and unpublished reports. Written documents appear in the list of references below.

Joyce Povlacs Lunde is Associate Professor of Agricultural Leadership, Education and Communication, and Educational Specialist, Office of Professional and Organizational Development, University of Nebraska-Lincoln.

REFERENCES

College of Agricultural and Life Sciences. (1991). *Integrative approach to curricula assessment and faculty development,* Fifth annual report, September 1, 1990–August 21, 1991. Madison, WI: University of Wisconsin-Madison.

—— (1992). *1992–1993 Undergraduate curriculum.* Madison, WI: University of Wisconsin-Madison.

College of Agricultural Sciences and Natural Resources. (1992). *New partnerships in agriculture and education: NUPAGE final report,* March 31, 1992. Lincoln, NE: University of Nebraska-Lincoln.

—— (1990). *Project Scholar: Priorities and plans for excellence in learning.* Lincoln, NE: Institute of Agriculture and Natural Resources, University of Nebraska-Lincoln.

College of Agriculture. (1990). *Project Sunrise third annual report.* St. Paul, MN: University of Minnesota.

Foster, R. (1992). *Summary report: Curriculum revitalization reporting meeting,* November 2–3, 1992. Battle Creek, MI: W.K. Kellogg Foundation.

BIBLIOGRAPHY

Association of American Colleges. (1985). *Integrity in the college curriculum: A report to the academic community.* Washington, DC: Association of American Colleges.

Anderson, P. (1985). What survey research tells us about writing at work. In L. Odell & D. Goswami (Eds.), *Writing in nonacademic settings.* (pp. 3-83). New York, NY: The Guilford Press.

Anderson, R.H. (1983). *Selecting and developing media for instruction, second ed.* New York, NY: Van Nostrand Reinhold.

Babb, E.M., & Bohl, L.P. (1969, May). *Manual for Purdue farm supply center management game.* EC-321, Lafayette, IN: Purdue University Cooperative Extension Service.

Banset, E.A., & Brink, D.M. (1993). Communication literacy across the sciences: Designing and evaluating writing assignments. *Proceedings, 45th Annual Reciprocal Meats Conference, American Meat Science Association,* 45: 27-35.

Barbour, D.H. (1987). Process in the business writing classroom: One teacher's approach. *The Journal of Business Communication,* 24, 61-64.

Bazerman, C. (1991). Review: The second stage in writing across the curriculum. *College English,* 53(2), 209-212.

Beach, R., & Bridwell, L.S. (Eds.). (1984). *New directions in composition research.* New York, NY: The Guilford Press.

Beck, M.A., Brink, D.M., Banset, E.A., Book, V.A., & Gilster, K. (1991). Writing in an animal science curriculum: A model for agriculture. *Poultry Science,* 70 (suppl.): 12.

Beckman, M.P. (1989). Interdisciplinary teaching in economics: How is as important as why. *College Teaching,* 37 (3),101-104.

Beford, M.S., & Stearns, F.C. (1987). The technical writer's responsibility for safety. *IEEE Transactions of Professional Communication,* 30, 127-32.

Bennett, W. (1984). *To reclaim a legacy: A report on the humanities in higher education.* Washington, DC: National Endowment for the Humanities.

Bjoraker, W.T. (1987). Concepts and philosophical issues in food and agriculture undergraduate education with basic guidelines for curricular planners. In *Curricular innovation for 2005: Planning for the future of our food and agricultural sciences.* Washington, DC: North Central Region RICOP Curricular Committee Project, U.S. Department of Agriculture, pp. 5-32.

Blatz, C.V. (1991). *Ethics and agriculture: An anthology on current issues in world context.* Moscow, ID: University of Idaho Press.

Bloom, B.S. (Ed.). (1956). *Taxonomy of educational objectives, handbook I: Cognitive domain.* New York, NY: Longmans.

Board on Agriculture. (1992). *Agriculture and the undergraduate: Proceedings.* Washington, DC: National Academy Press.

Boyer, E.L. (1990). *Scholarship reconsidered: Priorities of the professoriate.* Special report, Carnegie Foundation for the Advancement of Teaching. Lawrenceville, NJ: Princeton University Press.

Boyer, E.L. (1987). *The undergraduate experience in America.* Princeton, NJ: Carnegie Foundation for the Advancement of Teaching.

Brink, D.M., Banset, E.A., Beck, M.A., Book, V.A., & Gilster, K. (1991). Developing competence in written communication in an animal science curriculum. *Journal of Animal Science,* 69 (suppl.): 566.

Brink, D.M., Banset, E.A., Beck, M.A., Book, V.A., & Gilster, K. (1992). Partnerships to enhance communication competence of animal science graduates. *NACTA Journal,* 36 (September, 1992): 18-19.

Brockmann, R.J., & Rook, F. (Eds.). (1989). *Technical communication and ethics.* Washington, DC: Society for Technical Communication.

Bruffee, K.A. (1987, March-April). The art of collaborative learning. *Change,* 42-47.

Bruffee, K.A. (1983). Writing and reading as collaborative or social acts. In J.N. Hays, P.A. Roth, J.R. Ramsey, & R.D. Foulke (Eds.), *The writer's mind.* (pp. 159-170). Urbana, IL: NCTE.

Bunderson, V., & Inouye, D.K. (1987). The evolution of computer-aided educational delivery systems. In R.M. Gagne (Ed.), *Instructional technology: Foundations.* Hillsdale, NJ: Erlbaum.

Carnegie Foundation for the Advancement of Teaching. (1976). *Missions of the college curriculum.* San Francisco, CA: Jossey Bass.

Carroll, J.A. (1984). Process into product: Teacher awareness of the writing process affects students' written products. In R. Beach & L.S. Bridwell (Eds.), *New directions in composition research.* (pp. 315-333). New York, NY: The Guilford Press.

Chickering, A.W., & Gamson, Z.F. (1987, March). Seven principles for good practice in undergraduate education. *AAHE Bulletin, 39(7),* 3-7.

Chickering, A.W., Gamson, Z.F., & Barsi, L.M. (1989). *Seven principles for good practice in undergraduate education: Faculty inventory.* Racine, WI: Johnson Foundation, Inc. Wingspread.

Christensen, C.R. (1987). *Teaching and the case method: Text, cases, and readings.* Cambridge, MA: Harvard Business School Press.

Chudzinski, L.Z., Simerly, C.B., & George, W.L. (1988). *National assessment of faculty development needs in colleges of agriculture.* Urbana, IL: University of Illinois, College of Agriculture.

Clegg, S., & Wheeler, M.M. (1991). *Students writing across the disciplines*. Orlando, FL: Holt, Rinehart, and Winston.

Clemens, S. (Mark Twain). (1917). *A Connecticut yankee in King Arthur's court*. New York, NY: Harper and Row.

Clement, D.E. (1987). Human factors, instructions and warnings, and products' liability. *IEEE Transactions of Professional Communication*, 30, 149-56.

College of Agricultural Sciences and Natural Resources. (1988). *An analysis of core curriculum in the College of Agricultural and Life Sciences, University of Wisconsin-Madison*. Madison, WI: University of Wisconsin-Madison, CALS Curricular Revitalization Project, Office of Student Academic Affairs.

College of Agricultural and Life Sciences. (1989). *Coping with academic stress*. [Videotape series]. Madison, WI: University of Wisconsin-Madison Board of Regents.

College of Agricultural and Life Sciences. (1991). *Integrative approach to curricula assessment and faculty development, fifth annual report, September 1, 1990–August 21, 1991*. Madison, WI: University of Wisconsin-Madison.

College of Agricultural and Life Sciences. (1992). *1992–1993 Undergraduate curriculum*. Madison, WI: University of Wisconsin-Madison.

College of Agricultural Sciences and Natural Resources. (1992). *New partnerships in agriculture and education: NUPAGE final report, March 31, 1992*. Lincoln, NE: University of Nebraska-Lincoln, Institute of Agriculture and Natural Resources.

College of Agricultural Sciences and Natural Resources. (1992). *Project scholar: Priorities and plans for excellence in learning*. Lincoln, NE: University of Nebraska-Lincoln, Institute of Agriculture and Natural Resources.

College of Agriculture. (1990). *Project Sunrise third annual report*. St. Paul, MN: University of Minnesota.

Conley, D.M. (1991). Student perceptions of cognitive skill achievement in agribusiness management. *Agribusiness: An International Journal*, 7(2), 135-141.

Conley, D.M., & Simon, D. (1993). Testing for personality bias in evaluating agribusiness students. *Agribusiness: An International Journal*, 9(2), 119-127.

Conley, D.M., & Simon, D. (1993, August). *The management challenge of team formation in an agribusiness*. Selected paper for the annual meeting of the American Agricultural Economics Association, Orlando, FL.

Conrads, J.A. (1987). "Illustruction": Increasing safety and reducing liability exposure. *IEEE Transactions of Professional Communication*, 30, 133-5.

Cooper, C.R., Cherry, R., Copley, B., Fleischer, S., Pollard, R., & Sartisky, M. (1984). Studying the writing abilities of a university freshman class: Strategies from a case study. In R. Beach & L.S. Bridwell (Eds.), *New directions in composition research*. (pp. 19-52). New York, NY: The Guilford Press.

Cross, K.P., & Angelo, T.A. (1988). *Classroom assessment techniques: A handbook for faculty.* (Tech. Rep. No. 88-A-004.0). Ann Arbor, MI: University of Michigan, National Center for Research to Improve Postsecondary Teaching and Learning. Technical Report No. 88-A-004.0. Ann Arbor, MI: University of Michigan, Board of Regents. (Now available as Angelo, T., & Cross, P. [1993]. second edition. San Francisco, CA: Jossey-Bass.)

Curricular innovation for 2005: Planning for the future of our food & agricultural sciences. (1987). Madison, WI: USDA.

Davis, R.H., & Alexander, L.T. (1977). *Guides for the improvement of instruction in higher education.* East Lansing, MI: Michigan State University, Board of Trustees.

Dewey, J. (1975). *Moral principles in education.* Carbondale, IL: Southern Illinois University Press.

Dipardo, A., & Freedman, S.W. (1988). Peer response groups in the writing classroom: Theoretic foundations and new directions. *Review of Educational Research,* 58, 119-149.

Doheny-Farina, S. (1986). Writing in an emerging organization: An ethnographic study. *Written Communication,* 3, 158-184.

Driver, R.W. (1987). A communication model for determining the appropriateness of on-product warnings. *IEEE Transactions of Professional Communication,* 30, 157-63.

Duin, A.H. (1990). Terms and tools: A theory and research-based approach to collaborative writing. *Bulletin of the Association for Business Communication,* 53(2), 45-50.

Duin, A.H., Jorn, L., & DeBower, M. (1991). Collaborative writing—Courseware and telecommunications. In M.M. Lay & W. M. Karis (Eds.), *Collaborative writing in industry: Investigations in theory and practice.* Farmingdale, NY: Baywood.

Duin, A.H., Jorn, L.A., & Mason, L. (1994). Structuring distance-meeting environments. *Technical Communication,* 41(4), 695-708.

Duin, A.H., Lammers, E., Mason, L., & Graves, M.F. (1994). Responding to ninth-grade students via telecommunications: College mentor strategies and development over time. *Research in the Teaching of English.*

Duin, A.H., Simmons, S.R., & Lammers, E. (1994). *Decision cases for writing across the curriculum.* Minneapolis, MN: University of Minnesota, A monograph for the Center of Interdisciplinary Studies of Writing.

Ede, L., & Lunsford, A. (1986). Why write…together: A research update. *Rhetoric Review,* 5, 71-81.

Fillion, B. (1979). Language across the curriculum: Examining the place of language in our schools. *McGill Journal of Education,* 14, 47-60.

Forman, J., & Katsky, P. (1986). The group report: A problem in small group or writing processes? *The Journal of Business Communication,* 23, 23-35.

Foster, R. (1992). *Summary report. Curriculum revitalization reporting meeting, November 2–3, 1992.* Battle Creek, MI: W.K. Kellogg Foundation.

Freedman, S.W. (1984). The registers of student and professional expository writing: Influences on teachers' responses. In R. Beach & L.S. Bridwell (Eds.), *New directions in composition research.* (pp. 334-347). New York, NY: The Guilford Press.

Fulwiler, T. (1984). How well does writing across the curriculum work? *College English, 46,* 113-125.

Fulwiler, T., & Gorman, M.E. (1986). Changing faculty attitudes toward writing. In A. Young & T. Fulwiler (Eds.), *Writing across the disciplines: Research into practice.* (pp. 53-66). Upper Montclair, NJ: Boynton/Cook.

Fulwiler, T., & Young, A. (Eds.). (1990). *Programs that work: Models and methods for writing across the curriculum.* Portsmouth, NH: Boynton/Cook.

Gere, A.R. (Ed.). (1985). *Roots in the sawdust: Writing to learn across the disciplines.* Urbana, IL: National Council of Teachers of English.

Gere, A.R., Schuessler, B.F., & Abbott, R.D. (1984). Measuring teachers' attitudes toward writing instruction. In R. Beach & L.S. Bridwell (Eds.), *New directions in composition research.* (pp. 348-361). New York, NY: The Guilford Press.

Gragg, C. (1940). Because wisdom can't be told. *Harvard Alumni Bulletin.* Cambridge, MA: Harvard University.

Harl, N. (1985). *Implications of farm debtor distress: A challenge for land grant universities.* Paper presented at the Council of Agricultural Research, Extension, and Teaching. Arlington, VA.

Hart, F., & Turkstra, C.J. (1979, April). Senior projects supervised by consulting engineers. *Engineering Education,* 747-748.

Hartung, T.E., & Goecker, A.D. *Operation change: An action agenda for developing human capital to secure American agriculture.* Resident Instruction Committee on Organization and Policy. Washington, DC: Association of State Universities and Land-Grant Colleges [pamphlet].

Hoffman, G.J. (1991, December). *Undergraduate programs in the department of biological systems engineering, Nebraska.* One-on-one poster session presented at the meeting of the American Society of Agricultural Engineers, Chicago, IL.

Hoffman, G.J., DeShazer, J.A., Hanna, M.A., & Schulte, D.D. (1990, June). *Biological systems engineering: Future directions in Nebraska.* Paper presented at the meeting of the American Society of Engineering Education, Toronto, Canada.

Hoffman, G.J., DeShazer, J.A., Hanna, M.A., & Schulte, D.D. (1990, December). *Biological systems engineering vs. agricultural engineering: A curriculum with a difference.* ASAE Paper #90-5517 presented at the meeting of the American Society of Agricultural Engineers, Chicago, IL.

Hoffman, G.J., Jones, D.D., & Kocher, M.F. (1993, September). Are perceptions reality? *Agricultural Engineering,* 14-17.

Hoffman, G.J., Jones, D.D., & Martin, D. (1993, December). *Incorporating design into biological systems engineering.* Paper presented at ASAE Winter Meeting, Chicago, IL.

Holubec, E.J. (Spring 1993). How do you get there from here? *Contemporary Education,* 63(3).

Hoover, E.E., & Markhart, A.H. (1987). Horticulture—Managing a strawberry farm: A computer simulation. *Academic Computing,* 2(2), 32-33, 52.

Hoover, E.E., Markhart, A.H., & Nassauer, J. (1989). IBM computers for innovative teaching in horticulture and landscape architecture: Project AG01. In *Project Woksape final report.* (p. 27). Minneapolis, MN: University of Minnesota.

Hord, S.M. (1986). A synthesis of research on collaboration. *Educational Leadership,* 43, 22-26.

Hult, C.A. (1990). *Researching and writing across the curriculum, second edition.* Belmont, CA: Wadsworth.

Huot, B. (1990). Reliability, validity, and holistic scoring: What we know and what we need to know. *College Composition and Communication,* 41, 201-213.

I Want to Learn, Not Just Remember. (1989). In *Third annual report: Integrative approach to curricular assessment and faculty development.* Madison, WI: College of Agricultural and Life Sciences, Curricular Revitalization Project. p. 22.

Johannesen, R.L. (1990). *Ethics in human communication, third edition.* Prospect Heights,IL: Waveland Press.

Johnson, D.W., et al. (1991). *Cooperative learning: Increasing college faculty instructional productivity.* ASHE-ERIC Higher Education Report No. 4.

Johnson, D.W., & Johnson, R.T. (Spring 1992). Implementing cooperative learning. *Contemporary Education,* 63(3).

Johnson, D.W., & Johnson, R.T. (July-August 1985). Student-student interaction: Ignored but powerful. *Journal of Teacher Education,* 37(4).

Johnson, D.W., Johnson, R.T., & Holubec, E.J. (n.d.). *Learning together and learning alone.* Minneapolis, MN: University of Minnesota, Cooperative Learning Center [Workshop material].

Jolliffe, D.A. (1988). *Advances in writing research: Writing in academic disciplines.* Norwood, NJ: Ablex.

Jones, D.D., Kocher, M.F., & Hoffman, G.J. (1992, June). *Experience with a new biological systems engineering curriculum.* Paper presented at the meeting of the American Society of Engineers in Education, Toledo, OH.

Jones, D.M., Kocher, M.F., & Hoffman, G.J. (1993). Experience with a new biological systems engineering curriculum. *Proceedings, Midwest Section, American Society of Engineering Education,* 3B 1-14.

Jones, R., & Comprone, J.J. (1993). Where do we go next in writing across the curriculum? *College Composition and Communication,* 44(1), 59-68.

Katz, J., & Henry, M. (1988). *Turning professors into teachers: A new approach to faculty development and student learning.* New York, NY: ACE/Macmillan.

Kemp, F. (1988). *Stimulating creativity in the computer-based writing classroom.* Paper presented at the Computers in Writing and Language Instruction Conference, Duluth, MN.

Kidder, T. (1981). *The soul of a new machine.* Boston, MA: Little, Brown.

Kolb, D. (1985). *Learning style inventory.* Boston, MA: McBer and Associates.

Kramer, M. (1980). *Three farms: Making milk, meat, and money from the American soil.* Boston, MA: Little, Brown.

Krutz, G.W., Combs, R.F., & Parsons, S.D. (1980). Equipment analysis with farm management models. *Transactions of the ASAE,* 23(1):25-28.

Kuhn, T. (1963). *The structure of scientific revolutions.* Chicago, IL: University of Chicago Press.

Learned, E.P. (1987). Reflections of a case method teacher. In C.R. Christensen & A.J. Hansen (Eds.), *Teaching and the case method.* (pp. 9-15). Boston, MA: Harvard Business School Press.

Litzenberg, K., & Schneider, V.E. (1987). *Agri-Mass: Agribusiness management aptitude and skills survey.* Washington, DC: Agribusiness Education Project.

Love, G.M., & Yoder, E.P. (1989). *An assessment of undergraduate education in American colleges of agriculture.* State College, PA: Pennsylvania State University, College of Agriculture.

Lunde, J.P., & Hartung, T.E. (1990). Integrating individual and organizational needs: The University of Nebraska, Lincoln. In J.J. Schuster & D.W. Wheeler (Eds.), *Enhancing faculty careers: Strategies for development and renewal.* San Francisco, CA: Jossey-Bass.

Lunsford, A. (1989, April). *Short and sweet assignments that combine writing, reading, speaking, and thinking.* Paper presented at the National Testing Network on Writing Assessment, Montreal, Canada.

McLeod, S.H. (1989). Writing across the curriculum: The second stage, and beyond. *College Composition and Communication,* 40(3), 337-343.

McLeod, S.H., & Soven, M. (1992). (Eds.). *Writing across the curriculum: A guide to developing programs.* Newbury Park, CA: Sage.

Miller, F. (1989). The essence of agriculture. *Journal of Agronomy Education, 18(2):* 63-65.

National Commission on the Role and Future of State Colleges and Universities. (1986). *To secure the blessings of liberty: Report of the national commission on the role and future of state colleges and universities.* Washington, DC: American Association of Colleges and Universities.

North Central Region Curricular Committee Project. (1989). *Educating for a global perspective: International agricultural curricula for 2005.* Washington, DC: U.S. Department of Agriculture.

Odell, L. (1985). Beyond the text: Relations between writing and social context. In L. Odell & D. Goswami (Eds.), *Writing in nonacademic settings.* (pp. 249-280). New York, NY: The Guilford Press.

Odell, L. (1986). Foreword. In A. Young & T. Fulwiler (Eds.), *Writing across the disciplines.* Upper Montclair, NJ: Boynton/Cook.

Odell, L., & Goswami, D. (1984). Writing in a nonacademic setting. In R. Beach & L.S. Bridwell (Eds.), *New directions in composition research.* (pp. 233-258). New York, NY: The Guilford Press.

Paradis, J. (1991). Text and action: The operator's manual in context and in court. In C. Bazerman & J. Paradis (Eds.), *Textual dynamics and the professions.* (pp 256-278). Madison, WI: University of Wisconsin Press.

Paradis, J., Dobrin, D., & Miller, R. (1985). Writing at Exxon ITD. In L. Odell & D. Goswami (Eds.), *Writing in nonacademic settings.* (pp. 281-307). New York, NY: The Guilford Press.

Peters, D.S. (1982). Interdisciplinary teaching. *Alternative Higher Education,* 6(4), 229-241.

Phillips, J. A. (1984). *Machine dreams.* New York, NY: Dutton.

POD (Professional and Organizational Development Network in Higher Education). (n.d.). *An informational brochure about faculty, instructional, and organizational development: Prepared for faculty and administrators.* Ames, IA: Iowa State University, Professional and Organizational Development Network in Higher Education

Rabkin, E.S., & Smith, M. (1990). *Teaching writing that works.* Ann Arbor, MI: The University of Michigan Press.

Rachels, J. (1986). *The elements of moral philosophy.* New York, NY: Random House.

Reddish, J.C. (1983). The language of the bureaucracy. In R.W. Bailey & R.M. Fosheim (Eds.), *Literacy for life: The demand for reading and writing.* (pp. 151-174). New York, NY: Modern Language Association.

Regan, T. (1984). *Earthbound.* New York, NY: Random House.

Rorty, R. (1979). *Philosophy and the mirror of nature.* Princeton, NJ: Princeton University Press.

Russell, D.R. (1987). Writing across the curriculum and the communications movement: Some lessons from the past. *College Composition and Communication,* 38(2), 184-194.

Selection Research, Inc. (August 1990). *End-of-year evaluation report: NUPAGE project (second project year).* Lincoln, NE: SRI.

Simerly, C.B. (March 1990a). A national assessment: Faculty development needs in colleges of agriculture. *NACTA Journal,* XXXIV (1), 11-14.

Simerly, C.B. (June 1990b). Faculty development: A strategy for revitalization and change. *NACTA Journal,* XXXIV (2), 14-17.

Sledge, G.W. (1974). *Curriculum strategies for agriculture: An analysis of problems relating to the choice, preparation, and application of a curriculum.* Program and methods in higher education in agriculture. Paris, Oct. 14-18, 1974. Fifth Working Conference of Representatives of Higher Education in Agriculture. Paris, France: Organization for Economic Cooperation and Development.

Sledge, G.W., et al (1987). Futuristic curricular models and designs for the food and agricultural sciences. In *Curricular Innovation for 2005: Planning for the future of our food & agricultural sciences,* pp. 115-130.

Smelser, N. (1985). Evaluating the model of structural differentiation in relation to educational change in the nineteenth century. In J. Alexander (Ed.), *Neofunctionalism.* Newbury Park, CA: Sage.

Stanford, G. (1981). *Classroom practices in teaching English: How to handle the paper load.* Urbana, IL: NCTE.

Stanford, M.J. (1992). How to prepare decision cases. In M.J. Stanford, R.K. Crookston, D.W. Davis, & S.R. Simmons (Eds.), *Decision cases for agriculture.* (pp.42-48).

Stark, J.S., Lowther, M.A., Ryan, M.P., Bomotti, S.S., Genthon, M., Haven, C.L., & Martens, G. (1988). *Reflections on course planning: Faculty and students consider influences and goals.* Ann Arbor, MI: University of Michigan, School of Education.

Stonewater, J.K., & Stonewater, B. (1984). Teaching problem solving: Implications from cognitive development research (ED 240-918). *AAHE-ERIC Higher Education Research Currents.* Washington, DC: AAHE.

Strate, L., & Swerdlow, S. (1987). The maze of law: How technical writers can research and understand legal matters. *IEEE Transactions of Professional Communication,* 30, 136-48.

Study Group on the Conditions of Excellence in American Higher Education. (1984). *Involvement in learning: Realizing the potential of American higher education.* Washington, DC: National Institute of Education.

Task Force on Agricultural, Biological, and Environmental Core. (1988). *Final recommendations of the task force on agricultural, biological, and environmental core.* Madison, WI: University of Wisconsin-Madison, CALS Curricular Revitalization Project, Office of Student Academic Affairs.

Task Force on Agricultural Systems. (1988). *Agricultural systems task force policy statement.* Madison, WI: University of Wisconsin-Madison, CALS Curricular Revitalization Project, Office of Academic Affairs.

Task Force on Communication Arts and Foreign Languages. (1988). *Draft report: Final recommendations of the communication arts and foreign language task force.* Madison, WI: University of Wisconsin- CALS Curricular Revitalization Project, Office of Academic Affairs.

Task Force on the Humanities and Social Sciences. (1988). *Draft proposal three: CALS humanities and social sciences requirement.* Madison, WI: University of Wisconsin-Madison, CALS Curricular Revitalization Project, Office of Academic Affairs.

Task Force on International Studies. (1988). *Report of the international studies task force.* Madison, WI: University of Wisconsin-Madison, CALS Curricular Revitalization Project, Office of Academic Affairs.

Task Force on Mathematics, Statistics, and Computer Science. (1988). *Report of the task force on mathematics, statistics, and computer science core requirements.* Madison, WI: University of Wisconsin-Madison, CALS Curricular Revitalization Project, Office of Academic Affairs.

Tchudi, S.N. (1986). *Teaching writing in the content areas: College level.* Washington, DC: National Education Association.

Thompson, P. (1991). *Ethics in agriculture.* [AGSAT course]. College Station, TX: Texas A&M (Funded by Department of Agriculture, 1991-2).

Trimbur, J. (1985). Collaborative learning and teaching writing. In B.W. McClelland & T.R. Donovan (Eds.), *Perspectives on research and scholarship in composition.* New York, NY: MLA.

University of Wisconsin-Madison. (1990). *A mission statement for undergraduate instruction in the UW-Madison College of Agricultural and Life Sciences.* Madison, WI: CALS Curricular Revitalization Project, Office of Student Academic Affairs.

Verlotta, C. (1987). Safety labels: What to put in them, how to write them, and where to place them. *IEEE Transactions of Professional Communication,* 30, 121-26.

Wales, C.E., Nardi, A.H., & Stager, R.A. (1987). *Thinking skills: Making a choice.* Morgantown, WV: Charles E. Wales, Anne H. Nardi, and Robert A. Stager.

Walter, C., & Marstellar, T.F. (1987). Liability for the dissemination of defective information. *IEEE Transactions of Professional Communication,* 30, 164-71.

White, E.M. (1986). *Teaching and assessing writing.* San Francisco, CA: Jossey-Bass.

Whiteman, N. (1983). Teaching problem solving and creativity in college courses (ED 226-650). *AAHE-ERIC Higher Education Research Currents.* Washington, DC: AAHE.

Wiener, H.S. (1986). Collaborative learning in the classroom. *College English,* 48, 52-61.

Wilson, K., & Morren, E.B. (1990). *Systems approaches for improvement in agriculture and resource management.* New York, NY: Macmillan.

Young, A., & Fulwiler, T. (Eds.). (1986). *Writing across the disciplines.* Upper Montclair, NJ: Boynton/Cook.

INDEX